Praise for

EVERYTHING TRUMP TOUCHES DIES

"Scalpel in hand, a conservative strategist dissects Trumpism, the Washington, D.C., swamp, and the new GOP. The autopsy report isn't pretty. . . . Wilson's insider take is hilarious, smartly written, and usually spot-on. Somebody had to do it."

— *Kirkus Reviews*

"A searingly honest, bitingly funny, comprehensive answer to the question we find ourselves asking most mornings: 'What the hell is going on?'. . . . A fascinating, fierce, and fearless exposition of the political mess America finds itself in today."

— *The Chicago Tribune*

"His raw-brawling style and deftly articulated rage . . . have made Wilson an unexpected darling of the left, and a kind of Cassandra in steel-toed boots for his own party. . . . The book is a clarion call to conservatives about how 'Kim Jong Don's' reverse-Midas touch is 'an Orwellian erasure of what conservatism represents' that will define the party for generations to come."

— *The Week*

"Hear the sizzle? That's the sound of Wilson, Republican strategist and now Never-Trumper, burning the president, his family, cabinet, and GOP stalwarts."

— *Booklist*

fP

EVERYTHING TRUMP TOUCHES DIES

*A Republican Strategist Gets Real About
the Worst President Ever*

RICK WILSON

Free Press

NEW YORK   LONDON   TORONTO
SYDNEY   NEW DELHI

Free Press
An Imprint of Simon & Schuster, Inc.
1230 Avenue of the Americas
New York, NY 10020

First Free Press trade paperback edition February 2019

FREE PRESS and colophon are trademarks of Simon & Schuster, Inc.

For information about special discounts for bulk purchases,
please contact Simon & Schuster Special Sales at 1-866-506-1949
or business@simonandschuster.com.

The Simon & Schuster Speakers Bureau can bring authors to
your live event. For more information, or to book an event, contact
the Simon & Schuster Speakers Bureau at 1-866-248-3049
or visit our website at www.simonspeakers.com.

Interior design by Paul Dippolito

Manufactured in the United States of America

1   3   5   7   9   10   8   6   4   2

Library of Congress Cataloging-in-Publication Data is available.

ISBN 978-1-9821-0312-5
ISBN 978-1-9821-0314-9 (pbk)
ISBN 978-1-9821-0315-6 (ebook)

To Molly, Nora, and Andrew,
who took even the toughest of the last three years with grace,
humor, encouragement, great editing, and love.
Team Wilson, ride or die.

CONTENTS

PART FOUR: AFTER TRUMP

EVERYTHING TRUMP TOUCHES DIES

INTRODUCTION

Everything Trump Touches Dies

IF YOU'RE LIKE ME, THE TRUMP PRESIDENCY HAS TURNED you into a light sleeper.

Admit it. Some nights, when the world is quiet but your mind is racing, you check Twitter to see if he's started a nuclear war. Each morning, strung out from the fever dreams of Donald Trump and Steve Bannon performing a nude interpretive dance of Stephen Miller's "Triumph of the Wall," you wake up wondering if today's the day he's seen wandering naked on the White House lawn, screaming at clouds.

Come on. You know you've done it.

It's because you're struggling, like the vast majority of Americans, with the fact that our terrible, sloppy, shambolic president may just be insane. Not "Haha, he's so crazy" or "He's pretending to be crazy, but it's actually 87-dimensional quantum chess" crazy, but legitimately, clinically insane. I'd have to look up the *DSM-V* category to be more precise, but the term of psychiatric art I'm looking for is "shithouse-rat crazy."

Is crazy too strong a term? Perhaps instead you'd like to argue that a man with Donald Trump's dignity, stature, resolute self-control, deep erudition, and modesty presents as a perfectly rational national leader in every way. In that case, you'd be correct if the nation in question is some third-world hellhole—pardon me, I meant to use the new term of art, "shithole"—ruled by a President for Life with a penchant for elaborate military uniforms, missile parades, a high comfort level

1

with endemic corruption, relatives installed in positions of power, and a rumored taste for human flesh.

Donald Trump, the avatar of our worst instincts and darkest desires as a nation, sits in the Oval Office. I did what I could to stop it. I've watched the stalwarts of the Republican Party and the conservative movement slip into the sewage tank of nationalist populism with barely a ripple.

We failed to stop Trump in 2016, but that doesn't mean I'm going to sit by as the Nickelback of presidents wrecks my country. I'm not going to buy into "But Gorsuch" and "But executive orders" as a pale substitute for character, conservative governance, legislative accomplishments, and principle. Donald Trump is an objectively terrible president, in every sense of the word.

So how the hell did I get here?

As a rock-solid Republican Party guy stretching all the way back to the 1988 presidential campaign of George H. W. Bush, I've worked to elect Republicans and conservatives all over the country. I helped put a lot of them in office in red, purple, and blue states and districts, in races from the presidency on down.

I'm one of a handful of people your candidate or SuperPAC calls when it's time to drop the big, nasty negative ads, and I have a thick enough skin to take the criticism on behalf of the candidate once those ads are hitting the target. I'm the creator of some pretty famous— infamous if you're a Democrat or Roy Moore—attack ads. You've read and heard my work in speeches under the bylines of members of Congress, governors, and CEOs. I've run ads across the proverbial fruited plain.

After 2016, though, I've had a kind of political midlife change. No, I didn't get a 25-year-old girlfriend, a sports car, or a hair transplant.

When Trump slithered down the golden escalator in his eponymous tower in 2015, I felt bile rising in my throat. This guy? *This* jackass? I was quite sure nothing had changed about his blustering ego, fever-swamp birtherism, and con-artist modus operandi. Given the ideological underpinnings of Trumpism—slurry of barely coherent nationalism, third-world generalissimo swagger, and the worst economic ideas of the 19th century—I recognized he was an existential risk to the country, win or lose.

I had met Trump a handful of times. The first time was during Rudy Giuliani's 1997 reelection campaign for mayor of New York when my then-business partner and I were producing Giuliani's television ads. Trump later agreed to appear in a tourism film for the City of New York we shot. The general view inside Rudy World seemed to be that Trump was a loudmouth and a jackass, but enough of a City player to throw him the occasional favor. The next time was at a wedding at Mar-a-Lago for a mutual friend. Ironically the best man at that wedding was the governor of Florida at the time, one John Ellis Bush.

The last time I'd seen Trump in person was 15 years before while filming a gag bit for New York City's Inner Circle, where Trump motorboated Giuliani's fake breasts while the mayor was in his drag persona, Rudia. If you haven't seen it, don't Google it. If you have, I am deeply sorry. It's scarring. If you're looking for nightmare fuel, a pompous, bloated, and bewigged Trump kissing Drag Giuliani is the high-octane version.

Contrary to what Breitbart or Fox or Rush Limbaugh will tell you, I don't oppose Trump because I'm a Republican-in-Name-Only. I oppose Trump from the right, not the left, and as a constitutionalist, not as a globalist Soros neocon shill out to impose political correctness, sharia law, *and* full communism. Yes, I know that accusation is a roaring non sequitur, but welcome to rhetoric in the era of Trump. Their arguments are so consistently dumb, contradictory, and nonsensical that I have to believe there's a secret Word Finder App for Conservatives Who Love Donald but Aren't Smart and Want to Seem Smart to Other People Who Aren't Smart.

I supported Marco Rubio in the primary and worked for a pro-Rubio SuperPAC, but I would have taken any Republican in the field over Trump. Even Ted Cruz, and that says a lot. Like most sensible people, I dismissed Trump as a Roger Stone con game. Hell, I would have picked a random guy walking out of a bus station over Trump.

Everything about Trump's opening speech was moral poison to anyone who believed in any part of the American dream. Everything about his nationalist hucksterism smelled like the destruction of conservatism and a knock on the door of authoritarian statism.

So instead of toeing the party line, lining up behind a morally bankrupt and ideologically suspect Republican nominee, and being a good soldier, I decided that my principles and my country came before my party and politics. As a Republican, a conservative, and an American, I simply couldn't do it. I couldn't be a part of Trump's dismantling the party, the movement, and the nation I loved. I'm an O.G. anti-Trump Republican.

That Donald Trump isn't a conservative and is a Republican only as a flag of convenience was just part of my objection. Quite ironically for a cold-hearted, expedient political operative, I felt Trump lacked the moral and personal character to be the leader of the free world, to make the most consequential decisions, and to hold the lives and security of millions of Americans in his hands.

His tiny, tiny lemur-paw hands.

All this led, through a series of misadventures worthy of a Georges Feydeau farce, to my becoming one of the founders of the Never Trump movement. I'm an apostate in the era of Trump and Trumpism, and I have absolutely no regrets. I didn't make this choice lightly or trivially. Before you ask, I didn't do it because George Soros offered me a stack of gold bars and membership in the Illuminati. It cost me professionally, personally, and financially.

I could easily have pivoted, done the well-he's-the-nominee-and-party-über-alles act so many consultants and elected officials did, despite their loathing Trump just as heartily as I do. Some days, I hear Cypher's voice from the Matrix saying, "Why, oh *why* didn't I take the blue pill?"

If I'd been truly amoral, I could have easily spun up a ScamPAC called Americans Making America Great Again American Eagle Patriot Trump Brigade for Freedom Build the Wall Anti-Sharia PAC. AMAGAAEPTBFFBTWAS PAC would have dropped a few million fundraising emails to the obviously enormous ocean of credulous boobs who click "Donate" at the sign of a red hat and a sparkly eagle gif, and watched the donations roll in. I could have my volcano lair by now.

How far did I go off the Republican reservation? Well, although I'm still a registered Republican, every day is a moral and political stress test. I helped run Evan McMullin's independent bid for president. In an election in which neither of the major party options was at all palatable for a conservative like me, we wanted to offer voters something better. We wanted to give them a candidate and a message that honored the values for which this country ostensibly still stands: liberty, equality, the rule of law, and a reverence for the Constitution.

Old fashioned, I know. Conservative, remember?

I wasn't alone in understanding that there were two elections in 2016. The first election—the one everyone noticed—was in the usual partisan frame. It was Republican Trump against Democrat Clinton, and both sides ran to their corners and fought a political battle we've all seen before. Set aside for a moment why he won and why she lost. Those are *interesting* questions, but the frenzy of the visible election wasn't the most consequential issue.

The real election of 2016 was for the heart and soul of the Republican Party and the conservative movement and for the baseline values and norms a country needs to survive as a going concern in the democracy game. We've since learned that the consensus of the American intelligence community was correct. The election was shaped and manipulated by Russian intelligence operations altering the American political landscape, an endgame in the long twilight struggle.

Hypnotized by a celebrity con man vomiting out Steve Bannon's spittle-flecked, nationalist message to the furious and the febrile, Trump received virtually unlimited media coverage. GOP primary voters killed off a field of good men and accomplished leaders one by one in favor of Trump. Conservative leaders compromised their long-held principles again and again to favor Trump.

Republican voters had a choice between Trump's Troll Party and the Grand Old Party I knew. They chose the Troll Party.

It's a common, facile argument that the old GOP deserved death. After all, we weren't *perfect*. Just ask any talk radio host. We didn't produce enough Ted Cruz types to have a majority large enough to make the Purity Posse happy. We didn't throw Granny off the cliff, starve the orphans, return to the gold standard, and then put the womenfolk back in the kitchen. I get it.

As a party, we are flawed. All parties are. We frequently overpromised and underdelivered on free-market and conservative policy outcomes. We fell into the arms of DC's army of lobbyists and interest groups, most of whom are anything but conservative. For our base, the imagined best became the enemy of the good.

In my career, I have been a gleeful hatchet man for the GOP. I was willing to fight the ideological battles, large and small, in campaigns, on TV, in writing, and lately on social media. We had good years and terrible years. We elected presidents, took back Congress after decades, lost it, and took it back again. Our leaders ranged from bad to extraordinary. We pushed and pressed and worked to expand our reach because there wasn't an alternative.

Through it all, the GOP was the one party even vaguely amenable to limited-government conservatism, to at least some adherence to the Constitution over the social preferences of the moment, and to the constraints on government power that our Founding Fathers so cherished. The choice was an imperfect, leaky ship with tattered sails and a bickering crew sailing in the right direction or drowning in a sea of bigger and bigger government and surrendering to every liberal social whim of the day.

It was nice while it lasted.

Now the disease of Trumpism has consumed the Republican Party and put the entire conservative movement at risk. It has been hijacked by a bellowing, statist billionaire with poor impulse control and a profoundly superficial understanding of the world. The blazing, white-hot embrace of actual, honest-to-God stupidity has been as contagious as smallpox and as fatal as Ebola. This new creature, shambling toward its eventual political destruction, has reached a point where it supported an accused child molester for U.S. Senate.

Trump's Troll Party puts wild-eyed nationalist, anti-establishment ranting before the tenets of our constitutional Republic. Trump's party insists on ideological uniformity, obedience to the Dear Leader Kim Jong Don, even though Trump's policies are as mutable as his moods are mercurial. Whether you're a Republican from Florida or Vermont or Alabama or Montana, the Trump Party demands every candidate and elected official rigidly adhere to Trump's line, regardless of the regional differences that still mark the country.

All you have to do to stay in the good graces of this new political force is to swear Trump is always right. All you have to do is loathe with the fire of a million suns anyone who levies the slightest criticism of Trump. You must compromise everything you believe to praise and placate him. He is President for Life. Kneel before Zod.

No, thanks. Hard pass.

In 2015 I stood up and spoke out and found myself with a lot of new friends and a lot of new enemies, including a certain frequent tweeter with an exotic dead-animal hairstyle and a notoriously short temper. While no one—including his campaign staff—thought he could win, all the smart guys in the room (myself most certainly included) looked at the numbers and called it wrong.

Mea freaking *culpa*. We didn't factor in Jim Comey's last-minute surprise and a whole lot of help from the Russians. If you thought my biggest worry was that Trump would lose the election, you aren't paying attention.

Everything we Never Trump folks warned you of, including massive, decades-long downstream election losses, is coming. Alienating African Americans and Hispanics beyond redemption? Check. Raising a generation of young voters who are fleeing the GOP in droves? Check. Age-old beefs, juvenile complaints, and ego bruises taking center stage while the world burns? Check. Playing public footsie with white supremacists and neo-Nazis? Check. Blistering pig-ignorance about the economy and the world? Check. Pushing a tax bill that jacks economic inequality into the stratosphere? Check. Shredding the last iota of the GOP's credibility as a party that cares about debt, deficits, and fiscal probity? Check.

Immanuel Kant talks about the "unreal seen" (the phenomenon) and the "unseen real" (the noumenon). Well, the phenomenon of the 2016 election was about Donald and Hillary. It was a hell of a show, a political and moral spectacle, as is the current administration. The noumenon—the deeper, more real answers—come down to where this country, the GOP, and the conservative movement go, and whether we let Donald Trump take us there.

A brief word before we get the party started. In 30 years of politics, I had more scraps and scrapes with Democrats furious with my candidates taking their lunch money and ending their careers than I can tell you. Only rarely did I get a death threat I took seriously. Now, the threats are coming from the Trump base, and they never stop.

The harshest criticism I and many others in the Never Trump movement have experienced comes from the Trump right and its enablers. There is no hatred more pure, no anger more vicious, and no spleen more commonly vented than from the clumsily named anti-anti-Trump segment of the conservative commentariat.

We've been called traitors, RINOs, establishment shills, and betrayers of the conservative cause. Nothing angers them more than being reminded how they dismissed, diminished, and sacrificed the values they once fought for on the altar of Trump and Trumpism. Nothing is guaranteed to trigger a tidal wave of their fury more surely than a critique of their sudden moral and political flexibility after a lifetime of ideological purity and rigor. They're addicted to "But Obama" whataboutism, constant historical revisionism, cherry-picked chest-beating over ephemeral policy wins, and the grunting triumphalism of Trump's accidental victory.

I pity them. They've bet their honor, careers, and reputations on a man and a mob, not on a nation, a Constitution, a system of ideals, and a conservative temperament. I understand their defensive, pissy rage. That anger they feel each time we remind them of the gulf between conservatism and Trumpism is the pain of their souls trying to reenter their bodies.

There are three big reasons I'm writing this book.

First, when I look at what's become of the Republican Party, the conservative movement, and the United States, I feel like I'm visiting some dark, alternate universe. The party of Lincoln and Reagan and the movement of Burke and Buckley have been hijacked by a new strain of politics that is as dangerous as it is ludicrous: nationalist populism. I am a conservative who believes that the law and the Constitution must limit and bound the powers of the state. I believe in the power of law, not the power of the mob. I believe leaders are the servants of the people, not the contrary.

The current direction of Trumpist Republicanism is ideologically and philosophically repulsive to genuine conservatives. The adoption of the authoritarian statism designed by Steve Bannon, Stephen Miller, and their alt-right fellow travelers and embodied by Donald Trump should terrify the right. Instead, they're merrily on board with a lunatic with delusions of godhood, abandoning every principle they ever fought for and replacing them with *L'état, c'est Trump*.

There are a lot of books on the market decrying Trump from the left. Trump and Trumpism need a critique from the right that isn't just a long swoon and a reach for the smelling salts. I've forgotten more about conservative policy and philosophy than Trump will ever know and that the New Establishment has abandoned. Sure, I want to save the Republic from Trump and Trumpism, but I don't mind telling members of my party and movement to fuck themselves on the way there.

I'll admit I am also driven to write this book by a stirring bit of guilt. I've spent a career electing Republicans, defending the conservative movement and philosophy, and fixing the messes made by all-too-human elected officials. I am the guy you call when it's time to run the ads that end the campaign, in part because my skin is thick enough to endure the inevitable screeching and rending of garments that come when it's time to wade into the fight. You call me when you're in the back of the police car outside the shady massage parlor and you have to be on the floor of Congress to vote in 24 hours. I'm not some hand-wringing do-gooder, and if you've fought either by my side or against me, you know I'm down to scrap.

I helped fill that chest freezer full of red meat to throw out to the Republican base when the going got tough, often reducing the entire argument to the tactics of a single election-winning message, a single attack ad, a single oppo drop. And no, Democrats, don't get smug and morally superior; your team has our analogues, and your base loves the mirror-image red meat itself. I'm not here to apologize for leaving your candidates in smoking, radioactive craters.

Yes, I was part of dumbing-down the arguments, creating the Frankenstein monster of the post-2008 base, hoping that we could achieve the big goals of the movement that consisted—we thought—of more than just the Palin-Trump Axis of Idiocy. The old big tent of the GOP was always a rambling circus with evangelicals, foreign policy and national security conservatives, economic freedom warriors, and constitutionalists, all living in relative harmony. We knew the money came from one part of the coalition, the grassroots energy from another, the media heat from yet another. It was imperfect, but in the long march from the 1980s to today, we grew by thousands of elected officials all over the country.

The creature that emerged after Sarah Palin crawled from the political Hellmouth in 2008 kept growing, hungry not for policy victories that realigned the regulatory state, but for liberal tears, atavistic stompy-foot rages, and purity over performance. Her folksy charm became a furious whine, and the base of the party followed that tone.

In work for campaigns, associations, corporate clients with skin in the game of politics, and a constellation of SuperPACs, we fed the monster and trained it. I know how patronizing that sounds, the thought that we could activate and—call it what it is—manipulate voters. Well, we did. As the tools of data, targeting, and analytics improved, we got very, very good at it.

We kept feeding the monster. We rewarded its darkest impulses. We brought it out when the time was right. The portfolio of messages, political rhetoric, and communications venues we built constituted a suite of powerful political tools.

The tools of politics, like all tools, are morally agnostic. A scalpel in the hands of a doctor is a tool. A scalpel in the hands of a serial killer is a horror. Rational adults in both parties used the tools of persuasion, elections, and communications developed by other rational adults inside broad lanes.

Then Trump came along. We lost control of those tools, the party, and the movement. The monster is out of its cage, and its new trainers (both here and in Russia) encourage only its dumbest, darkest, most capricious, cruel, and violent behaviors. This book is, I hope, one of a number of poison darts in the neck of the monster.

The problem in writing this book is time; every day brings some new outrage, scandal, excess, or moment of historic dumbassery by this president. That said, deadlines wait for no man, so I trust you'll pardon this volume for not chronicling every moment of President Death Touch's misrule.

Let's get started.

PART ONE

THE ROAD TO
THIS SHITSHOW

What to Expect When You're Working for Trump

(A Tragedy in Five Acts)

– ACT I –

It all starts out so well.

You're going to join the Trump administration. You're on the team. You're Steve Bannon or Rex Tillerson or Scott Pruitt or John Kelly or Michael Cohen. You're Reince Priebus or Jared Kushner, or even Ivanka. Perhaps you're someone lower in the food chain, and you're going to show those RINOs who's the boss now.

You're a breath of fresh air in a fetid, corrupt hellhole only Donald Trump can reform. Donald Trump loves you, and his 50 million followers love you through the associative magic of Twitter. You bask in his reflected glory. You're on the starting line. Even if you were skeptical at first, you're swept up in the charisma and the adoration. Nothing can go wrong.

Donald Trump couldn't be more complimentary, and the Trump-centric new right media draws you as a towering hero of our times, a giant in the constellation of warrior princes and shield maidens surrounding the savior of America. Even the conservative press who were skeptical of Trump's temperament opine, "Well at least we've got people like X in the administration. He's so solid and so smart. Just imagine what he'll get done."

After all, Trump beat everyone (maybe even you) in the Republican Primary. He beat the hated mainstream media. He beat Hillary Freaking Clinton. Trump doesn't play by the rules, and neither will you. Democratic critics are like mosquitoes.

There's a champagne brunch with your lobbying firm partners the Sunday after you're nominated. Everyone is flush with victory, and you're feeling like everyone is going to do well (that profit-sharing plan still holds while you're on leave from the firm, after all) while doing good for the country. You love this president, and this opportunity, and all the things it's going to do for your career.

You're going to Make America Great Again.

1

VICHY REPUBLICANS

SOME SAY DONALD TRUMP IS THE PRICE THIS NATION IS paying for too many years of partisan bickering and division. Some say 'Merica's forgotten workin' men rose up in a single, inchoate scream of rage at a system that for too long provided them with nothing but empty promises, bad trade deals, and government-subsidized carbs. Some claim it's from a generation weaned on talk radio, Fox News, and the comments sections of a million Tea Party websites. Some say it's a sign of a merciless God testing us to the breaking point.

I still think it's because we didn't let that old gypsy woman vote when she couldn't produce a photo ID back in 2012.

All those reasons fall short of the mark, though, don't they? By now, it should be clear that Trump's election was a sign of the coming Apocalypse, soon to be followed by a rain of blood, seven years of darkness, and a plague of frogs. That may be exaggerating slightly, but we do have a plague of Pepes, the cartoon frog meme that is a favorite symbol of Trump's alt-reich fan base, and there's an odds-on chance that our grandchildren will hear this tale while hunched over guttering fires in the ruins of a radioactive *Mad Max*–style hellscape.

The Trumpian heroic narrative is simple; powerful alpha male warrior descends golden escalator. Forgotten Americans rise, don red helmets. Evil sorceress Hillary is defeated in single combat. Great feasting and rejoicing by the unwashed masses follows. Swamp is drained and all live MAGA ever after.

The truth is, as you might imagine, more prosaic, more horrible, and more human.

The mythology of Donald Trump's rise to the Oval Office is rich in Trump-aggrandizing explanations that ignore the enablers, normalizers, media fellators, ideological arsonists, and moral ciphers who make up Washington's and New York's political and media culture. They're the proximate reasons Trump was able to overcome the field of almost a dozen serious Republicans, and Ben Carson.

No, MAGA-hat fans, you didn't simply rise in your mighty millions and elect The Donald all by your deplorable selves. You had help, much of it from the very elites you so revile. ("Revile" means hate. Sorry. I know you're in an oxy stupor much of the time, so I'll try to move slowly and not use big words.)

Yes, Trump's election shocked the world, but the forces, conditions, and players who enabled and empowered Trump's rise to the Republican nomination and the presidency have been with us all along. They're perfectly explicable, if honestly embarrassing, to the world's longest-running democracy.

For all that Trump voters claim to hate the swamp and the coastal elites who populate it, they owe the reptile-American population a note of thanks. The hated New York, DC, and media elites helped Trump more than they'll admit. I'll leave Russia's role in the 2016 campaign to the many outstanding books on the topic, and to that Mueller fellow.

It was the cable networks (and no, not just Fox), the elite media, inert major donors, a monied horde of lobbyists, and the professional conservative activists who ditched principle for revenue, clicks, ratings, and transitory influence. They enabled, empowered, and elected Trump and continue to do so with their rolling coverage of his every presidential distraction strategy.

Without a particular confluence of their attention, resources, and focus, the Trump clown show would have been like every other kooky email chain forwarded by your mom or the contents of some narrow-gauge but high-cray Facebook group like Tea Party Patriots Against the Soros Moon Base. (I know you're about to search Facebook for TPPASM. The question isn't whether that's a real group. The telling factor is that in this era you think it *could* be.)

The swamp played its role and does to this day; Washington's culture is nothing if not resilient, adaptable, and resistant to change. I lived in it for years and watched it grind down the most idealistic people into the venal, smug, insular elites America loves to loathe. Washington is the drug-resistant syphilis of political climates, largely impervious to treatment and highly contagious. Donald Trump may have infected Washington with his own nationalist STD, but Washington returned the favor.

In early 2015 the DC political class of lobbyists, staffers, associations, think tanks, and the rest of the Washington ecosystem viewed Donald Trump as a political impossibility. He was the vulgar clown prancing and bellowing on the national stage, but never for a moment someone they could take seriously. The Old Order money liked Jeb Bush. The optimists liked Marco Rubio, the purists Ted Cruz. The 348 GOP candidates on the campaign trail, on the early debate stages, in the political scrum that was the 2016 GOP primary were almost all experienced, successful, and well-staffed. They were, by and large, Serious People. It was the quality of that divided field that let the political version of Gresham's law sweep Trump into a position where Washington and national Republicans made the most consequential and destructive compromises in modern political history.

As the election progressed, it took an array of insiders from the GOP and the conservative movement to legitimize and normalize Trump for the Republican base voter beyond the howling edge of the Fox viewership. These men and women were Vichy Republicans, eager to shred their principles for a chance to touch the fringe of Trump's golden wig, eager to bask in the celebrity glow of his spray tan.

Some Vichy Hall of Famers aren't people you might directly associate with the Old Guard, Locust Valley Lockjaw Republican elite. Oh, no indeed.

Many were the purest of the Purity Posse. You know, the "we'd-rather-have-a-pure-minority-than-a-squishy-majority" types.

These were conservative stalwarts dedicated to purging the RINOs, the impure, the accommodationists, the compromisers, and anyone who would vary from the Limbaughian-Levinist doctrine. (I made that up, but you can imagine seeing it in a history book about some schism in early socialist thought.) The people in Washington's elite conservative political circles who looked down on Republicans who tried actually to govern and to live in the real world of political give-and-take were some of the first to let go of their alleged principles when Trump came calling. His skill at causing others to abase and destroy their reputation is peerless.

There's so much blame to go around, it's hard to know where to start, but the Vichy Republicans needed one man in a key position to become their Marshal Pétain. They needed one man to ensure the Trump takeover of the GOP, no matter the cost. They found him in the wee form of Reince Priebus.

REINCE PRIEBUS

Historians will recognize Reince Priebus as the man who could have killed the Trump virus early. Instead, he incubated it. He kept feeding it nutrients when he should have been killing it with bleach and hot, cleansing fire.

Reince Priebus is a man so inoffensive, so meek, so self-effacing, and seemingly hammered most of the time that his judgment on Trump led to a series of mistakes, missteps, capitulations, pratfalls, and bad reads of the political terrain that legitimized Trump for far too many mainstream Republicans. Mr. Wisconsin Nice was ultimately the Marshal Pétain of the GOP.

Not long after Trump entered the race, Priebus feared Trump would bolt the party, run as an independent, and wreck the GOP's chances against Hillary Clinton. He absurdly believed that if he convinced Trump to sign a GOP loyalty pledge, Trump would support the party after he lost the primary and that the oath would moderate some of Red Hat Don's more grotesque excesses.

So Priebus went to Trump Tower with a cheesy parchment that looked like it was extracted from a bin of discount award certificates at Office Depot and run through a knockoff-brand inkjet printer and had Trump sign it. The chairman of the party of Lincoln got rolled like a rube off the cheap bus to Atlantic City on a Friday night. What Reince saw as a solemn oath, Trump saw as a reality-TV stunt.

I know what you're thinking. Had Reince been recently thawed from a cryogenic chamber, deep in the Earth? Was he part of some religious cult that forbids television? Could he not read? How could anyone have missed Donald Trump's famous disregard for contracts, agreements, debts, obligations, commitments, payment schedules, and marital vows? How could anyone not suffering from a diet of lead paint chips and head trauma possibly believe that one gimcrack piece of paper would constrain Trump in any way at all?

Well, Reince Priebus did, and party tribalism, Russian information warfare, and Hillary Clinton's inept campaigning took it from there. He was too trapped in the ichor of Trump's smarmy world to escape it. The fixed smile and dead eyes Reince showed at every event weren't an affirmation of his decision; they were a cry for help. Reince kept playing Tina to Trump's Ike, knowing Trump had played him and knowing Trump loathed him.

I remember seeing Priebus at one of the last of the 2016 primary debates in Miami. I took my son into the spin room to watch the festivities, and there he was: a rictus grin, a thousand-yard stare, the certain knowledge that Trump was going to be the nominee and he'd done nothing to stop it.

Could he have stopped it? Yes, at four or five different inflection points. Did he want to? Perhaps.

Perhaps a strong chairman with a clear vision for the future of the party could have. But here's a dirty little secret of national political party chairs: they generally suck at their jobs, and Reince fell under even that low bar. In the era of SuperPACs, powerful House, Senate, and governors' committees, and independent expenditures, their role has become disintermediated and minimized. They're largely a conduit to sluice money around the campaign finance system. There was a reason I used to joke that I wanted Debbie Wasserman Schultz to be Democratic National Committee head for 1,000 years, and it wasn't because I found her to be politically intimidating or effective.

Few party chairs leave a meaningful legacy, though, for good or ill. Reince, however, will be remembered as the man who sold the GOP to Trump on the cheap. To his ironic credit, Priebus had ordered the infamous post-2012 Republican autopsy report, which called on the GOP to modernize, approach Hispanic voters differently, and reform itself.

Reince was later briefly "rewarded" by being given the thankless position of White House chief of staff. To date, the shortest-serving chief of staff in modern times, he survived less than six months of grueling, internecine battles for which he was entirely overmatched. By the end, between Donald Trump's Twitter sprees, Steve Bannon's private and public warfare with him, Jared and Ivanka's class disdain, and an unmanageable White House, Reince was utterly broken.

He tried to recruit a cadre of RNC operatives to the White House and to impose a paper flow and scheduling system on President Ungovernable. That worked out about as well as expected; the handful of RNC aides, congressional staffers, and Washington hands he brought in were shredded, ignored, and rolled over by the Chaos President. They were immediately the subject of endless leak campaigns to Breitbart and alt-right bloggers clinging to Trump's world like pasty white lampreys.[1] Priebus wasn't Patient Zero for the Everything Trump Touches Dies effect, but he was the first of the DC political folks to go. For the Washington establishment, losing Reince hardly seemed like a loss at all; he'd been unable to deliver the certainty, structure, and compliance they desired. It was a sign in the age of Trump of Washington's along-for-the-ride powerlessness that he sank without a trace and to few signs of regret from the people who counted on him to impose sanity on the Bedlam of 1600 Pennsylvania.

After departing the White House, Priebus returned to his law firm, started cooperating with the Mueller investigation, and slowly, painfully tried to reframe history. The Kenosha Ninja tried to cast himself as the hero of the piece, as all men do in retellings of their story. "No president has ever had to deal with so much so fast: a special counsel and an investigation into Russia and then subpoenas immediately, the media insanity—not to mention we were pushing out executive orders at record pace and trying to repeal and replace Obamacare right out of the gate," he said.[2]

Oh, is *that* what it was, Reince? Self-delusion runs deep, and the desire to rewrite history is always with public men and women. Perhaps—and work with me here—Reince might have had a scintilla of self-awareness and a little self-deprecating appreciation for the fact that Donald Trump's entire portfolio of problems weren't some externality or deus ex swamp. Donald Trump created them, full stop.

The vital importance of a White House chief of staff who can handle the pressure, handle the principal, and handle the politics has never been clearer. If Priebus had come to this job in the ranks of the very best chiefs of staff in the past hundred years—Andy Card, Leon Panetta, Jim Baker—it could have been a different story.

However, Priebus was too weak to do the job and too blinded to know that the mistake he made at the beginning would destroy his career and reputation. His fellow Wisconsinite Charlie Sykes put it best: "I see him as kind of a tragic figure. What began as a matter of duty on his part—the decision to go all-in on Trump—ended with this scorchingly obscene humiliation. It's sad, but it's the result of choices he made. It's not like he wasn't warned."[3]

PAUL RYAN

Paul Ryan's enabling of Donald Trump is a tragedy for conservatives in three acts. Ryan is a genuinely bright, curious, thoughtful conservative of the Jack Kemp school. He was the end product of three generations of increasingly sharp conservatives who emerged from the long march to broad national Republican power. Ryan was a man who had the conservative movement wired into his very DNA and could articulate the principles of limited government, personal responsibility, fiscal discipline, balanced budgets, and strong national defense without the ugly, grating edge of a Newt Gingrich. He could fight and win legislative battles without the doofy passivity of a Dennis Hastert or a Bob Michael.

After rising to Speaker of the House, Ryan was selected in 2012 to serve as Mitt Romney's running mate. The reaction in the conservative firmament was beyond rapturous. In what had to be the most insanely subspecialized example of Rule 34, Ryan was even the subject of erotic fanfic by conservative women. "My desires are unconventional . . . mostly reducing marginal tax rates."

Paul Ryan was like a man created in a laboratory to sell conservatism and the Republican Party to the American people in the post-Obama era. Then he embraced and enabled Donald Trump.

I'll grant you, Ryan's love wasn't as slobbering and over the top as many displayed. While he declined to endorse Trump with the usual ring- and ass-kissing demanded of others, he also never took steps as one of the most senior leaders in the party to signal to his caucus and to Republicans across the nation that Trump was as dangerous to the Republican Party as Ryan privately believed.

Trump didn't like Ryan for failing to display the level of obsequious ass-kissing of, say, a Ted Cruz. Ryan didn't dislike Trump enough to choke him out. Ryan assumed Hillary Clinton would win, and he didn't want to inflame the restive Republican base any more than the talk radio screamers and online arsonists were about to do in the wake of the 2016 election. This was Ryan's most consequential mistake.

When the infamous *Access Hollywood* "pussy grabber" story broke, Ryan put on a hangdog expression and said, "I am sickened by what I heard today. Women are to be championed and revered, not objectified. I hope Mr. Trump treats this situation with the seriousness it deserves and works to demonstrate to the country that he has greater respect for women than this clip suggests."[4]

When I read that, I could hear my grandmother's honey-dripping southern voice in my head saying, "Oh. Bless your heart." Ryan then disinvited Trump from a Wisconsin Republican Party event and said he'd no longer defend Trump or campaign for him after the statements. I'm sure that stung a man incapable of feeling guilt or remorse of any kind. As we'll discuss later, this was one of the ur-moments of the Ryan strategy of "furrowed brows and deep concern."

By then the die was cast. Ryan had let Trump become so powerful in the Republican caucus that his fourth-quarter beefing had little impact. One close advisor to the Speaker told me that Ryan had played the game mainly to keep his restive, fractured caucus in line. That's not the whole story, though.

Ryan wanted something, and he sacrificed his reputation to get it. More than life itself, Paul Ryan wanted a massive corporate tax cut and a sweeping set of entitlement reforms. His calculation had little to do with Trump, and everything to do with those two dreams. Like many men who see only one path to historical consequence, the Devil knows the one thing they desire above all else. The idea that Trump was the only way he'd achieve his goals corrupted Paul Ryan. The Speaker passed his tax bill, only to discover that it wasn't the economic or political miracle he had imagined.

The tax bill, combined with the ludicrously overblown 2018 budget, left Ryan lost and clearly miserable. Both were masterworks of gigantic government giveaways, unfunded spending, massive debt and deficits, and a catalogue of crony capitalist freebies that would have Hayek spinning in his grave. He had foolishly allowed Devin Nunes to manipulate the probe of Russian interference into the U.S. elections into a Fox News ratings machine. A Ryan aide told me that he had allowed Nunes to run buck wild to keep the small but vocal Trumphadi caucus in line. He thought it was a valuable steam valve to relieve political pressure, but it was really a Get Out of Jail Free card for Trump and his associates hip deep in Russian influence.

It's hard to reconcile the Paul Ryan who rose through the conservative and Republican ranks with the Paul Ryan who let Trump run rampant. He'll have plenty of time in his retirement to contemplate his existential angst over what he enabled and how he allowed Donald

Trump to destroy the Republican Party and the conservative principles he swore to protect.

TED CRUZ

Ah, Ted Cruz. Long a poster boy for the Purity Posse, Cruz was the
alpha-dork Senate Conservatives Fund Texan elected in the wake of
2012. He came into the 2016 race with all the conservative purist cred
in the world. He was the darling of the Mercer money clan, had talk
radio singing hosannas on how he was the leader of a bold conservative tomorrow. All those qualities were in inverse proportion to his,
um, less obvious personal and physical charms.

More than almost any other member of the 2016 field, Ted Cruz
helped normalize Trump, burning his credibility to a toasty crisp.
Cruz, who would later hear Trump accuse his father of complicity
in the assassination of John F. Kennedy and stood meekly as Trump
insulted Cruz's wife. He told Fox News, "I like Donald Trump. I think
he's terrific, I think he's brash, I think he speaks the truth." Ted even
lost the support of his longtime sugar daddy, Robert Mercer, and nod-
ded politely through it all. In 30 years of political life, I have never seen
a politician engage in acts of greater self-abnegation and humiliation.

"Many of the Republican candidates have gone out of their way to
take a two-by-four to Donald Trump. I think that's a mistake," Cruz
told Tim Alberta of Politico.[5] Now, Ted is a bright guy. There's no
question he's much, much smarter than the average bear. However,
like quite a few smart people, Cruz has a massive blind spot when it
comes to playground bullies, which I'm sure has obtained for the entirety of his life. Trump saw him from the jump as a mark.

The Tragedy of Ted Cruz sounds like a Marlowe play. The Faus-
tian bargain Cruz made in his efforts to win over Trump voters has
reduced him from Republican Party rock star to something akin to a
Trump World house pet: tolerated, occasionally praised, but mostly
kept out of sight lest he soils the carpets. Ever ambitious and taken
with his own perceived cleverness, Cruz still clings to two rather obvi-

ous dreams. The first is that of every man or woman who warms a seat in the Senate: the White House. The argument there is that he can be the thinking man's Trump, a follow-on that smoothes the rough edges of nationalist populism and leads the nation into his glorious vision. His ambitions are boundless and obvious.

The other desire Cruz allies whisper is that he's the logical choice for Trump's next Supreme Court pick. However, if Cruz for one moment believes President Trump is going to put the son of the man who killed JFK on the Supreme Court, he's got another thing coming. That's held for Anthony Scaramucci.

CHRIS CHRISTIE

Chris Christie started political life as the great, pasty-white hope of the *Acela* Republicans. A moderate but tough-minded, shit-talking Republican with a stellar record as a prosecutor won the governor's race in Blue Jersey, and the conservative world cheered. He rocked the same kind of confrontational swagger and sounded like his tough-talking counterpart across the Hudson, my old boss Rudy Giuliani, though as the heaviest presidential candidate since William Howard Taft, Christie looked like Giuliani ate another Giuliani.

It soon became clear that Christie's role wasn't to run a campaign for the presidency but to become Donald Trump's hit-manatee. His greatest moments of notoriety in an otherwise featureless campaign came during the debates, where Christie heaved his massive snark at Marco Rubio and others, then stood like a well-fed dog, to bask in Trump's approval.

A former chairman of the Republican Governors' Association, Christie brought to the table more credibility than many. He helped normalize Trump, and as a Republican who won in a deep-blue state like New Jersey he could make the case that Trump could win there, and in the Northeast.

In February 2016 Christie abandoned his race for the White House and made public what had been obvious: he was in the tank for

Trump all along. All Christie's work for Trump ended as all sacrifices to Umber Moloch do; with humiliation and abandonment. He was never seriously considered for his dream job: attorney general of the United States. After an enthusiastic endorsement from Christie at an airport hangar rally, the most humiliating hot-mic moment imaginable gave Christie a preview of his coming irrelevance. When Christie finished his sweaty, bellowing intro, Trump leaned in and said, "Go get in the plane. Go home."[6]

After torpedoing Marco and endorsing Trump, Governor Shinebox was dissed and dismissed by Trump and savaged inside Trump's world by both Steve Bannon and Jared Kushner.

Christie is a lesson about just how little loyalty Trump displays and how little concern he has for the deadly political poison associating with him represents. The governor who helped normalize Trump and wreck his primary opponents ended his tenure in New Jersey with approval numbers approaching the single digits and a political career deader than that thing Trump calls his hair.

NEWT GINGRICH

Newt Gingrich, a man with a low tolerance for those he considers his intellectual inferiors (which is to say, everyone), was one of the grandest tigers in the conservative jungle. The architect of the famous Contract with America and generalissimo of the 1994 House takeover, Gingrich was a singular figure in the Republican rise to national power and a keeper of the holy tablets of economic conservatism. Without Gingrich, it's arguable there would have been no Tea Party. Without Gingrich, the Fox News style of base-only messaging wouldn't have become the defining style of the conservative caucus in the House. Gingrich helped usher in a broad, Republican-leaning fundraising establishment on K Street and helped popularize and professionalize a constellation of think tanks, associations, and consultants who extended the Republican gains of 1994.

Gingrich was a policy entrepreneur from the start, writing book after book of techno-optimistic conservative ideas. He was and is a frequent talking head on the Fox News channel, reaching millions. I remember reading his *Window of Opportunity* in the summer of 1984, wowed by his embrace of high technology, space travel, and industry and his leveraging America's edge in the sciences to win the battle against state tyranny as embodied in the Soviet Union. Good times.

He had become a kind of Republican éminence grise, seen everywhere and with a hand in a hundred political pies. He was always the smartest guy in the room, even if it was only in his head, and he had a constant, persistent dedication to his own hustle and branding.

When it came to Trump, Gingrich started twerking faster than a five-buck stripper. He put his considerable conservative credibility and media skills to work Trumpsplaining how Donald's apostasies to conservative policy and principle were *just* fine. His tireless defense of Trump left eyes rolling among those who knew him. As far as ideologies go, the men had nothing in common. Gingrich had one; Trump didn't. The only similarity in the two men was a chain of broken wedding vows and bitter ex-wives.

Newt always had his detractors, and he's blown it more than a few times by outplaying his coverage on issues like the Clinton impeachment, but he was a marquee conservative saying Donald Trump was one of us. To the Fox News demo and Republican base voters (but I repeat myself), this was a solid gold endorsement. He's remained all-in, writing a book called *Understanding Trump* (no, it's not a pop-up book) and becoming one of the leading voices supporting Trump on *l'affaire russe*.

Why did Newt do it? It's a mystery why he walked away from every stated conservative belief for Trump, but he must have known he was the longest of long shots for the vice presidency, even though his allies floated the prospect to a few credulous reporters. He earned his keep, however, scoring the ambassadorship to the Holy See for his wife, making her the first Vulcan American to hold the post.

Who knows? Perhaps Newt's lifelong ambition to be governor-general of the American Moon Base will finally come true.[7] He's got to rebuild his reputation somewhere.

ROGER AILES AND RUPERT MURDOCH

Roger Ailes died before he knew what he had wrought. His control of the Fox network was the single most powerful weapon in Trump's media arsenal and remains so today, even after his death. Rupert Murdoch, the canniest media mogul of our time, wasn't about to get in the way of the billion-dollar-a-year profit center Roger had built.

The political moment in which we find ourselves is a product of Roger Ailes. The overt echoes of Nixon's 1968 campaign and administration are crisp and constant. Ailes understood the feelings of a middle class beset by change and built campaigns and messages to stoke the anxiety, outrage, and passions of an audience that wasn't part of the coastal media, political, and economic elite. During Nixon's 1968 campaign Ailes realized the political utility of casting the news media as the enemy of the American people and all the not-so-subtle codings embedded in that attack.

Roger's genius for television was simply unrivaled. He was a rare combination of political and media skill, deeply understood America's cultural divides, and intuitively sensed the rising social primacy of entertainment in our politics. It was Ailes who helped reshape Nixon's disastrous 1960 television image of sweaty weirdo to 1968's image of feisty scrapper for the Forgotten American. Ailes didn't do it with policy; he did with the power of television.

It's impossible to overstate the power of Ailes in shaping the conservative media ecosystem. He wasn't just a singular genius in creating television; he understood it had replaced many of the other institutions that once mediated American politics. Roger wasn't the first warrior in the long-running conservative enterprise to push back on the perception of a hostile, liberal media, but he was by any standard its most successful general.[8] He found a market that was underserved and created a product that became a multibillion-dollar powerhouse on our political landscape.

Trump and Fox weren't allies at the start of the campaign. Rupert Murdoch infamously viewed Trump as nothing more than fodder for his tabloid media operations, like the *New York Post*, calling him a "phony" and later "a fucking idiot."[9] (Fact check: true.) After Trump's infamous attack on Senator John McCain's war record, Murdoch tweeted, "When is Donald Trump going to stop embarrassing his friends, let alone the whole country?"[10]

CNN journalist Tom Kludt called them "frenemies with benefits" and noted, "In Murdoch, Trump might see the man he aspires to be; mogul, patriarch of a closely held family empire, dinner party-host to the world's elite."[11]

Murdoch hit Trump hard, and Ailes rose to the defense of the network's Megyn Kelly when Trump famously attacked her for bleeding from her . . . wherever.[12] Murdoch touted support for Cruz, Rubio, Bush, and Carson in tweets in 2015, but to no avail. Even if Murdoch and Ailes had wanted to elect a different Republican, by late 2015 it was clear that the Fox audience was all in, and the emergent property of all pro-Trump voters was hatred and abandonment of anyone or anything in his way.

Ailes and Murdoch weren't about to compromise shareholder value for something as inconsequential as the White House. They rode the wave, deciding to profit from the nation's loss. The audience of the largest cable news network in the nation generated more than $1 billion in profit in 2016, and nothing was going to stand in the way of that.

Once Fox was put in service to Trump, the game was over for the other Republican candidates. The House That Rupert Built would under Ailes and his successors become Trump TV, providing him with instant, fawning coverage, 24/7 live shots, and a well-watched evening lineup that shouted itself hoarse in support of The Donald. It was an in-kind political contribution worth billions. Who cared whether they believed a word of it? Their audience took it, as the kids say, both seriously and literally.

It's a tautological question as to whether the Fox audience of today coalesced around Trump's political momentum or the political momentum of Trump coalesced the Fox audience. In the end, the leadership of the network was stuck in a prison with a version of the Watchmen's Rorschach: "I'm not trapped in here with you. You're trapped in here with me."

Before his death, Ailes was forced out of Fox News for a decades-long, endemic pattern of sexual harassment, an early play in the #MeToo movement. The legal mess is a story in and of itself, but Ailes managed to leave behind a cadre of key deputies who continue the status quo at the network.[13] That status quo is all Trump, all the time.

MIKE PENCE

For a man who was once referred to as saying Donald Trump would be unacceptable as president, Mike Pence came around to Esoteric Trumpism in a big way.[14]

Pence was a safety blanket for Christian conservatives, as far right as any governor has ever been, and for Indiana, it worked. Long a staple of the conservative movement, he combined generic central-casting politician looks, rigid ideological purity across the board, and the personality of a basket of wet laundry. For all the ideological boxes he checked, Mike Pence lacked even a politician's contrived passion when it came to the fieriest debates.

A reliable back-bencher for his first few years in the House, he served from 1988 until 2011, rising to lead the GOP conference. He made friends, quietly. He just . . . was. A quick campaign for governor of Indiana in 2012 and easy reelection in 2016 meant Pence was a man people talked about because he'd punched every résumé ticket in order, but not as some shooting star in the GOP world. Sure, Pence signed the most strict abortion law in the country, as well as the controversial and later-reversed Religious Freedom Restoration Act, but on one was beating down his door to run for national office. Pence is also part of the New Reefer Madness crowd, a strict drug warrior who fought to take away judicial discretion in drug sentencing in cases in Indiana. Calling Pence a stern, Daddy Party conservative barely scratches the surface.

And yet, being a man who wears his moral qualifications on his sleeve—he famously will not spend time alone with a woman other than his wife, even in a professional setting—Pence found himself lured into the Trump campaign's orbit by none other than Paul Manafort. How did one of the slimiest creatures in the DC Swamp earn the God Squad seal of approval and win over Mike Pence as Donald Trump's running mate?

After a typical Trump reality-TV selection process—Will Chris Christie get a rose? Will Rudy stay on the Island? Will feisty Newt Gingrich flip over a table?—Manafort's machinations played out, leaving Pence the last man standing. There was more a sense of resignation and inevitability than joy.

In just two paragraphs of the *New York Times* coverage of the Pence selection the reporters managed to use the words "workmanlike," "sturdy," "dependable," and "standard."[15] It was a sign that the First Showman was going to be the star of the show and Pence would be the understudy relegated to Midwestern dinner theater.

Pence spoke fluent, perfect conservative like a native because he was one. Trump would always be the fat, loud, crass American tourist bellowing, "co-mo say dee-chay gluteno free-o?" Presidency or not, he will never truly understand the signals and signifiers of the conservative movement. In contrast, Pence was a relief to evangelicals, social conservatives, and Washington insiders. He was . . . safe.

Pence's hopes of being a true star in the Trump White House were quickly dashed. His utility extended to breaking ties in the U.S. Senate and the usual VP duties of weddings, campaign appearances, and funerals. Because of Trump's enormous, delicate ego, Pence has been forced to recalibrate the role of vice president. I missed the part in Article II, Section 1 of the Constitution about kissing the president's ass 24/7, but apparently Pence found it.

CPAC

If you're not a conservative, it will be hard to understand just how important the American Conservative Union and the Conservative Political Action Committee annual conference was to the movement. I use the term "was" advisedly, because as soon as the CPAC leadership got a hit of Trumpism, it deviated from literally every value it had worked for over the long march and embraced him with vigor.

Let me give you a quick and dirty look at CPAC before we go too much further. A conference of conservatives may sound to the layperson like some boring God Squad event where middle-aged dudes in suits sit in seminars about the benefits of entitlement reform on long-term sovereign debt loads. Nothing could be further from the truth.

Lest any of you think that conservatives believe in no sex before or outside of marriage, CPAC is a place where young conservatives go to engage in some mindless, consequence-free fucking. People there are rather more likely to be swiping on Tinder than reading *National Review*. It's a place where the m4m Craigslist ads suddenly pop with lines like "Clean-cut free-market conservative seeks dirty liberal bear." It's the Rumspringa for Hillsdale students, Young Republicans, College Republicans, and conservative activists from across the nation.

CPAC and the ACU were always in a scramble for the unicorn intersection of American politics and celebrity. They were always seeking celebrity special guests that could draw a crowd. Arnold Schwarzenegger was about the pinnacle of celebrity at the conference until CPAC's majordomo Matt Schlapp decided to bring Trump in 2011. It was both a preview of Trump's campaign to come and an early warning signal of the deathwatch of the GOP.[16] Trump combined a few things that the CPAC audience loved: fuck-you swagger, a confrontational attitude, and an entertaining show.

I'm sure the first outing was a win-win for the host of a popular reality-TV game show and the ACU. He was a good draw, but no one thought he was really part of the conservative movement. At the grassroots, this was an era when the Ron Paul CPAC machine could still stack a straw poll, and when the conservative movement was flush with the 2010 victory.

When Trump returned in 2013, he and Sarah Palin had longer speaking times and better slots on the schedule than Paul Ryan, Marco Rubio, or Rand Paul, all of whom were at the time considered the future of the GOP.[17] It was another missed signal that the entertainment wing of the GOP was going to do everything it could to put crowd-pleasing yahoos front-and-center at CPAC's annual conclave.

The conservative apparatus was infected with Trumpism for a host of reasons, but in a blistering essay in March 2016, Matt Cover hit the essential blunder of the entertainment wing and the CPAC conservatives right on the head:

> To aid their growing grassroots campaign, [conservative] Movement leaders began inviting Donald Trump into the fold, giving him prime speaking slots at the Conservative Political Action Conference (CPAC) and other grassroots events. They hoped to leverage Trump's celebrity and rhetorical skill to help push their message into the broader media environment. It would prove a disastrous blunder.
>
> Trump, ever the narcissist and self-promoter, stole the Movement's intra-party revolution away from Cruz and his Washington allies. Trump's superior celebrity and mastery of modern media have allowed him to seize on the ignorance created by the Movement's phony "anti-Establishment" campaign.
>
> He has, with frightening skill, channeled the misplaced frustration and mistrust carefully sown over the past seven years by Movement organizations and entertainers.[18]

The rest of the professional conservative establishment, from Grover Norquist's Americans for Tax Reform to the Heritage Foundation, group after group, abandoned any pretense of adhering to their formerly held beliefs and became cheerleaders for Trump.[19] Did some see this as an uncomfortable bow to the inevitable? Surely. The small-dollar donors to these groups were always more fringe and less sophisticated than their Washington leadership. They watched the Fox coverage, saw their social media landscape, and decided that embracing Trump and nationalist populism would, at the least, let them live to fight another day.

LOBBYISTS

It must be the broad masochistic streak among lobbyists that keeps legions of dominatrices in business in Washington, DC. For all their disdain of Trump as a clown, a joke, and a human train wreck, they sat quietly at first as he dumped his vitriol on them.

At the beginning of the 2016 election campaign most of them expected a Hillary win, and even Republicans didn't see that outcome as the end of the world. Hillary was explicable. She was transactional. She was, in short, their dream date. At a minimum, they could scare the hell out of their clients with Hillary, leading to higher fees and bigger battles. They could work around (or even quietly with) Hillary, monetizing the threat she posed to their clients, dragging out legislative fights year after profitable year.

As Trump's ego, shallow understanding of the world as it exists beyond the *Fox & Friends* bubble, and obvious, full-frontal venality became clear, they sensed that if Trump did make it to the Oval Office, it would be a golden age on K Street. The man was crony capitalism in human form and subject to the kind of flattery in which the lobbying community excels.

If you've spent much time around lobbyists, you know the spiel: "Why, yes, Donald! You are the tallest, most handsome, smartest man in the room, and this room on your beautiful Trump-branded property (which I will use for all future meetings) is the classiest and most elegant room I've ever seen. Is that real gold? So luxurious! Sex with my wife? Feel free!" In short, they recognized that Trump might be a master con man, but his tells, blind spots, ego needs, and vanity could put them in the driver's seat.

So as much as Trump insulted and demeaned Washington's Republican swamp dwellers and promised to crush their lives and incomes, these masters of passive-aggressive behavior bowed meekly and slipped their necks into the leash the moment he was nominated. They were "topping from the bottom" with Trump, but he didn't understand how they played him and still doesn't.

This transition wasn't as difficult for the lobbying community as you might think. Lobbyists have seen the ebb and flow of political power in DC for generations and switched smoothly when a majority party becomes a minority party, or even when the ideological temperature warms or cools. They're supposed to do this; their job is to advocate for their clients with the people in power.

Many of them do have ideological foundations and long-term party affiliation, but it was understandable, if a little frustrating, to see people who months before were shoveling money to Hillary or Jeb or Marco or Ted suddenly become born again Trumpers, their bespoke MAGA hats resting uncomfortably on their $400 haircuts. With majorities in the House and the Senate, they saw that the path to success was to strap on the rhetorical and financial knee pads and worship at the foot of the Orange One.

These people are a million miles from the lives and experiences of the average Trump voter, and they're precisely the kind of lifelong politicians and corrupt insiders whom residents of Trump Nation blame for everything from illegal immigration to Obamacare to the return of Zima. The DC types suddenly hoisting overpriced cocktails in the Trump Hotel hadn't changed their views; they'd just raised a flag of convenience with a golden T in its center.

Could they have turned their considerable resources and energies to defeating Trump? Absolutely. Their clients are the lifeblood of major donor money and command many billions. They could have darkened the sky with the ashes of the Trump campaign in the early primary if they'd chosen to do so.

Instead, they advised their clients in corporate America to hold their fire. They sat quietly and watched the world burn.

MAJOR DONORS

The major donor community too could have stopped Donald Trump in 2015. It would have cost them almost nothing. If they'd chosen to hammer Trump with ads, early and often, the spring primary elections of 2016 might have looked a lot different.

Instead, they played the dumbest game of political calculus I've ever seen. I witnessed this line of thinking iterated among a dozen megadonor conversations and email chains within days of Trump's descent down the gold-plated escalator in Trump Tower. It went something like this:

"Well, I'm with Jeb now, but we're going to wait to hit Trump until he takes out Marco."

"Well, I'm with Marco, but we're going to wait until he takes out Jeb and Ted."

"Well, I'm with Ted now, but if we attack Trump we're really attacking the voters Ted needs to beat Marco."

On and on it went, reductive as hell and dumber than dirt. Most legitimately believed Trump would self-destruct and their chosen candidate would rise. In fairness, we all thought Trump's self-destructive tendencies would end him. But in my case, I knew he needed a push off the ledge. Sadly, I'm not a billionaire (I know, right? It's a source of constant frustration) and couldn't fund a national ad effort against Trump.

The people who could have stopped him elected to sit on their hands.

Some donors worried that Trump would target them personally. Some worried their brands or businesses would suffer when a man with tens of millions of rabid Twitter followers turned his ire on them with his weapon of choice: ragetweets.

They were right about that, but for the wrong reasons. His social media attacks were powerful but ultimately inconsequential to corporate bottom lines. They also thought that if they poked the Orange Bear he'd become so enraged that he'd outspend their candidates by putting his own money in the race. That's where they got it really, really wrong.

There has always been a single, central signifier in the myth of Donald Trump, whether as a developer, a casino operator, a reality-TV host, a branding pitchman, or a presidential candidate: the idea that Trump is wealthy to the tune of his oft-claimed $10 billion. His branding depended on it, no matter how many Not Our Kind, Dear and Not Quite Our Class signals his vulgar affect sent to people with real money.

Everyone believed it. Hell, even I believed it. Combined with Trump's utter lack of transparency regarding his fantasy finances and his refusal to release his tax returns, even wealthy megadonors had little to go on. *Forbes* was skeptical, calling out Trump's financial bullshitting, but political professionals neglected to perform due diligence and simply assumed he could bring serious cash to the game.

By August 2015 I was working to convince major donors of Trump's long-term, existential threat to the country and the party. We thought he would be a destructive force and likely throw the race to Hillary Clinton.

One moment from that period sticks with me as a turning point in my thinking about Trump's money: a major Wall Street donor—a hedge fund manager who had survived 2008, 2000, and 1987 looking like a genius—laughed when I told him we'd need to mount a serious and fully funded effort to take on Trump if he chose to self-fund.

My friend scoffed at the very idea that Trump was worth even a quarter of the mythical $10 billion, much less that he was liquid to the tune of more than $200 million. "He's not a billionaire. I'm a billionaire. He's a clown living on credit."

However, in a year of voter disenchantment and outsider cachet, the mythic tales of Trump's business prowess and his alleged wealth deeply impressed his fans and even convinced many Republican megadonors that Trump was an unalloyed business success, a man of global financial consequence uncorrupted by the venal horrors of the campaign finance system.

His claim to being self-funding was a home run in campaign focus groups. By late 2015, everyone in politics had heard a variation of this message a hundred times in focus group interviews and on social media: "Mr. Trump isn't a politician. He's rich, and no one owns him." Because 35% of the GOP believed the marketing of the Trump brand (amplified by America's addiction to reality television), the power of Trump's alleged billions cast a long political shadow.

The specter of Trump's money haunted the other presidential candidates in the Gang of Seventeen, who largely and until far too late pulled their punches, lest he unleash a media firestorm paid for from his pocket. That fear of Trump's resources sent Reince Priebus scurrying like a terrified Hobbit to the Barad-dûr of the Trump empire to beg the Orange Lord to sign a pledge that he wouldn't run as a third-party candidate. The thought that Trump could easily fund a third-party bid was a cheap form of political blackmail against the donors and the candidates, and it worked. It was a classic Trump con.

Aside from a few newsworthy catches like Sheldon Adelson, Trump the candidate never managed to convince the donor class that he should have their support. After his election, of course, the money rolled in, and the donors who despised and mocked Trump were quick to write checks to the inaugural committee.

Almost to a man, they loathe Trump with gusto. I went back to review a memo I sent to donors in July 2015. In it, I warned, "We can spend a few million now to stop Trump, tens of millions if we wait until the Fall of 2015 or hundreds of millions in the Spring of 2016 . . . or just wait until he destroys the GOP and [we will spend] several billion to rebuild our party brand and to undo the damage a generation of far-left governance will cause. Your call." When I saw a six-figure donation to the Trump Inaugural Committee from a major donor with a robust dislike of Trump, I tweaked him in a playful email with a copy of that memo attached.

His four-word response by text message was "Yeah. Fuck me, right?"

Men like my friend aren't uncommon in the major donor community. Some are so wealthy that Trump's actual net worth was a rounding error to them, but they weren't as a rule bold enough to put their money on the line to defeat him. A few still comfort themselves with the knowledge that the tax bill will pad their bottom lines nicely. Some hope that someday, somehow he'll stop tweeting and won't get us into a nuclear war.

Many still quietly regret their inaction. Those who don't yet, will.

THE REPUBLICAN CONSULTING CLASS

As a Republican consultant for over 30 years now, I don't expect you to love me. Honestly, I expect you to think of me as being morally ambiguous, politically opportunistic, vicious, spiteful, and committed to my bottom line before anything good or wholesome. Spoiler: mostly true. This has never been a business—particularly my former niche of campaign advertising—informed merely by a deep sense of wonder at the miracle of our Republic. Just win, baby.

As consultants, we're supposed to be a few steps ahead of the curve. We're paid to put knowledge and foresight about the secret desires of voters into action, and to play a strategic game for our candidates and clients over a span of years. Perhaps it's a sign that I've become as jaded as a Vegas stripper that even I was stunned by how the Republican consulting community went from being almost universally opposed to Trump, and operating with the ability to see where he'd lead the party, to cheerleading for Trump as the next messiah, proclaiming his glory to their clients.

A lot of them are smart enough to know better and are more engaged with the actual issues so that it's hard for them to simply play dumb, pretending Trump isn't a liability. Those folks knew from the jump that Trump wasn't one of them, and never would be. They knew a flag of convenience when they saw one; they simply didn't give a damn.

It's a question that's haunted me since their collapse in the era of Trump: Were they faking then? Or are they faking now? Is the mere course of "Just win, baby" expedience for the election cycle, or is there ever a point where they say "No mas"?

From all of the Vichy Republicans, Trump demanded a fundamental compromise. He demanded they look back on their records of 10 or 20 or 30 years in public life and say, "What I really meant was . . ." and then launch into a gusher of praise for Donald Trump.

He demanded they bend and bend until their bones snapped, pretending on friendly conservative media outlets like Fox that Trump's actions, character, and policies are from the mainstream of conservative thought, and ranting about fake news to the rest of the media. In the campaign, they enabled Trump. In government, it's more of the same, just louder and dumber. They've engaged in an Orwellian erasure of what conservatism represents. We have always been at war with East Asia.

Perhaps all of this gave the Vichy Republicans and their allies a moment's pause from time to time, but most seem to have turned in their principles at the door.

What to Expect When You're Working for Trump

(A Tragedy in Five Acts)

– ACT II –

You breeze through your confirmation hearings, greased by Mitch Mc-Connell's desire to avoid angering the Tweeter In Chief. Democratic critics are like mosquitoes: small and annoying but of little consequence.

You didn't really have to do much more than show up. Hell, you thought it would be easy, but not this easy. The few perfunctory questions from the Republicans were mostly about how much you loved them and they loved you. The Democrats were a little harder, but really, you were back at the BLT Prime restaurant in the Trump Hotel by 5 p.m.

Everyone's there. Scaramucci, holding court. Reince and Walsh and their old-guard types are at a table, all consumed by their iPhones. Kellyanne. Bannon being Bannon, sitting in a booth with that creepy little beanbag Matt Boyle. Spicer already looks like he's had a couple, but wouldn't you? Damn mainstream media. Jared and Ivanka breezed in and out again after a single sugar-free Cosmo each. You don't know Don Jr. well yet, but you also don't want to interrupt him when he's chatting up a frankly spectacular blonde who sure as hell isn't from Washington.

You like it. It's the New Establishment of Donald Trump's Washington. These are the people you'll fight side by side with for the next eight years. Your old business partners from your lobbying firm are there every night, in the same booth, with a rotating cast of luminaries from Trump's orbit. They're bringing in so much business, and you're happy to play the role of the Big Man. Your aide, who is probably too smart for her own good, tells you this is like the Algonquin Hotel of the Trump era, and you wonder what she meant. You think she's being sarcastic and you don't like it, but this is a night to celebrate.

You knock back a last Pappy Van Winkle, say your good-nights, and roll out. Tomorrow morning, that big black Suburban with government plates is going to roll up in front of the house you bought in Georgetown to appease your latest wife and take you to your office.

*It's time to get shit **done**.*

2

FURROWED BROWS AND DEEP CONCERN

BY NOW YOU'VE ALL BECOME FAMILIAR WITH THE CATA-logue of Republican excuses for Donald Trump. You've watched them politely look away from Trump's excesses, missteps, racist asides, and other lunacies and utter excuses of such spectacular banality that it takes a moment to process how truly mendacious their words are in the face of reality.

Trump has broken some essential political survival mechanism in Republican elected officials, and it's hard to see how many of them will recover; over and over Republicans have failed a basic political common sense test on Trump. The excuses they make for him are so out of proportion to the reaction he deserves. In the face of incompetence, they display indifference. In the face of corruption, they engage in epic whataboutism. In the face of instability, they blame inexperience.

To understand how Trump has changed the GOP for the worse, it's important to recognize the tribal divisions inside the Republican Party today. The following typology should help:

A TYPOLOGY OF CONGRESSIONAL REPUBLICANS

1. The True Believers

While the GOP base is still largely positive about Donald Trump, the actual number of fire-breathing, 24/7 members of the Trumphadi caucus is astonishingly small. The True Believers in Trumpism overlap heavily (and ironically) with the Freedom Caucus, the group of hard-right Republicans who claim to believe in limited government, personal freedom, balanced budgets, and the elimination of debt and deficits. These are the Steve Kings, Mark Meadowses, Devin Nuneses, and Jim Jordans of the world.

I could write more about them, but honestly, they're tendentious and boring and will be the first up against the wall, come the Revolution.

2. The Opportunists

In the Senate Mitch McConnell and Lindsey Graham play Trump's game in pursuit of their own ends. Both men have agenda items they want to move: in McConnell's case on the economic front, and in Graham's on foreign policy. They're both entirely aware of who and what Trump is and quite overtly play to his weaknesses to keep him out of their knitting. Their praise of Trump isn't some esoteric mystery; it's a cost of doing business and a way of distracting the Toddler in Chief with shiny objects.

There are a dozen opportunists in the House Trump camp, young, full of hustle, eager to get on Fox News. They only *look* like the aforementioned True Believers. They're not; these guys are conning the con man. One example is Matt Gaetz of northwestern Florida's 1st Congressional District. You've seen Matt on a hundred cable news shows. Young, dark haired, and slowly going to seed, he looks like a frat boy wearing his father's suit.

Matt comes from a political family; his father was president of the Florida Senate, and Matt served in the Florida House from the tender age of 22. He has an eye for the main chance and a nose in the wind.

As full-time Trump cheer squad members, Matt and others have worked the Con Man in Chief like champions, playing to his vanity, giving Fox News the kind of pro-Trump talking head action money can't buy, but it rings more than a little hollow. The ambitions of the Opportunist class are vividly apparent. In the meantime, Matt and the others are harvesting cash from building out their email lists of the credulous Trump fan base.

3. The Cowards

Every week at least a couple members of Congress call me as their father confessor to admit their sins and avow their hatred of Trump. They are publicly loyal to Trump for three reasons: FOMT, FOTB, and BTP. These three acronyms explain all of their behavior.

FOMT: FEAR OF MEAN TWEETS Donald Trump's superpower is his ability to turn his 50 million social media followers into an unguided, deafening weapon against anyone he targets. Folks like Jeff Flake, Ben Sasse, Dean Heller, and others who have been attacked by Donald Trump on social media find their phone lines jammed, their email inboxes filled with poorly capitalized and grammatically disastrous screeds, their social media accounts flooded with Trump memes, and their ability to communicate suppressed in a tidal wave of hate and death threats. The fear of Trump tweeting a member of Congress with an attack is ever present and terrifies them into silence.

FOTB: FEAR OF TRUMP'S BASE Somewhere along the line, members of the Trump base became objects of terror to members of Congress. One congressman told me of a moment when he was mildly critical of Trump in a town hall meeting, and within minutes people were posting threats to his Facebook page, blowing up his phone, and mentioning how they hoped he'd support Mr. Trump (the "Mr."

is always a tell) because otherwise how would the congressman's kids grow up without a father?

These aren't Republicans as we once knew them. They're more feral, more fierce, and wildly less conservative. The narrow line between statism and conservatism is in the rearview mirror of their ratty, clapped-out beaters. They're angry at everything, all the time, and they increasingly believe in vivid conspiracy theories that members of Congress with an ounce of sense won't touch with a ten-foot pole.

BTP: BUT THE PRIMARY! The fear that Donald Trump will cause a Trumpcentric primary challenger to run against an incumbent Republican member is constant and sharp. When Steve Bannon was still in the Trump orbit, he was promising to field Trumpish challengers to every Republican running for Senate, save Ted Cruz. Members have told me over and over that they live in terror of one tweet from Trump praising some nutcase, causing their primary to become a reality-TV show called *Who's More Trump?*

The Cowards are by far the majority in the Republican caucus; even as they defend him publicly, they loathe him privately. Many of them are part of a large number of 2018 retirements. If you're ever looking for Profiles in Chickenshit, these members are your finest exemplars.

4. The Rationalizers

You've heard all the variations: "We've gotta pass X." "He's new to this." "That's just Trump tweeting. We'll work it out in private." "He's not a typical politician." "He's settling into the job." Those excuses are as common as they are untrue.

The Rationalizers' permissive parent style of governing works about as well as letting your kid subsist on a diet of cookie dough and television. Kids need discipline, and when Donald Trump's Rationalizers talk about his unfocused, childlike behavior, it's never with any parental firmness or authority. "I wish he'd stop tweeting so much" is the equivalent of "Little Donald is so bright, but I wish he'd focus in class." "The president isn't a conventional politician" translates as "We hope Donnie will channel his creativity, and stop setting fires and dissecting roadkill in the kitchen."

Paul Ryan was the leader of the Rationalizer caucus, desperately trying to derive order from Trump's chaos. Ryan wanted to manage Trump so that he and the GOP caucus could run on the tax cut, the economy, and infrastructure. All of these messages went out the window, and Ryan owns his share of the blame. Too often he behaved as if he were some deferential junior VP at a Trump resort and not the leader of the House of Representatives in a coequal branch of government. The idea, popular among the Rationalizers, that a diet of their ass-kissing and deference would make Trump a normal president who responded to normal political cues was always a mistake.

5. The Retirees

Retirement frees Republican members to speak the truth—and boy do they ever. It's a damn shame they had to wait until they declared they were done with leadership to speak the awful truths about Trump, but it's also a small reminder that some conservatives still believe in something more than the Maximum Leader.

Jeff Flake's amazing floor speech on the risks of Trump was roundly mocked in the Trump-right media but will go down in history as a moment when, under terrible pressure, an American politician took the hard road, told the truth, and called out a member of his party.

When it comes to trifling chickenhawk no-account pudknockers like Donald Trump, John McCain left his last fucks on the floor of the Hanoi Hilton. In an era where political heroes are thin on the ground, McCain's almost never pulled a punch with Trump, and even in the twilight of his life, McCain is still swinging for the fences. Trump's attacks on McCain fall flat because one man is a hero to millions, the other only in his own mind. After his diagnosis of brain cancer in the fall of 2017, McCain's light has been fading, but his fire and fight never did.

Even Trey Gowdy, Chairman of the House Oversight Committee and scourge of Hillary Clinton's role in the Benghazi attack, was born again hard after announcing his retirement. Gowdy, once a hero of the Trump right and the Fox News set, became anathema when he finally called bullshit on the White House's lawlessness and chaos.

THE FIVE STAGES OF TRUMPSPLAINING

Imagine a world where Hillary Clinton or Barack Obama sat in a White House meeting and casually brought up a willingness to ban assault weapons, belittled fellow party members for being afraid of the National Rifle Association, and just threw out the idea of bypassing due process to seize firearms.

What would happen? I'll tell you what would happen. The GOP, every conservative publication, and every single Republican member of Congress would be tearing their damn hair out. The wailing and lamentation would shatter the heavens.

But Trump did all those things on February 28, 2018, when he sat in a Cabinet Room gun control roundtable in the wake of the Park-land, Florida, school shooting. It was a moment Second Amendment advocates and NRA supporters were waiting for; they had worked their hearts out for their guy, and with the most consequential push for sweeping gun control in a generation, they needed him to stand firm on their issue.

So, of course, gun-rights advocates, NRA members, and rank-and-file conservatives were aghast when Trump ran into the waiting arms of Dianne Feinstein and other pro–gun control advocates. Shocker, I know. The man he claimed to be on the campaign trail—a rigid, uncompromising fighter for the Second Amendment—disappeared. Even Breitbart News, the house organ of Trumpism, ran a "Trump the Gun Grabber" headline. A few days later, Democrats who thought they could touch Fecal Midas and get away with it were disappointed when he flipped on gun control again and did virtually nothing.

This weathervane political positioning caused the same kind of whiplash for Republicans during the disastrous Obamacare repeal fight; in that debacle, the president described one version of the congressional GOP repeal plan as "mean" while berating Republican members of the Senate and House via Twitter and calling legislative audibles at the worst possible moments.

It again happened over DACA, the Obama-era executive order protecting children brought here illegally from deportation; the build-the-Wall-and-ship-them-home version of Donald Trump sat in a room full of legislators and said he'd support the "clean DACA bill," sans border security provisions. White House advisor and immigration hawk Stephen Miller looked as if he was about to crap out a kitten, and House Majority Leader Kevin McCarthy had to correct the president sharply. For just a brief moment, Senate Minority Leader Charles Schumer and House Minority Leader Nancy Pelosi probably couldn't believe their luck. Pelosi must have been thinking, "He can't be this stupid." Trust me, Nancy, he is that stupid. Until Republicans' apoplectic responses penetrated even Trump's consciousness, Trump was ready to make a deal right that minute.

Trump is a creature almost preternaturally aware of the media climate around him and of the shifting moods of the public. In event after event, he is obviously influenced by what he sees on television. For him, ideology and philosophy do not mediate politics; television mediates politics. More specifically, television is the only place where the coverage of any crisis, story, or issue reflects on his mental brand image. He thinks he is, or at least should be, the star of every story.

These examples are hardly unique, and they certainly don't cover every single time that Donald Trump opened his mouth and blew up his party or conservative orthodoxy during his campaign and first year in office. Even more corrosive is the rhetorical, ideological, and political gymnastics required of Republican leaders, conservative media, and the conservative movement every time Trump straps verbal Semtex to his body and hits the detonator. He's President Hold My Beer Watch This, and everyone stands riveted to the spot, waiting for the calamity.

Stage 1. "Oops, I Pooped Myself"

This is how it always begins.

Trump verbally soils himself in public with an embarrassing state-ment, lunatic theory, early morning golden-toilet tweet, or throwaway line he thinks will make him look good on the next round of cable news coverage. He does this because he sees everything through the narrow, blinkered framework of his role as a reality-TV game show host and pitchman, but everyone, friend or foe, still seems surprised, every time. He never seems to realize the impact of his words, the damage he's about to cause, or the mess he forces others to clean up.

This includes wild departures from conservative ideology, fiscal re-ality, American tradition, common sense, and the established models of physics. The elevator-drop sensation when Trump screws the pooch in the press has left Republicans numb, shell-shocked, and sleepless. It's why time seems to dilate in the age of Trump; a month is a week and a week is a year and JESUS CHRIST WHAT DID HE JUST TWEET?

Stage 2. So Stupid, It Burns

Republicans in Congress, Trump's media allies, and his more intelli-gent supporters instantly feel a pain akin to being set on fire and then dunked in acid. In Trump's Cabinet set-piece meetings, you can al-ways see the grim looks on their faces the moment he steps in it. Their downcast eyes lock on the White House notepads placed on the table before them. The suddenly rigid postures and thousand-yard stares of Republican leaders in these moments are inadvertently hilarious.

You can almost hear the mental gears turning, grinding out ra-tionalizations and excuses to reconfigure whatever batshit lunacy just sprang from his brow like Bad Idea Athena. You can watch them mort-gaging one more fraction of their dignity and sanity as the man they praise as the Perfectly Normal and Totally Not Insane Best President Ever Who Unlike All the Losers Before Him Is Making America Great Again has done the impossible by lowering the bar a few more notches.

Stage 3. "But Her Emails"

His media myrmidons recognize that he's done it again and know their next 48 hours will be spent crafting a series of high-wire, hot-take absurdities in defense of the indefensible. These stories almost always include a portfolio of excuses for this president as someone who "isn't a traditional politician" and "is new at this." They defend it as "Trump being Trump" and unleash a wave of epic whataboutism. The land echoes with cries of "But Obama!" and "But Hillary!"

You can count on Trump-right rodeo clowns like Sean Hannity to dredge up old favorites from their fantasy catalog. "Why isn't Robert Mueller investigating Bill Clinton's love child?" "Were Hillary and Huma Abedin secretly gay-married by George Soros?" "Tonight, Sebastian Gorka will join us to rip the lid off the secret mosque Barack Obama had built under the Rose Garden!"

These appeals to raw partisan tribalism work in our current political climate and the lurid, fanciful horrors described by Trump's defenders start to snap MAGA voters and votaries back into line. Why, without Trump's straight talk and disruptive nature, we'd be hip deep in Antifa supersoldiers, ISIS terrorists, pedophiles, and MS-13 gangbangers! Only Donald's force of will is holding back an invasion of wily Chinese and rapey Mexicans and stopping the local shawarma stand operator from detonating his bomb vest.

A casual listener or reader would think Kenyan communist Muslim sleeper agent Barack Hussssssein Obama is still in office. From these breathless stories, it would be easy to imagine President Hillary Clinton is running roughshod over the land in her attempt to impose sharia-compliant cultural Marxism (Don't ask. They don't know what it means either), all while opening a chain of pedo-friendly pizza restaurants.

Stage 4. Magical Rationalization

When all else fails, it's time to go for the magical thinking defenses of Trump. "You just don't get him, man." "He's a dealmaker, not a politician." "Trump's got this." "He's playing 47-dimensional quantum chess, RINO." "So much winning!" It's a living, breathing embodiment of the Emperor's New Clothes, except his followers never get to the crux of the parable.

They race to frame Trump's absurdities into some kind of explicable fact pattern, to find some secret, subtle strategy where none exists. The idea that Trump always has some deeply considered game plan, some rationale for every action, some hidden endgame in mind is, of course, ludicrous, but it doesn't stop this defense from being run through the Trump-friendly media channels on the far right on an almost daily basis.

Michelle Goldberg of the *New York Times* wrote a fabulous piece about the ultimate Trump conspiracy. "The Conspiracy Theory That Says Trump Is a Genius" beautifully captures this odd element of the Trump cult's magical rationalization. His supporters believe in their hearts that Trump is a deep thinker, a master planner, a strategist nonpareil. This late-stage element of defending Trump is wearing increasingly thin. Reality is, as they say, a heartless bitch.

Stage 5. Waiting to Exhale

In this stage, the scope of the latest political pratfall is clear, and even his allies have to face reality. They start to quietly pick up the pieces, redacting, patching, revising, and extending remarks and deploying all the other tools of the political janitorial staff. After Paul Ryan, Mitch McConnell, or desperate, terrified White House staff have cleaned up his mess enough to walk around without wearing Wellies and Trump-splained his more crazy assertions, more intelligent Trump supporters heave a quiet sigh of relief and recognize they've dodged one more bullet.

Then a delicious amnesia sets in, and the cycle repeats itself. Trump springs some rhetorical turd on them, leaving his followers surprised when his next political disaster, policy malapropism, or self-inflicted wound embarrasses them and the nation. Loving Donald

Trump somehow prevents them from believing it can ever happen again and that Trump won't do the same thing in a day or two on some new issue or some new crisis. Lucy always pulls the football away at the last second. The Scorpion always bites the Frog.

By now they should know quite well that Donald Trump has only the most tenuous appreciation for the power of the office of the president. They should know he is both uneducated and uneducable. Trump is no fan of briefings that don't come in graphic-novel form or of knowing the specifics of legislation or policy proposals. They should know he is malleable, crass, and dishonest, and that all he cares about is serving his swolt ego.

The fact they still act surprised and go right back into the five-stage pattern speaks volumes about how far they've fallen, and how little they care.

THE POLITICAL COSTS OF KISSING TRUMP'S ASS

Why does Trump kill all that he touches? In part because he requires every man and woman in his orbit to destroy themselves to remain in his good graces. He requires every person near him to constantly stoke the mighty bonfire of his narcissism and to ramp up the praise until it butts into pure idolatry. It isn't enough for Trump to have support; he breaks down every relationship into its most protean form.

All politicians are inclined to some degree of narcissism. It's a necessary offset to the endless small indignities. All politicians, no matter their public image, are needy bitches. Donald Trump takes that hunger, that constant, gnawing desire for love, affirmation, and praise to a level unknown in American political history. One doesn't become president without a healthy ego, but no president has been more obsessed with being the center of attention and praise. It's a sick addiction and a driver for so many of his pathologies.

He also requires a degree of moral and ideological flexibility where nothing that came before matters. Nothing today can be expected to persist. Everything Trump says is mutable, subject to instantaneous revision, no matter the political cost to those defending him. Virtually every Republican elected official has learned that Trump is a man of moods, of ephemeral interests, and with little regard for the record. For Trump, the past isn't prologue; it simply doesn't exist. Nothing he says, does, or promises is real for longer than his gnat-like attention span can hold it in his wee brain.

I've been around DC and American politics quite a while now, far longer than the average bear. I'm struck over and over again how little sense of dignity and self-preservation today's DC Republicans have.

Yes, Trump blew up the old rules, but there's only one thing you have in politics at the end of the day, and that's your reputation. How you behave, what you do, who you work with and for, all still matter, even in the reign of King Donald the Mad. Are we still back in the days of the more genteel Bush 41 era? Of course not, but imagining a Reagan, Bush 41, and Bush 43 demanding the kind of abnegation Trump requires is impossible.

Do the "good guys" working for Trump understand this? We may never know. They steadfastly refuse even to consider that enabling Trump doesn't keep the rabid wolves like Bannon out; it just releases Trump to act on his id. In doing so, it widens the gap between Republicans and the rest of America dramatically. No, Paul Ryan isn't a skirt-chasing, Putin-philic, lavishly corrupt scumbag. Mitch McConnell isn't a pussy-grabbing, porn-star-screwing maniac. (Get that image out of your head, I dare you.) Even so, the stench and politically radioactive ichor of Trump covers them and every other Republican.

The perception grew from reality; Ryan and his cohorts will, in fact, defend any outrage. This vicious cycle gave Trump a sense that no line is too far, no outrage is too grand, no lie is too egregious. He didn't learn that the rule of law and the Constitution bind even the mighty powers of the president; he learned Dad and Mom were at the beach house and left the car keys and a credit card on the kitchen table.

Where were the people who would put country over party? Nowhere in Congress, that's certain.

What you can find in Congress is any number of Republicans willing to trash-talk the president off the record. GOP members I've spoken to in the past year and a half have repeatedly told me they loathe and fear this president. One member told me, "You know that scene in *The Hunt for Red October* where the guy torpedoes his own submarine? 'You fool! You've killed us all!' That's him." Another member, writes the *Resurgent*'s Erick Erickson, said he sees Trump as "an evil, really fucking stupid Forrest Gump." These aren't the purple-state squishes of Trump fans' imaginations. These are—or, at least, were—rock-ribbed, red-state, red-meat conservatives.

That Trump continues to receive praise from them instead of condemnation, and cheers instead of catcalls is an element of his disastrous first year in office. It's an endorsement of his shock-jock leadership style and a permanent mark against the one group of men and women who could have stopped that behavior and yet utterly refused to take responsibility for doing so.

It's hard to imagine a scenario where Republicans could embarrass themselves more thoroughly than they already have, but Donald Trump will drag them down time and again, no matter what they believe about him. He is the eternal Loki, a trickster god drawn to, listening only to what Edgar Allan Poe calls "The Imp of the Perverse."

It's become a bit exhausting reminding them that the world doesn't have to be this way. Over and over they touch the hot stove, ignore the angry howls from their constituents, and continue to defend the indefensible.

What to Expect When You're Working for Trump

(A Tragedy in Five Acts)

– ACT III –

No sooner have you settled into your comfortable office and begun to Make America Great Again than you notice that Donald Trump's ardor has cooled, his praise has become mere tolerance, and your glory suddenly tastes a bit sour. Watching him in action, you quickly learn one thing about this king's mercurial moods and white-hot temper: it's best to turn the praise and ostentatious displays of loyalty up to eleven every day.

You notice that the president isn't just a one-way street but that he also demands that his allies do things that aren't, you know, appropriate. He doesn't care about the statutes or those ethics rules that were designed for the unwashed little people. He wants his wishes fulfilled, tout de suite. You saw his incandescent rage after Jeff Sessions recused himself over the Russia investigation—you quickly correct yourself: witch hunt—and you don't want to ever be on the receiving end of those tweets.

In the meantime, life is good. There's no adult supervision. You're in charge of your fiefdom. Sure, you could order a conference table from

Ikea, but why not have one that requires a hundred acres of pristine rain forest lumber be cut down and built by an army of slave labor instead? If you're going to MAGA, don't you deserve a security detail large enough to overthrow a third-world nation?

While it's fun blowing through traffic with lights flashing and sirens blaring, except for all the small liberties, you really have almost no actual power. There's rarely an actual agenda or program from the White House. Mostly, you're chasing the rabbit of the president's daily whims and interests. Some days he'll announce a policy solidly in your department's ambit via tweet. You won't know it's coming. The White House staff won't know it's coming. Like a plague, it just appears, sudden and deadly.

From the lowest Hill staffer to the most isolated GS-9 in the bureaucratic hinterlands, no one in Washington likes that. Washington hates surprises, disorder, and things outside the lanes and traditions. As a cabinet member or senior aide, it makes your hackles rise, but what can you do? Sure, you'll keep tweaking the regulatory stuff and going through the Kabuki dance with Congress, but you know you're mostly along for the ride.

Right about this time is when you start quietly asking friends, "Is leaving after a year okay? Or is it eighteen months?"

3

RUNNING WITH
THE DEVIL

AMERICAN EVANGELICALS SOLD THEMSELVES TO TRUMP
for 40 pieces of silver. A degenerate, unrepentant man who represents
everything evangelicals have railed against for generations bought
their loyalty for nearly nothing. It remains one of the most remarkable aspects of the campaign of 2016 and of the presidency of Donald
Trump.

Trump's personal depravity isn't a secret. His amoral, deeply vainglorious nature isn't hidden under the proverbial bushel; it is the sum
of his entire character. His religious beliefs and ties are, at their very
best, loose. One author describes Trump's faith as "nonchalant Christianity."

In Iowa, Trump said, "When I drink my little wine . . . and have
my little cracker, I guess that is a form of asking for forgiveness, and I
do that as often as possible because I feel cleansed. I think in terms of
'Let's go on and let's make it right.'"[1]

I'm not entirely sure which doctrinal strain of Christianity that
represents, but I believe it emerges from the First Church of Greed,
Manhattan Synod. Trump's only faith is in himself, and his only God
is Mammon. His obsession with money and the trappings of wealth
don't exactly scream out that this is a guy who will pass through the
eye of a needle, but perhaps I'm just not up on my Prosperity Gospel.

I know many evangelicals. No, I'm not doing the "my black friend" for the God Squad. I mean it. I know a *lot* of evangelicals. I'm not one, but many I know are some of the most good-hearted people you could ever hope to meet. They live their faith, do good works, give generously to their communities both in time and tithing. They once had standards and applied them to their politics. I didn't always agree with those standards, but they had them.

Until 2016. That was the year political and professional evangelicals went off the cliff with a candidate who was a walking, talking, porn-star-screwing offense to their every belief. Suddenly, nothing mattered. The TV pastor class of Jerry Falwell Jrs. were out building their own version of the golden calf statue the moment Trump slithered into their megachurches. I'm not enough of a biblical scholar to give you the perfect reference, but something about the road to Hell being broad and smooth comes to mind.

Sure, there were hints in the political ecosystem that not all the members of the God Squad were, shall we say, living their beliefs. During a statewide primary election a few years back, a prominent evangelical said of my candidate, "Well, I know he's 100% pro-life, but he's not very vocal about it." This guy's favored candidate in the race had two restraining orders against him and was so far to the right that he was utterly unelectable, but—it's a miracle!—had generously donated to the construction fund for said evangelical's megachurch.

Another prominent evangelical leader's conduct with his multiple girlfriends over the past two decades led to his having the nickname "The Strangler." One evangelical who frequently rails against the sin of gay marriage may have a pretty young thing for a wife, but she lacks the one physical aspect that truly makes him see the face of God, which is to say, a penis. I know people, and church people *do* love to talk, Proverbs 11:13 aside.

It should have been a preview, but all of a sudden, Donald Trump came along and washed away all the prior disqualifiers. All the things evangelicals had said for generations that made a candidate anathema were suddenly *just* fine.

Let's review, shall we?

Many evangelicals told me that casinos and the venal, sinful atmosphere they create are deeply corrupting moral influences. Apparently not. Donald didn't run his casinos with even the thin veneer of the family friendliness of modern Vegas. The Trump Taj Mahal in Atlantic City was a humid, grim dump fleecing seniors of their Social Security, just like Jesus preached in the Gospel of Skeeze. It looked, felt, and smelled like a strip club–cum–low-stakes roadside casino. Every surface was sticky, and you did *not* want to know why. I can't recall which book of the Bible says, "Thou shalt take Granny's Social Security check and collect it for the LORD's slot machines."

I was taught that divorce was a calamitous social evil, and to be avoided at all costs. Apparently not. I mean, Trump has only had two of them *so far*, both caused by rampant adultery, but MAGA, right? Is that from the Book of Gorsuch? I think it might be.

Fucking—pardon me, *dating* porn stars while your wife is pregnant and then paying them hush money is frowned upon in modern Christianity, yes? Apparently naming the right court nominees expiates that particular sin in the eyes of the God Squad. Oh, he did it more than once? Well, forgiveness is next to Trumpishness when it comes to evangelicals handing out moral mulligans.

Being a goddamned degenerate pussy-grabber with a lifetime of adultery, venality, and dishonesty is not, to my knowledge, one of the core tenets of the Christian faith. I can't find it in either the Old or New Testament, and I'm not sure which book of the Apocrypha the "pussy grabber" exception comes in, but as noted earlier, I'm no biblical scholar.

Trump has opened entirely new theological avenues. Until now, forgiveness was always available, as long as repentance was in the mix. There is literally not one aspect of Trump's behavior as a citizen, a husband, and as a man that shows the slightest scintilla of repentance for anything, ever.

It used to be that supporting candidates who backed abortion, ever, was a permanent stain, a terminal moral and political disqualifier, and made one an ally of industrialized infanticide. Now? *Mirabile dictu!* Trump gave Schumer, Pelosi, and Hillary Clinton hundreds of thousands of dollars over the years. No big deal. It's the Divine Miracle of Amnesia!

After Trump entered the race, evangelicals were strangely incurious about his history with abortion, for he had been staunchly pro-abortion until 2016. Our oppo researcher dug up a telling quote from a 2016 interview with Maureen Dowd. When asked by the *New York Times* columnist if, during his swinging bachelor days in New York City, he had ever been involved with someone who had an abortion, Trump sneeringly replied, "Such an interesting question. So what's your next question?"

One last note on abortion is relevant to a story told to me before Trump joined the race. A close friend of Trump's, one of his most passionate defenders today, explained to me why Trump would never enter the presidential contest by telling me, "The last conversation Trump ever has with one of his girls is when she calls and says, 'Don, I'm late.' Or when he gets bored with her. At that point, Cohen and his people take over. NDA, payout, go away. It's all in Cohen's office. He can't have that come out." This was well before Stormy Daniels was a household name.

The Cohen in question is, of course, Michael Cohen, the now-notorious sleaze consigliere for Trump's wandering hands and penis. Imagine being a man who spends many of his waking moments working to cover up, pay off, intimidate, and silence women. Given that Cohen's degree from a strip-mall law school may not be good for much else, I guess we can't begrudge him the work, but Cohen became famous in 2018 when the aforementioned system for handling Trump's version of bimbo eruptions became public knowledge, and his role in the notorious Stormy Daniels affair reduced him to a national laughingstock.

Evangelicals have been a core part of the Republican coalition since the 1970s, but the era of Trump makes it perfectly clear that they have no problem at all with big, intrusive government powers and executive orders being deployed to shape social policies they find desirable. Trump understood how to parlay their sense of beleaguered social and political inferiority into a message claiming that he would aggressively pursue their ends even if it meant ignoring that pesky Constitution and the will of the people.

Barack Obama kicked our ass down the street twice by growing the Democrat coalition. It's a zero-sum game, and every gain for them is a loss for us. It's a cliché, but you grow by addition, always and only. Too much of the evangelical political agenda became associated with exclusion, alienation, and a disconnection with the society at large.

Changing hearts and minds in a society that has passed them by on many issues is boring and hard work. They'd rather compromise with a candidate who will nominate their preferred judges than uphold their values. Instead of working to change society through moral suasion, exemplars of faith, or even just better communications, they'd rather trust the federal government in the hands of Donald Trump to deliver their desired social end states. Call me crazy, but I thought that was the other team's modus operandi.

Evangelicals are the dead-enders of the Trump world, a phenomenon explained by both demographics and geographic distribution; the southern and Midwestern states where they live are Trump country, writ large. He is their Golden Calf, and the leaders of the Evangelical movement repeat daily, "This is your god, who brought you up from Egypt."

Despite being a majority in the American religious landscape, they continue to feel as if they're under constant attack from secular culture, the media, and the government. They've lost battles in the court of public opinion over gay marriage that had been a core part of their messaging since Anita Bryant in the 1970s. Trump brilliantly plays that sense of alienation, promising as he always does to be their avenger—a flawed vessel for their agenda, but their vessel nonetheless.

What to Expect When You're Working for Trump

(A Tragedy in Five Acts)

– ACT IV –

Uh-oh.

Now you've done it.

You were just trying to be on the team and promote the MAGA message. You punched all the "This President is so amazing" buttons your press aide got from Sarah and Kellyanne. You tugged your forelock, subsumed your ego, and promised bigly successes across the board.

Then the question came out of left field and you made a huge, devastating mistake; you actually answered it. You damn fool.

Mueller? Russian sanctions? Climate change? The tax bill? The ludicrous plan to build a Wall? It doesn't matter what it was; it's that your statement got attention . . . more attention than the president did that day.

Now you're sitting in the dark in your Georgetown town house, plowing down your third Olde Ocelot on the rocks, feeling as if gravity has switched off and your career is about to end in a blaze of Twitter fury from The Donald. You sleep fitfully, if at all.

In the morning, though, the reviews are good. It seems like you actu-

ally did something right for an administration that needs all the wins it can get. You get a little bounce in your step until a new, icy realization settles in your gut.

There is only one star in this firmament, and that star is Donald Trump. The favorable attention about how smart, insightful, driven, strategic, or effective you are is rage-bait for Trump, and even if you don't end up on the receiving end of his fury that day, the second you become a star for even one moment longer than the president, the game starts to wind down.

4

THAT'S WHY YOU GOT TRUMP

DEAR DEMOCRATS: THIS CHAPTER IS FOR YOU. SURE, MY Republican and independent readers may still glean some amusement or information from it, but I hope you'll pay attention. Here's the truth: Democrats are bad at politics.

No, really. You're holistically bad at politics both on election day and in the cut-and-thrust of Washington, and your lack of skills is often Trump's best ally. This chapter will look at why that is true and give you a bit of unsolicited advice. Because you really, really need it.

You'll object, I know. You'll race right to the fact that Barack Obama beat the GOP in two blowout national elections, and you're right. By all means, rest on those laurels, but how have you done since then?

It's been a goddamned train wreck, and you need to face that. Since 2008, you lost a presidential race to Donald Trump. Donald Fucking Trump. You've lost 11 governor's mansions and 12 Senate seats, reflecting the post-Trump wins of Ralph Northam in Virginia and Doug Jones in Alabama. You lost 69 seats in the House of Representatives.

Most important, you've lost almost 1,100 seats in state legislatures, which largely control the redistricting process and which produce the "farm team" candidates who will run in the future. They help build the local and state party cadres of activists and volunteers who knock on doors, make calls, and do the grunt work of the campaigns. Facebook, Twitter, Snapchat, memes, and the other modern appurtenances of campaigning are necessary, but not necessarily sufficient.

Trump hatred is good fuel for your voters, but it's not quite enough to get you over the hump and into the majority again. You need to buckle down, get the data, targeting, and operational things right again before you'll win back even part of what we took from you. You'll have to run candidates who don't fit the top-down standards of Upper West Side Democrats.

Let's have some real talk about Hillary Clinton: she was a catastrophically terrible, horrible, crap-tier candidate, and she always has been. Democrats will sputter about her accomplishments, her stature, her work as a senator and secretary of state and still look away from the hard truth of politics: sometimes politicians have the Gift; sometimes they don't. Hillary never did. Not once. Not for a moment. Her campaign team mastered one trick; the elite media psychological warfare game that blinded the press to just how god-awful she was as a candidate.

I watched the birth of Hillary Clinton's elected political career. It wasn't pretty. As the communications strategist in Rudy Giuliani's doomed U.S. Senate race against Hillary in 1999 and into the spring of 2000, when Giuliani left the race, I had a ringside seat.

It was the terrible aftermath of the Monica Lewinsky scandal that put Hillary in contention for the seat. Her position as the Wronged Woman came screaming out of every focus group we conducted. New Yorkers, seeing her as a feminist champion (an arguable point, but we'll fight that out another time), were ready to give her a chance because Bill had treated her so execrably. We also knew the voters of New York thought she wasn't particularly relatable, credible, or engaging.

She had one stroke of political luck in her entire life: Rudy's (ahem) troubled marriage to Donna Hanover had been Page Six and gossip fodder for years. In early 2000 it collapsed in a public, messy wreck that kept the campaign team in a state of spin frenzy in an attempt to shut down a story that had been a long time in coming. Rudy's bad news got much, much worse; after being diagnosed with prostate cancer, he withdrew from the race.

Rudy's replacement was the affable but doomed Rick Lazio, who ran an affable but doomed campaign. It was never even close to being a serious competition. You can't beat a celebrity without a celebrity, and Rudy was the only person who could have defeated her. Hillary could have run the remainder of the race from a hot tub and won. She phoned in her 2006 reelection and got her head handed to her by Barack Obama in 2008. We know how 2016 ended.

Hillary's unnatural affect and clunky style never worked. She operated from behind a brittle shell of caution, overthinking, scar tissue, and the gnawing fear that a dead hooker would turn up in Bill's bedroom. I know this will anger Hillary fans, but inertia alone is not enough to win the White House, and that was what drove more than a few voters to back her. Never a gifted, graceful, or natural speaker, Hillary's constant mental self-auditing was always visible: "I will now run Human Interaction Subroutine 54.1, warm smile followed by sincere chuckle."

Without using the phrase "first woman president," try to name the actual predicates of Hillary's campaign. Unless you're an HRC campaign insider, you can't. There was never a there there for most voters outside of the usual partisan autopilot. She was a Democrat, and tribal gravity being what it is, she ran up the numbers any generic Democratic candidate would.

Some of you will object, saying, "But she won the popular vote!" Yes, she did, but those aren't the rules of the game, whether you like it or not. Democrats have long enjoyed the Blue Wall in the Electoral College, in which California, New York, Massachusetts, and a handful of other large liberal states give them a handy edge, but just as Bill Clinton famously "picked the lock" on the GOP's Reagan and Bush–era Electoral College map, Hillary took that advantage for granted in Wisconsin and elsewhere.

While we're on the subject of the GOP's secret weapons, I'll name another: Nancy Pelosi. Nancy Pelosi may raise a metric crap-ton of money for the Democrats, but she sets the rest of America's teeth on edge. Ever wonder why we stuck her in candidate and SuperPAC ads against you until Trump came along? Because it worked for a long, long time; only Trump has made her more palatable.

Nancy Pelosi doesn't test well with focus groups, to put it mildly. Before my liberal friends howl, this isn't sexism. It's long-term, ob- served data from dozens of focus groups and surveys over the years. She scans as harsh, shrill, partisan, and out of touch to Republicans and—importantly—an enormous swath of independents. We used her against you because she's a convenient shorthand for the things many Americans see as culturally and socially disconnected from their lives. It's not nice, but it is politics. She has also, to put it bluntly, lost a step in the past few years. The rest of the House and Senate Democratic leadership isn't much better. I know you all love Aunt Nancy, but it's time for her to retire to a farm upstate after you win the majority in the fall of 2018. The Democrats desperately need a younger, smoother, smarter set of public faces for their party if they're going to compete. In a perfect world, we'd be fighting over policy and not worrying about appearances. This is quite clearly not a perfect world.

Middle America scans the cliché New York–Boston–San Fran- cisco liberal sneer as a judgment on their lives, their values, their faith, and their culture. Do the great unwashed sometimes deserve it? Sure. Would it help expand the brand if you didn't rub things in their face that may be normal in Berkeley but repulsive in Middle America? More than you think.

The siren song of "the first" is the Democratic Party's greatest temptation. The First Woman. The First African American. The First One-Legged Furry Aficionado. You love the *branding* of shattering the blah blah blah. Sorry, my eyes glazed over.

Stop it. When it's a genuine first—someone who has put in the work, done their time in the vineyard, made the long crawl up the political mountain—their accomplishments should speak for themselves. Recruit candidates who have done things in the world, built businesses, fought in our wars, accomplished something more than doofy do-gooderism at nonprofits. Think "best," not "first." Too often "the first" comes across as a novelty more than substance.

Just as I've called down the fire on my party for adopting an ideological monoculture after 2010 and their current cult-like devotion to Trump juche, you need some tough love. Another reason we took over 1,100 legislative seats from you over the past 15 years is your top-down ideology. Florida is not Vermont. Michigan is not Wyoming. New York is not North Carolina. As long as you insist on a single set of national standards for your party candidates, you limit the regions, states, and districts in which you can effectively compete.

If every Democrat has to be adamantly pro-abortion and can never, ever even begin to express a moral qualm about the subject, you're going to have trouble reaching meaningful chunks of the Catholic electorate and Protestant evangelicals. Even in cases where the Democrats could pick up seats with a pro-life candidate, the party, its allies, and its leadership will almost always pick a losing pro-abortion candidate instead. Government-funded drive-through abortion on demand at the end of the third trimester is a great message in Manhattan and Seattle. For the Pittsburgh suburbs and among conservative Catholic Democrats in Wisconsin? Not so much.

Abortion also becomes one of the definitional characteristics of what it means to be a Democrat. For your base, that works, but you keep missing the nuance. Americans are divided on the issue but have reached a broad if tacit social compromise: tolerance for the practice, but with a sea of moral qualms and conditions.

And yes, I've done work for pro-abortion Republicans in places where a pro-life GOPer would never survive. We had to fight inside our party primaries to win, so you're not alone in facing this kind of compromise.

If you're mad at me for touching on one of your most sacred cows, you might want to get a glass of Chardonnay before reading the next section. Yes, ideological rigidity on abortion costs you votes in the aggregate outside of coastal enclaves, but it's nothing at all compared to guns.

Do you want to know how we beat you, over and over and over? This is going to sting for my Democratic friends, but one of the easiest ways for people on my side to disqualify you with large chunks of American voters is the subject of guns. I know, for you gun control is a central article of the liberal faith.

I know that Parkland convinced you that Everything Changed. As telegenic as the Parkland kids are, guns are wired into America's DNA in a way they, and you, don't grasp.

I'm not saying you don't come at it from a well-meaning perspective or reasons that seem perfectly cogent in your head. You see violence caused by people and ascribe it to the tool they used. You genuinely believe that you can regulate it away. Bless your hearts. You genuinely think gun control is a winner at the polls and a decisive voting issue. It's not. Gun control and gun violence make it into the top 10 of any Most Important Problem polling question panel for about a minute after a tragedy like Parkland, then fall back to where they usually live: in the 1 to 5% range. Jobs, the economy, the direction of the nation, and national security still drive voter decisions. Gun control hasn't, and doesn't.

Most of you don't understand guns and the role they play in America's culture away from the coasts. You can't grasp that the millions and millions of Americans who own guns, hunt, shoot for sport or pleasure, or carry for self-defense hear your attacks on guns as attacks on *them*. Most of you Democrats still don't realize the way you speak about guns is a signifier of political hostility to Americans who long ago made up their minds on the matter. You conflate them with the people who commit these crimes, and you do it constantly, tendentiously, and with the worst goddamned nanny-state condescension.

In an ironic twist, about 35% of the 1.4 million people in Florida who have a concealed-carry permit are Democrats. You guys don't even understand your own base.

I can hear your objections already. "What about Parkland? Las

Vegas? Sandy Hook? What about . . . ?" I get it. No one thinks crazy people should own guns, including the staunchest NRA member. I'm not arguing policy with you. I'm telling you what the real politics are, and they're not what you think. First, you're fooling absolutely no one with the phrase "sensible gun safety." We all know perfectly well that phrase came out of a focus group. You say that, and red state voters hear "gun confiscation." You conflate criminals and the insane with lawful gun owners and users, and you can't imagine why my side doesn't think you're reasonable. Let me use an esoteric, technical polling phrase for you: Americans fucking love guns.

Your position on guns is poison to one group you might consider winning once in a while: almost every white male in the country over the age of 35.

Democrats also miss a key element of the NRA debate. You can hate the NRA and call it a domestic terrorist organization all you want, but unlike Moms Demand Action, they deliver something for candidates beyond campaign cash; they deliver committed, passionate, single-issue, do-or-die voters. They organize, they do the hard work of campaigning, they mobilize. It's not about their money; it's their effort and turnout.

Democrats are missing a massive market opportunity in the era of Trump, one that could move votes and donations that could rebuild their party. It'll take some work, but there is a clear pathway for the Democrats to become the party of fiscal sanity, probity, and responsibility.

I find it hard to write those words, but it's true. Under Trump, the GOP wholly abandoned any pretense that we cared about the debt, the deficits, or borrowing trillions of dollars to fund our political wish list. Fiscal conservatism is a dead letter in my party, and there's very little stopping the Democrats from picking up the mantle. We once roundly mocked the Democrats as the liberal "Free Shit" party, but with Trump writing checks like a drunken sailor blowing his entire paycheck on hookers in Olongapo after three months at sea, we've lost that privilege.

All you have to do is face down your own Free Shit Caucus. Looking at you, Bernie Sanders. Democrats ended their years in the wilderness with Bill Clinton, who ran as an economic and political centrist. He pushed the party to the right, and in the famous formulation of James Carville, "picked the electoral lock." The economic future of the country is going to be radically different than the recent past; there's an opportunity, for Democrats bold enough to move back in the center of the economic spectrum.

The Republicans certainly have abandoned it.

What to Expect When You're Working for Trump

(A Tragedy in Five Acts)

– ACT V –

You're not naive. You've been to the rodeo a time or two, and you know DC is filled with crafty, shitty people who hate your success. What you didn't expect was that the friendly fire now raining down on you was going to come from inside the White House.

What you didn't count on was that every faction inside the White House would be leaking about you, shitting you out to every reporter with Signal or Confide. Jared hates you, though he keeps giving you these weird come-hither looks in cabinet meetings. Ivanka hates you because Jared keeps giving you the aforementioned looks. Kelly hates you because he's mad at the world. Miller hates you because you look like a meal he could digest for a week after he unhinges his snake jaw.

What you really didn't expect was that the president himself would get on the phone at night with Maggie or Jonathan or Michael and crap all over you. You can imagine him, stalking around the residence, his sweaty, doll-size hand gripping his phone while sniffing out, "Say 'The president has lost confidence in him.' Yeah. Do that."

Now comes the moment you've been dreading. You know the hammer is coming, but you hope against hope that Trump won't humiliate you.

Then, there it is. The tweet. You read it through a narrow, gray tunnel as your vision constricts. You're out.

You know what happens next: the people who loved you yesterday will now rip you to shreds. Reading Breitbart's headlines about you (to say nothing of the comments section) is like watching a pack of wild dogs tear apart the corpse of your reputation. You know Tucker and Laura and Sean and Rush—once such good friends—will blame you, not Trump.

It can't get worse. Then it does.

A story breaks about your departure, and as you watch the White House Press Room briefing, Sarah Huckabee Sanders responds to a question about you with "Well, we didn't really know him that well. He was never the president's first choice for that position. He was barely part of Cabinet meetings. The only time I recall seeing him was when he was getting coffee for other people. He might have been just a volunteer. We really didn't get a sense he was that important to the president."

You blindly fumble for the remote control as you feel yourself disappearing, fading out of memory, a ghost of the Washington you thought had changed forever.

Calls and emails to people who loved you just days ago go unreturned. You didn't get the book deal your wife hoped for. You can't get Fox to return your calls about being a contributor. Your old partners at your lobbying firm or PR shop or PAC are cagey, offering to get dinner "one night soon, somewhere away from downtown so we can talk."

This is rock bottom, right? Wrong.

As you're sitting in your office packing your few belongings into a shipping box, your soon-to-be-ex-assistant pings your intercom. "Sir, it's Mr. Mueller's office on line two. It's urgent."

You realize that asshole Rick Wilson was right all along: Everything Trump touches dies.

PART TWO

VICTIMS OF THE CURSE

Inside the Oval Office

(A Comedy in Five Acts)

– ACT ONE –

You hate the idea at first that this is all one big reality television show, but it doesn't take too many weeks to see that's just what it is. You really wish you'd watched more of The Apprentice *when it was on. You'd try to catch up, but as a very young White House staffer it's honestly just too much of your limited six hours a day of downtime.*

Lord knows, you're grateful to be working here. You know that previous White Houses were stacked with Harvard, Yale, and Princeton types, and as a recent graduate from the University of Alabama, getting this chance was more than you could have dreamed. Luckily, your momma's cousin's best friend met Mike Huckabee at Seaside one summer and that got you a VIP invite to the big rally in Mobile and you met Mister Lewandowski and off you went. You'd done an internship with Jeff Sessions when he was in the Senate, and somehow that was good enough to get you here. It sure wasn't your 3.1 GPA.

Maybe it was just luck. Your daddy's car dealership meant he was always a solid donor, and he liked Mr. Trump from the start. That didn't hurt. They seem real sensitive around here to who was with the president early, and who joined the Trump Train later.

Your moment comes early, when POTUS himself is outside the Oval, yelling at Sean Spicer. "Don't you own a goddamned dark suit? Where do you buy suits like that, Walmart?" You're walking down the hallway with papers for Mr. Priebus, and trying to not make eye contact, but POTUS eyes you from head to toe. He approves.

"See, Sean? See?" he squawks, glaring at you. "What's your name?"

You tell him, barely squeezing out you name, "John Fairhope, Mr. President."

"See, Sean? Antelope here wears a dark suit with a good tie. You look like a fucking schlub," the leader of the free world says angrily. Spicer's eyes are dead, his skin pale and beaded with sweat. You try really, really hard not to breathe.

The president swings his gaze to you again and says, "Where do you work, Tone Loc?"

You stammer out, "I'm working in the chief of staff's office as a deputy assistant for . . ."

He interrupts, "Not anymore!"

Your life just changed.

You don't know it yet, but not for the better.

5

WHAT WE LOST WITH TRUMP

DONALD TRUMP IS A TERRIBLE PRESIDENT. THAT'S NOT an aesthetic judgment. That's not a partisan judgment. It's a simple tally of his incompetence, recklessness, and the costs he's imposing on the nation he was elected to lead.

I'm not talking about the usual Washington problems, but the bigger, more sweeping costs we face as a nation. The predicate of Never Trump wasn't simply that he couldn't be president; it was that he *shouldn't* be president. A brief look at the tally of our diminished state follows.

LEADERSHIP

Presidential leadership has that ineffable, know-it-when-you-see-it quality, a quicksilver property that ebbs and flows with the arc of lives and fortunes of the men who hold the highest office in the land. It's either there, or it isn't.

We saw it in George Washington, not just in the battles he waged and won and the example he set as a leader, but in his dignified departure from power and his return to Mount Vernon after sacrificing so much for so long. He led during the time of our greatest early adversity and never let the power of office or position overtake him.

Sometimes it's a determination to do the right thing, damn the consequences, the anger, and dissent it will cause. Abraham Lincoln's Emancipation Proclamation almost ended his presidency, and eventually cost him his life, but he never wavered. He led in word and action, demanding incalculable sacrifice to prevent incalculable harm to the Republic.

It was John F. Kennedy's call rallying a nation facing down communism, that "we shall pay any price, bear any burden, meet any hardship, support any friend, oppose any foe, in order to assure the survival and the success of liberty."

It was Ronald Reagan, standing tall and resolute before the Brandenburg Gate, rapping out the cadences of the end of 70 years of Soviet oppression, confident that our way of life, our values, and our system were superior to communism.

It's FDR in the well of the House, dragging a nation from the opiate stupor of comfortable isolationism and unleashing our military and industrial might in a devastating war to end the threat of Nazism, fascism, and Japanese militarism.

It doesn't always come from a crafted, perfect speech.

Sometimes it's a haggard, strained George W. Bush mounting a fire truck in the smoking ruins of the World Trade Center, throwing his arm around a firefighter and telling a grieving, angry nation, "I can hear you! The rest of the world hears you! And the people—and the people who knocked these buildings down will hear all of us soon."

These are just a handful of examples in the long, brilliant catalogue of American presidential leadership. Their styles were different, but all were grounded in our national character. Their leadership skills rose to meet the responsibilities of the office.

Leadership takes two things Donald Trump notoriously and evidently lacks: character and an ability to engage in political acts that go beyond oneself. He is almost completely obsessed with the spectacle of Trump, the performative presidency that is about his ratings, his appearance, his coverage. These are small, shallow things and anathema to selfless national leadership.

To be sure, every president has pondered his legacy and his role in history. They are still human, after all. But Donald Trump ponders only how *Fox & Friends* covers the previous day. Presidential leadership has never before been about tweeting, preening, or boasting. It hasn't been an endless exercise in self-fellation, until now.

DIGNITY

Who could have imagined that a man of Donald Trump's spectacular vulgarity, vanity, and gimcrack gold-leaf aesthetic would turn out to be a president without a shred of dignity? Who would have thought a man with a grasp of history derived solely from movies and television would be unable to channel the wonder and power of this nation in times of crisis?

Who could imagine that a serial adulterer with a desperate need to have his manhood validated and who engaged in a string of risible, sleazy affairs would become an international laughingstock?

Who could have foreseen that the faux billionaire up to his ample ass in debt to God knows who would look at the White House as a way to nickel-and-dime the taxpayers and the GOP into bumping up his revenue stream at his hotels and golf courses?

Spoiler: everyone, ever.

Those of you who hoped the awesome power and majesty of the presidency would draw Trump away from decades of tawdry, low behavior were in for a rude surprise. George Washington embodied presidential dignity in a way that was transferred by some providential magic to almost every man who has held the highest office. Not so with Trump.

Henry Cabot Lodge once wrote of our first president:

Washington cared as little for vain shows as any man who ever lived, but he had the highest sense of personal dignity, and of the dignity of his cause and country. Neither should be allowed to suffer in his hands. He appreciated the effect on mankind of forms and titles, and with unerring judgment he insisted on what he knew to be of real value. It is one of the earliest examples of the dignity and good taste which were of such inestimable value to his country.[1]

Donald Trump is like a monster from the laboratory of a jackass mad scientist, built to represent the perfect antithesis of Washington's example. In almost every aspect of his demeanor, speech, and affect, Trump is a clownish figure, a deserved magnet for mockery. From his absurd hair construct to his ludicrous ego to his pathetic, whiny need to have his alpha-male status affirmed every moment, Trump is the least dignified president since William Howard Taft held a Jell-O-wrestling contest on the South Lawn.

His Liberace-meets-Saddam decorating style has always screamed out "Not Quite Our Class, Dear," and his personality is the very opposite of commander-in-chief material. Trump is the living, shitty embodiment of a culture that's more Real Housewives and less Shining City on a Hill.

No man is perfect in this regard, but even by the standards of today, Donald Trump's grasping, horrid ego reduces him to a clownish figure, easily, eminently, and, most important, deservedly mockable. He is always too conscious of how he looks on the small screen of the television rather than the vast stage of the world; everything about him screams need, insecurity, false bravado.

Why does dignity matter in the president? Because at some point in every administration, history comes knocking. Tragedy strikes. The nation looks to the man they elected to lead them and whispers, "Now what?" Large and small, natural disasters, terrorist attacks, crises require a president to be a moral leader, to guide, to heal, to comfort, to direct the painful energies of a hurt nation into a positive direction. Trump can't stop looking in the mirror, a self-obsessed Narcissus in a fright wig.

TRUTH AND FACTS

Post-truth American politics goes beyond the traditional best-spin model of political communications both parties have embraced for generations. Setting the Trump campaign's endless torrent of bullshit aside for a moment, the tragedy of a presidency and a party that will argue endlessly and fruitlessly about basic, incontestable facts is a truly terrible sign of the corrosive nature of this man and his machine.

I've been behind the glass watching enough focus groups to know that very few Americans trust *anyone* in Washington. Their hatred of politicians is transpartisan. Their baseline position is that Washington is full of lying liars who lie. Trump took that to levels no one could have imagined before, and we're going to regret it at home and abroad.

On the domestic front, no one in Washington trusts Donald Trump, not even his staff, his allies in Congress, and certainly not anyone else in the legislative or political process. He's a serial liar of such infamy that any promise he makes is known at once to be conditional, ephemeral, and deniable.

More Americans believe Donald Trump is dishonest than believe that of any president since Nixon; roughly two-thirds of Americans view him as being untrustworthy across almost all survey data sources. That's hardly a distinction any resident of the Oval Office desires.

Facts, as Reagan famously said, are stubborn things. Truth and honesty are vital pillars of presidential leadership; they create an ineffable reservoir of goodwill for the moments when the man in the Oval Office can't tell Americans all the details of a military or law enforcement operation. They are a buttress against attacks on his programs, his intentions, and his statements.

Leadership demands trust. Trust that the president will keep his word, do as he promises, and deliver on commitments. Donald Trump, the Münchhausen of presidents, is a notorious serial liar and fabulist. He is a man who has boasted about his own dishonesty in life, marriage, and business.

VISION

Describe Trump's vision for America without using a slogan. I'll wait.

You might argue that Trump has a kind of negative vision, a mental landscape of threats, horrors, imagined enemies, Fox News bogeymen, and other members of his nightmare closet, but beyond his infamous, vague catchphrase "MAGA," there's not much to latch on to when it comes to presidential vision. His base quite evidently loves having their fear centers endlessly stimulated by his constant drip of apocalyptic, conspiratorial rhetoric, and revels in triggering the snowflake libtard RINOs, but Trump's actual vision for America is a dimwitted slogan, not a plan. "Make America Great Again" is a retrospective, pessimistic throwaway, a callback to an imagined past. It's superficial boob-bait that isn't matched up against a plan, a program, or a vision beyond *L'état, c'est Trump.*

Left or right, most presidents have some kind of end point, some shape of the American landscape they want to see. It's the fundamental programming layer of their plans, policies, and rhetoric. Trump's MAGA line is as dazzlingly superficial as the rest of his mental processes, and aside from a Wall to stop Mexicans and some form of amorphous swamp-draining, you'd be hard-pressed to lay out a Trump doctrine. Domestically, it's a mishmash of news of the week. Internationally, Make America Great Again is translated as "Cede American leadership to Russia."

One person in Trump's orbit understood the need to articulate a broader vision than "Look at my bigly hands, America," and it was Pollyanna Conway. From time to time, she could convince him to read words on a teleprompter or draft a tweet for him that made him look a little less self-absorbed, but Trump's vision is for his brand, his company, and his bottom line, not the United States of America.

OPTIMISM

For Americans, the future is always coming, shiny, amazing, and prosperous. The Founders were, at their base, optimists. Every generation of Americans has held onto the idea that we're getting better, moving toward the music of our better angels, fixing the bugs, hacking in new code, and building a better tomorrow. The Down-note Trumpism is fundamentally pessimistic; it's a picture of America in decline, of evil foreigners beating us at trade, of problems only a strongman can solve, and the idea that the amorphous "left" is winning all the battles. This isn't Reagan's sunny optimism; it's depressingly small and limited in scope. The Trump Train stops in a podunk future that looks like 1930, not 2030.

Big, visionary, prospective leadership has always been informed by the bullheaded optimism that defines this country. We aren't just passengers; we're builders, dreamers, doers, fighters. No challenge is too big. No problem is too complex. Every time the world thinks we can't, we *do*. "America, *fuck yeah*" has become "Daddy, save us!" in the age of Trump.

It's one of the things I find most depressing about Trump. He's trained his docile followers to believe in an America that is weaker, sadder, and smaller than we really are. I remain militantly optimistic about America, our rich talent and our amazing, messy, wonderful, ridiculous, crazy, passionate people. It's too bad a central tenet of Trumpism is to run down the people of this country and describe a nation so lost and weak it requires an authoritarian strongman.

FOCUS

Donald Trump has the attention span of a gnat on meth. If he was stonked to the gills on Adderall, he might achieve the attention span of a toddler. This is a man with a notoriously shallow intellect, and a marked inability to stick to a consistent line of thinking. It's hard to determine if he simply can't remember what he said at any given moment, or whether the bright-and-shiny objects around him are too much of a distraction.

Because his governance style is a combination of tabloid beefing, tweet rages, and pick-the-worst-policy games, it takes the hallucinatory belief by his followers that Trump is merely playing multidimensional chess, pursuing some secret, brilliantly considered scheme to MAGA . . . right up until he changes the subject again. In Trump we will never have a president able to marshal his and the nation's attention on any challenge. This is a feature of Trumpism, not a bug.

He depends on the constant, endless chaos and static of exploding our attention span, pinballing from one crisis to the next. You can imagine him saying "I don't want to talk about Mueller. How about I bomb Syria instead?"

UNITY

Trump has divided us in ways no American of good faith can countenance. He is the ultimate us-versus-them president, a man who stokes partisan tribalism, racial animosity, and political division for sport. He relishes division.

He flirts with racial forces that no sane president would do anything but rebuke and shun. He refuses to make even the most tangential moves toward bipartisan harmony. He encourages a paranoid, constant war with the media. He wrecks the rule of law, ignores the traditions of presidential leadership, and never fails to stoke division when he should bring the country together.

The only unity emerging in the era of Trump is on the negative side: he has drawn people together in vocal, constant, furious anger. No modern political figure, left or right, has had more people hate him with a mad, burning passion than Donald Trump.

RHETORIC AND INVECTIVE

I love a good scrap. I always have. Politics should have a spectrum of rhetorical engagement, from profound philosophical discussions down to a good verbal street fight. Hell, if you've ever seen me on television, you know I'm an equal opportunity asshole who doesn't mind mixing it up. This tradition of hot rhetoric in politics stretches back to the Founding Fathers, who could name-call, smear, and drop ye olde oppo like champions.

Trump-era name-calling is just as tiresome and juvenile as it is nonsensical. It's not that I mind fighting with Trump's cheer squad, bot armies, pet journalists, and allies; it's that it's so rarely a fair fight.

Snowflake. Social Justice Warrior. RINO. Libtard. Cuck. I could go on, but you've seen them a hundred times if you've been anywhere near social media since the rise of Trump. A party once defined by the smart articulation of a conservative worldview that sought to limit the power of the state, ensure the primacy of our values, and advocated for free minds and free markets now plays a kind of Hannitean bingo. Random insults from a playbook so sub-literate it barely rises above pictograms are strung into some stochastic pattern and blurted out over the nearest social media timeline.

With the rise of social media as the Trump world's primary communications domain, you can reliably expect any argument to end with variations on the theme of "Did I trigger your liberal cuck tears, snowflake? What about Benghazi? What about her emails? What about Obummer's long-form birth certificate? Mueller's the traitor, traitor. You want sharia communism, don't you? How much is Soros paying you? You're the real racist, shill."

Baffled? Don't be. Trumpism exists in the shallow end of the rhetorical pool. The very, very shallow end, where its users ignored the "No diving" sign and still suffer some rocking head trauma from the experience.

Their reliance on these simple chains of concatenated insults betrays the reality that something much more profound is wrong with conservative and Republican thought. Movements depend on ideas and an underpinning philosophy. The Word-Finder Republicans aren't making arguments; they're just venting, pecking like chickens for tiny fragments of snark, hoping to seem witty without actually possessing even the slightest wit.

Their efforts to insult their betters aren't exactly a towering intellectual effort, but what can one expect from people quite obviously raised on a diet of plastic-jug vodka and lead paint chips or from those credulous enough to follow a man whose central rhetorical tendency is to berate his opponents with middle-school nicknames?

I know this reeks of elitism in the era of Trump, but would it be too much to ask that before Trump fans sling #MAGA insults they learn the distinction between "you're" and "your"? Would it take too much time from *Real Housewives of Appalachia* to learn even the bare basics of English grammar, spelling, capitalization, and punctuation?

Everyone makes spelling and grammatical errors. Hell, I promise you there are going to be some in this book. For most people, those mistakes are occasional bugs. For Team MAGA, they're a core feature. A Tweetdeck or Chrome "Your Indifferent Grammar Is Killing Me" plug-in would help. Perhaps it's time for Microsoft to bring back Clippy, the pop-up icon that suggests things like "Are you sure you want to tweet this, moron? You used 'you're' instead of 'your' in this tweet."

Comedy is hard. Wit is harder. Stringing together a recycled package of 20 or so insults over and over is right up the intellectual alley of the average Trump fan. Bonus points for #lots #of #MAGA #hashtags.

Inside the Oval Office

(A Comedy in Five Acts)

– ACT II –

As the Deputy Special Under-Assistant to the President for Unspecified Duties, you have an office so small, your elbows touch the walls. Your desk is barely the size of a milk crate, and you have to engage in some gymnastics to get to your chair. It would be a cliché to say your office in the West Wing is a closet, but this would make a closet look palatial.

You pinch yourself, though, every morning.

You're working in the White House. For the president. In the West Wing. You've made it to the locomotive on the Trump Train and you're never going to look back. No one knows quite what your job is . . . including you. The president yelled at Reince that he wanted you promoted because "He looks the fucking part. Get me guys who look the fucking part, REINCEY." The president hasn't given you a nickname, good or bad, but you're at work every morning, looking sharp and ready to MAGA.

Hope Hicks eyeballs you for the first few days, wondering if you're trustworthy. Kellyanne Conway keeps walking past your office and eyeballing you. She can't decide whether to ignore you or devour you. Her eyes remind you of those gators you'd see floating in the Mobile-Tensaw River back home.

Jared asks one day, "So, Fartloaf, where did you go to school?" When you tell him Alabama, his eyes glaze over and he wanders away, whispering "Alabama. Interesting." The next morning, Ivanka stands in the door of your office, sleek and groomed to within an inch of her life. You can't quite parse her expression.

Her voice is like honey. "Jared tells me you're Daddy's mysterious new ideas man. Thank God, because entre nous"—she drops to a whisper that makes you feel both trusted and slightly aroused—"all of Bannon's public ideas are terrible, and the ones he talks about when he and Miller and Gorka get drunk are probably war crimes."

She rests her perfectly manicured hand on yours. It's cool, almost preternaturally so. She stares into your soul and says, "We're going to be friends, aren't we, Fairlane?"

You manage a croak, "Of course, Mrs. Kush—"

"Shhh. Jared only calls me that when he's in the punishment box. Call me Ivanka. . . ." She slides a business card across the tiny desk. "And do call me."

6

THE MEDIA

CONSERVATIVES WAGED WAR ON THE MEDIA FOR DEcades, and the media won. Far from spelling the end of the mainstream press, Trump's election gave the national, professional mainstream media a moment and a mission that has produced a golden age of journalism. The *New York Times*, the *Washington Post*, the *Daily Beast*, the *Atlantic*, the *Los Angeles Times*, CNN, and MSNBC are expanding their audiences and prospering like never before.

The inverse of the ETTD curse has been a blessing for the national media, as reporters have rediscovered a commitment to working sources, breaking news, and kicking down doors to get stories. Trump combines uniquely newsworthy behaviors: a constant flirtation with the edges of the law; a clown-car administration staffed by the corrupt, the creepy, and the craven; and a temperament better suited to an asylum than to the Oval Office.

For decades, the rallying cry on the right was "But the liberal media!" It was the quickest route to explaining any failing on the right flank of our politics. Failure to repeal Obamacare? Liberal media. Americans' stubborn love of Medicare and Social Security? Liberal media. The cancellation of *Firefly*? Liberal media. Duh.

"If only we could overcome the liberal media monoculture, the truth and strength of our ideas would finally break through" was the spoken and tacit assumption in every battle. "If only we could really be heard on economic matters, on foreign affairs, and on race, the

Republican Party and conservatism would finally get a fair hearing in the minds of the American people" was a common argument. It wouldn't have to be a zero-sum game of replacing one set of biases with another; the rightness of our ideas would carry the day.

Uh huh. How'd that work out?

Yes, the mainstream media often deserves a kick in the ass so hard they would reach orbital velocity for their professional missteps, insularity, ideological blinders, vast self-regard, and occasional outright malice against conservatives. Yes, they make mistakes large and small, every day. Reporters and editors have every human flaw and weakness that everyone else has. There are ideological bad actors in the media, as in every other institution.

However, as a justification for every one of Trump's failings, reveling in their misery falls wildly short of the mark. A movement that once took pride in its intellectual rigor and was graced by the ideas of Burke, Hayek, Weaver, Friedman, Kirk, and Buckley today views the feces-flinging by Breitbart and in a constellation of kook-right conspiracy sites that would make Lyndon LaRouche blush as highbrow conservative commentary.

It's not an argument for mainstream media malpractice, Obama, Clinton, social justice silliness, George Soros, or the Pentaverate to say that imitating the worst behavior of the press doesn't exactly honor the ideals we claim to serve or elevate the conservative message. Instead, it makes a mockery of our ideas if we believe a Trumpcentric media monoculture is a positive outcome and that screaming "Fake news!" is a substitute for advocacy and argument.

Yes, in 2008 the press lost their damn collective minds. The first Obama campaign benefited from a tidal wave of largely uncritical adulation. The superlatives flowed in a ridiculous, flowery stream of praise that bordered at times on the creepy. Yes, "the One" was a media absurdity. I remember emailing a reporter this snarky note after reading one of her pieces: "Are you practicing writing 'Mrs. Katherine Obama' in loopy script in your mash book?" (Name withheld to protect the embarrassed.)

They spoke and wrote about Obama in terms so glowing and so toadying that it was easy to caricature the journalist class of 2008 as a group of fangirls squeeing and fainting at his every utterance. That nearly mindless rah-rah remained a constant element in Obama's coverage until he walked out of the Oval Office. Conservatives rightly mocked it, but the smarter types recognized it as an example of the normative power of media and pop culture. The two had combined in one fell swoop to overcome Barack Obama's thin résumé, his lack of experience, and questions about his ideological underpinnings. Donald Trump wasn't the first celebrity president. Yes, the press treated Hillary as Her Majesty the President-in-Waiting Glass-Ceiling-Shatterer-for-the-Epoch and ignored her terrible campaigns and clunky persona and the defective-robot affect she displayed on the campaign trail.

That's no excuse for the coverage of the 2016 Republican presidential campaigns or of this presidency, where coverage was driven by *Infowars* and Breitbart. Trump fans aren't looking for up-the-middle coverage; they're looking for partners in the fake news explosion that helped Trump win the election. If being a Republican means buying into stories so obviously, barkingly insane that they sound like Roger Stone's conspiracy rantings after a three-day meth bender, then we don't have a political party; we have an inpatient mental health facility. To remind you once again, a meaningful fraction of Republicans believed that Hillary Clinton was running a global child sex and cannibalism ring from the basement of a Washington, DC, pizza restaurant.

If conservative media is to mean something outside the narrowest confines of the base, it needs to be honest, direct, and critical of our failings. Conservatives who legitimize the creepy authoritarianism, unalloyed racism, and apocalyptic religious and cultural war fantasies on the pages of Breitbart, Gateway Pundit, and the dog's breakfast of other Trump fan "news," they're not building conservatism. They're creating a filter bubble as wrongheaded and as dysfunctional as the one they imagine exists at the *New York Times* or MSNBC.

Good journalism ought to matter on the right and not fall into the slavish corruption of basic journalistic practices in service to the preferred narrative. Good writing and reporting ought to matter. As for my friends in the mainstream press, you're not off the hook. No matter how much Republicans claim to hate the media, let's be very clear: without the active participation of the mainstream media in the Greatest Scam on Earth, Donald Trump wouldn't be president. The mainstream media helped elect him through its constant attention to his every utterance.

Why did they do this? Didn't they hate Trump and love Hillary? Sure, quite a few thought he'd be easy meat for Hillary in the general election, but as with everything, money explains most of their behavior. Finally, the networks had a presidential election that had all the draw of professional wrestling and all the heat of a table-flipping, hair-pulling reality-television show. CNN president Jeff Zucker had produced Trump's *The Apprentice* and knew good television when he saw it.

Rupert Murdoch had already pushed Fox into a position where it would net more than a billion dollars, but CNN had long lagged behind Trump State Television's profits. In 2016 CNN's ratings and gross profits spiked sharply higher, crossing the $1 billion mark for the first time in its 36-year history.

Donald Trump, as heinous as he is as a person, a leader, and a president, is must-see television, and American cable networks made several billion dollars proving that Americans love reality television, the more vulgar and loud the better, even when the fate of the nation is involved.

Inside the Oval Office

(A Comedy in Five Acts)

– ACT III –

The first early morning call is a little shocking. It's 5:54, and you're clearing in through White House security. You've been in line for fifteen minutes already. While you're walking through the mags, your phone beeps with a blocked number. You answer.

The president of the United States bellows, "Fruitloop! Listen to this Tweet idea! Listen!" He reads it and your mind is blank. Something about a witch hunt, Mueller, Crooked Hillary, and the Wall. It was so fast, you could barely process it. Then the president is back: "Do you like it? I like it! Should we do it?"

You respond the only way you know how: "Yes, Mr. President. It's a great one!" or something similar. You honestly can't think of another way to do it.

Moments later, everyone in the line ahead of you is staring at their phones. Those who aren't are dragging their handsets out of purses and pockets.

At 6:01, the president sends out a tweet saying "Crooked Hillary, who could not win an election due to LOW STAMINA now directs a witch hunt against me! Ironic! Crooked Hillary is the witch! Get on your broom and ride back to Mueller (MR WITCHHUNT)." Several more follow, and your guts turn to water. By the time you're in your office, it's on every network.

Sarah Sanders stands in the door of your office, heaving. "You little shit. He says you wrote that tweet." She's livid, her eyes practically rolling and her nostrils flaring.

"He called me about . . ."

She interrupts, "I know he called you. He told me. I can tell you one thing, after the shit with Spicer and Scaramucci, I'm still here and they're not. I'll survive you, too. I'd better not hear any leaks about how you're the new wonder boy."

She won't listen to your innocent explanation, and you know you've made an enemy without trying.

You've been on a couple trips now, and a reporters are starting to wonder who you are. It's awkward, because the truth is that reporters terrify you. You know people around you leak—a lot. That weird little Wolff guy is always in Bannon's office. Reporters are everywhere in this White House, and it's obvious that it won't go well in the end.

So you keep your mouth shut.

7

THE TRUMP BASE

FOR TRUMP, HIS FAMOUS "I LOVE THE POORLY EDUCATED" line was a throwaway, but for those of us watching the Trump Party's metastatic growth in the summer and fall of 2015 and early 2016 it was blindingly obvious. As much as Trump apologists want to gussy it up with some pseudo-intellectual cruft, the hot core of Trumpism is a group of Americans who are the perfect marks for a con man like Trump: anxious over economic and social status markers in a changing world. Sure, they're looking for a place for both their anger and uncertainty to be heard, but they're also looking for someone to blame.

If there's a sharper critique of America's failed education system than the breathless, mindless Trump voter, I can't name it. Given the dumbing-down of the American educational system in the past fifty years, graduating from high school now means you can draw air in and out of your lungs. Schools are long on feelings and short on critical thinking, to say nothing of civics, economics, or reading comprehension. It's not a point of pride any longer. The weaknesses, vagaries, and generally terrible nature of our alleged education system is a longer topic for another time, but where was Trump's support strongest? You guessed it.

You know the rest, and since base demographics are partly political destiny, the demos tell the story. Trump supporters are older, whiter, less educated, and more southern and Midwestern than the mean, and their income ranks in the average range. They love God, television, and Fox News.

Economic anxiety and stagnation are two of the ostensible drivers of Trump Party membership. "The poor get everything for free and the rich get all the tax breaks"[1] in many ways perfectly captures the Troll Party belief set. They're not entirely wrong, but quite a lot of "the poor getting things for free" applies to them. Food stamps, disability, Medicare, Medicaid, and Social Security dependence aren't exactly foreign concepts to many Trump voters.

It speaks to the fact that Trump's notorious base is impervious to reason and immune to irony and is still a deep mystery to many who aren't Trump supporters. They are willful, petulant, and full of point-less defiance. They've become defined by an obsession with Trump as the sole remedy for the offenses imposed on them by a rotating cast of villains and evildoers. In the process, they've become easy marks for every flavor of conspiratorial lunacy and gimcrack appeals to their worst instincts.

I know I'm not supposed to mock Trump's base. It's elitist, and cruel, and . . . oh, who am I kidding? Honestly, at this point, it's almost a moral imperative to slap the stupid out of them. So I'll dispense with the brief, obligatory nod to their hard workin', God-fearin', 'merican salt-of-the-earth values and return swiftly to being an elitist asshole. Because, by God, they've earned it.

There's an entire journalistic enterprise these days trying to tell people who don't sit in trailers all day watching reality television whilst shoveling down corn syrup–and-soy-based salty-sweet Walmart-brand bacon-cheese snax into their maws about how the Other Amer-ica is the Only Real America. As a corner of political anthropology, it's fascinating, but it's been repurposed as an excuse for Trumpism, including its most hateful pathologies.

We're supposed to be the "no excuses" Daddy party, remember? Imagine your teenager says, "Dad, I'm going to get a lip piercing and some fierce face tattoos." A responsible parent says, "Whoa, back on that, kiddo. This is an unwise life decision." When your teenage daughter says, "Dad, I know I'm only fourteen, but Roy says age is just a number, and he's, like, a judge, and he's thirty-two, and I love him," the correct response is not to nod in approval but to reach for a shotgun.

So Trump's base voters shouldn't get a free pass from the right lane. They don't get a pat on the head because of bullshit "economic anxiety" or NAFTA or whatever other ouchies they got from the brown people and the robots they think took their jobs. They don't get to scream about welfare queens and then sit idly shoveling down Oxycontin like candy while waiting for their EBT cards to recharge and their disability checks to hit. They don't get to bitch about triggered, liberal snowflake social justice warriors while nursing a set of grievances that lead them to spittle-flecked outrage at the slightest challenge to their worldview.

This isn't simply some elitist rant. It's the tough, parental love that Fox and talk radio never gave them. It's the switch to the backside when they start quoting *Infowars* unironically, something that might have corrected the conspiracy craziness a lot earlier in the process. The political correctness culture that makes so much of the left utterly fucking insufferable is all about punishing wrong thoughts. Sadly, the Trump right is just as intolerant of people who vary from their narrow set of beliefs and values as the most fervent Social Justice Warrior on the left. They're just as dedicated to suppressing speech they dislike; ask Michelle Wolff or any NFL player who took a knee to protest police misconduct.

It's not the top-level values of the Middle American voters who came out for Trump that bother me. It's their contradictions, moral blindness, and embrace of the tantrum over the idea and rage over principle. I'm not blaming them entirely, either. Like many others in the professional political class, I missed a huge signal in their behavior and their affect. We always thought of conservatives as having a certain level-headed, rational underpinning.

We were so, so wrong.

Fanatical MAGA voters who elected Trump are more like Obama voters than we wanted to admit. We should have seen this coming because people like me helped grow them as a political force. Let's get this mea culpa out of the way: After the 2010 elections, we learned to motivate and activate Tea Party voters, even for candidates who weren't perfect fits for Tea Party purists. We knew they were out there, and we identified them, targeted them, and motivated them.

We just didn't understand they weren't waiting for a conservative revolution. They were instead waiting for a strongman, a caudillo, a Saddam.

They didn't really care about fiscal conservatism. These were "conservatives" unmoved by arguments about the debt, the deficit, or the Constitution. They didn't really care about reducing the size of government. In the end, they were just angry at a changing America, a changing economy, and at people who didn't look or sound like them. Fed by Fox News, talk radio, and weaponized Facebook feeds custom-designed to engorge their feelings of fury, resentment, and impotence, they were looking at a world that was evolving socially, technologically, and politically at a Kurzweilian rate.

In short, those voters we groomed since 2010 were perfect marks for Donald Trump, political con man of the century: pissed off, hair-trigger, and punitive as hell.

One early-warning sign, like the faint radar echoes presaging a bomber attack, came early on in the Trump campaign. It was in the form of a single picture the great news photographer Mark Wallheiser took at a Trump rally in Mobile, Alabama, on August 22, 2015. You know the one; Trump supporters, wild-eyed and hypnotized, reaching across a rope line to touch The Donald.

Even controlling for the fact the rally was in Mobile, that look of cultlike devotion and the intensity of the crowd should have been a clearer signal. Yes, the elite GOP's instant not-our-kind-dear reaction was in part our insularity, but . . . that look. That sign. One woman was holding her child with an expression that said: "I offer my infant as a sacrifice to you, Lord Trump. Devour him at your leisure."

In many long years in politics, I've never seen that look for any Republican candidate, ever. I'd seen something close to it in the eyes of Obama's fans, most certainly, but even for candidates with passionate followings that white-hot I-won't-be-ignored bunny-boiler cray is like a political unicorn. Marco had his fans, as did Scott Walker, Jeb Bush, and Ben Carson. Even Ted Cruz had his . . . oh, never mind. The Paulites were famous for a certain kind of, shall we say, overly dedicated fan mostly of the late-twenties still-a-virgin libertarian variety. This was new territory.

The obsession with Trump was crazy-ex-girlfriend multiple-restraining-orders loony, and for a while it was fun to ignore it, to write it off as the reddest red-staters fanboying the celebrity candidate they knew so well from TV. The rallies, the stage show, the hats, the pure, unadulterated fanaticism wasn't simply about the election itself; it was about a decoupling of the Republican Party from ideas and ideals and its new attachment to the Dear Leader. We didn't see it coming soon enough.

We should have taken the illness more seriously, like the people who know that the bite on the hand is the first sign of the zombie apocalypse. Deal with it fast, or everyone is going to end up in a mindless, undead cannibalistic rage. The post-thought Trump supporter made the most rabid Obama fandom look tepid in comparison.

For all our mockery and indifference, we didn't see that there is a deep strain in American political life that isn't seeking party rigor or ideological purity or even an independent iconoclast but the safe reinforcement of the pack of people just as pissed off as they are. We underestimated the deep human psychological need to be part of a movement based not on hope but on channeling the comments section of the nuttiest blogs.

That's what Trump gave them. He was an avatar for their anger, their impotence, and their blamestorming for everything wrong in their world. For once in their shallow, sad, TV-inflected lives they felt like they were the cool kids. That picture said it all; Trump was offering himself up not only as the avatar for their anger with the existing administration but as something more, something protean and dangerous.

As the months of 2015 dragged on, I came to realize that Obama and Trump fanatics were two sides of the same personality-cult coin. The cognitive dissonance between what the Trump faction hated about Obama and what they loved about Donald was notable, and after Trump's victory, even more striking in that Obama's fans seemed pretty happy just to elect him. They weren't, as a rule, even angrier after the election. The odd parallels in fanaticism are striking.

Trump fans hated Obama's cult-like followers, with their mindless stares of adoration, their impervious barrier between emotion and reason, and their instant fury when confronted with the facts about his record, his history, or his philosophy.

They reviled "Hope" as shallow and superficial but embraced "MAGA" with gusto. The conservative conceit of being the party with a robust philosophical underpinning from Burke to Buckley was guilty of the same kind of shallow love of a stunt-casting celebrity candidate that they mocked in the Democrats of 2008.

Conservatives at the time despised Obama's obviously empty promises to credulous, low-information voters on the left and the center. They loved it from Trump and still do.

They furiously blasted Obama for soft-pedaling his positions on single-payer health care, gay marriage, gun control, and abortion to get elected, and that the media let him slide on a catalogue of political sins. Trump fans took this to an entirely new level.

They mocked Obama's promises of millions of new jobs in the clean energy sector but adored Trump's gauzy, anachronistic promises to bring back millions of jobs in dead industries like coal, buggy whips, and witch-finding.

They hated how Obama rode into office on the wave of constant attention from the mainstream media. They loathed how the press played along with his game, draining the life out of every other candidate by describing him as an inevitable juggernaut, an unstoppable political force, and a game-changer who was tapping into something deep and powerful in American political life. Bless their deplorable little hearts, they loved it from Trump.

They hated how Obama's naive ignorance of the real and brutal world of international affairs was papered over by his hollow promises to make the world respect the United States again. But Trump's Russia-inflected win, nuclear brinkmanship, and diplomacy-free MAGA-with-MOABs? Beloved.

They hated Obama's casual disdain for people who weren't from a major city where, you know, all the rich, smart, educated, liberal people like him live. But they loved it from Trump. Trump is about as Heartland America as I am a Lapp reindeer hunter.

They hated Obama's elite credentialism and how he wielded his Harvard and Columbia degrees to browbeat his aspiring-class opponents from outside the meritocracy and how he used them to cow an already docile press. But they loved it from President Best Mind, who bellowed his alleged Wharton credentials every chance he got.

As much as Republicans hated when Obama slipped and had a smug expression that felt like he was mocking the stupidity of the unwashed, they loved Trump's sneering japery.

Republicans hated Obama's cadre of glassy-eyed, creepy advisors, with their combination of over-the-edge ideological fervor and deadender stares of adoration for the Glorious Leader. But they loved the misfit-toy collection of weirdos, former golf caddies, Russian-tied sleazeball consultants, reporter-punching thug campaign managers, dissipated bullshit artists, and Pepe Army sleeper-cell members who followed in Trump's wake.

They hated Obama's support for bailouts, too-big-to-fail, and heavy-handed, taxpayer-funded government intervention in industries, but they loved it from Trump, a man promising to keep his boot on the throat of companies that didn't cooperate with his America First agenda.

They hated Obama's comfy alliance with Harry Reid, Nancy Pelosi, and the odious Clinton family enterprise, but they shrugged at Trump's lifetime of donations to the most liberal Democrats in the country.

They hated Obama's cavalier disdain for private property rights, but they loved it from Trump. "He's a businessman" was the universal cry to excuse any sin.

Everything that set their teeth on edge, raised their hackles, and made them loathe Barack Obama is there in Donald Trump. Every aspect of the con game Obama played on America in 2008—the obsessive focus on one base issue (for Obama the war in Iraq; for Trump, immigration), the cult-like obsession, the instant attacks on apostates, the willful ignorance of his history and his beliefs—is present in Trump.

Everything they despised in Obama's political character and behavior they love from Trump.

Part of Trump's dark appeal struck on the common idea that only he could redress the wrongs of the past and only he could avenge them. The future they experienced was one of international dangers on every side, domestic upheavals, cultural and social fluidity, and endless, savage economic destruction. They saw Wall Street and Washington as ravenous, heartless, and hungry for their last scraps of self-worth and net worth.

The master con man saw what the marks wanted and gave it to them. Over and over, he framed arguments about "the way things used to be." In his beer-hall style rallies, Trump talked about "knocking the hell" out of people. His was the language of the brawler safely behind the cordon of security, but it was effective nevertheless.

Stephen Miller and Steve Bannon smoothed out the rhetorical edges on the nostalgia campaign, seamlessly merging with their vision of nationalist populism. Trump soon promised a return to coal mines, steel mills, ironworks, town criers, and the village blacksmith. While most modern presidents looked back 20 or perhaps 30 years in their retrospective visions, Trump took it all the way back to the '50s.

Mostly the 1850s.

It was irresistible to people raised in a climate of rapid change and fed a constant stream of "the liberals are destroying you" cable news. More than any presidential candidate in the past, Trump let them speak their hatreds aloud. It was Muslims. It was the crafty Mexican army of immigrants, coming to take their jobs, pillage their suburbs, flood their streets with taco trucks, and impregnate their womenfolk. It was the Chinese, implacable and inscrutable. He left it to his alt-right allies to whisper in the darkness, "It's the Jews. It's the blacks."

His base loved it. They ate it up with a spoon. If Trump had proposed repealing child labor laws to allow kids to mine coal, they would have roared their approval at sending the little tykes down-pit with hammers and pickaxes.

Trump promised his base a world where they could all go back to the 1950s, where a high school graduate could get a job down at the local steel mill that would support a family. It was a cruel lie, and he knew it. He promised a return to American manufacturing prowess not based on innovation, disruption, and competition but by using trade deals and immigration policy and in which Washington picked winners and losers. He promised punitive measures against anyone who resisted.

The unsubtle code (and let's be honest, Trump voters don't really *do* subtle) was that America would be safer, whiter, straighter, more Christian. We'd be isolated from the evils of the world by walls and warriors. It was one of the most striking and dishonest sales pitches in American political history, and that includes William Howard Taft's promise to fight an MMA match with Elihu Root to settle the Ballinger-Pinchot affair.

THE WALL IS IN OUR HEARTS

The Wall. You know, the Wall that was going to span America from the Pacific to the Gulf of Mexico? That wall that Mexico was going to pay for?

"I will build a great, great wall on our southern border, and I will have Mexico pay for that wall, mark my words."

A staple of rally after rally, call-and-response after call-and-response, the Wall became a singular, powerful, and incredibly stupid signifier in the Trump Con. Those of us not easily taken in by simple state fair carny tricks realized right away this was boob bait for the rubes. It had so many embedded meanings, mostly about brown people and the threat they posed to the virginal white daughters and high-paying jobs of America's heroic, beleaguered white working class. It was classic Trump pitchmanship: promise an impossible project, get someone else to pay for it, and leave investors holding the bag when it never gets built.

When the early models for Douchehenge were unveiled in the fall of 2018, many of Trump's fervent supporters believed the job was practically done. The Master Builder would protect them with ramparts and towers, like some medieval warlord drawing his serfs inside the castle walls as Goths or Franks or Mongols approached. Trump would pretend the Wall was going to stop the Bad Things and Brown People, when in reality he barely bestirred his round ass to do any of the political things needed to make a deal to build the wall. The Democrats offered the easiest path possible by offering to fund Donnie's pet project in exchange for a DACA fix. It's telling that for Trump the issue was never worth any compromise with the hot nationalists around him.

Of course, the Wall as a signifier was always more important than a wall qua wall. It was a way of making racial animus acceptable. It was a method for Trumpites to distance themselves from actually having to see Mexican immigrants face to face, to attach a story to a statistic. The Wall was magical thinking writ large, ignorant of history, economics, immigration, and the American story.

A common trope of the Wall crowd was "Without borders we don't have a nation." The alt-right and immigration hard-liners loved this theme and repeated it endlessly. Trump's ideological architects—Miller, Bannon, Gorka, and Coulter—never understood that the propositional nature of America was always bigger and more powerful than their blinkered, racial interpretation of this country. They weren't protecting what we are and can be; they're just second-order effects of a decline in the idea and ideals of America. Call me a cockeyed optimist about the power of this country to not only welcome but also *create* new Americans, but I still believe that we are a system, not a race. We are a nation of universal ideals and principles, not just a few lines on a map or a wall in the desert.

MUSLIM BANS, MASS DEPORTATIONS, AND OTHER MAGA FANTASIES

Trump's promises of Muslim bans and deportations were perfect fodder for the Breitbart set. In their conception of the world, every Muslim is one YouTube video away from strapping on a bomb vest or taking control of an airliner. The argument that we are in a war of civilizations with an implacable, global Muslim enemy has become deeply wired into the conservative worldview promulgated by Fox, Breitbart, and other Trump-friendly media.

Once in office, Bannon and Miller cooked up Trump's now infamous Muslim ban, which went about as well as expected for people with no knowledge of government or the law. Breitbart and other Trump-right media outlets were in paroxysms of joy. The ban was shot down by the courts off and on for the next year, with subsequent iterations getting a long series of boot-to-the-head smackdowns. The travel ban was fatally flawed, but that didn't stop the Camelot of Stupid from pursuing it until the last dog died. There are a dozen other ways to stop Islamic terrorism, but why not just engage in trolling by executive order instead?

Of course, Muslim terror is a painful and serious reality in the world. We've fought an almost 20-year global conflict since that terrible day in September 2001 and lost almost 5,000 military and 3,000 civilian lives in the process.

What Trump and his allies don't want you to know is that when it comes to violence on our shores the alt-right and white supremacists have been running neck and neck with Al Qaeda. In this country for the past two years, they'd prefer to isolate, segregate, and persecute Muslims.

In an interview with Chuck Todd on *Meet the Press* in August 2016, Trump promised to deport the Dreamers and their families. Todd, incredulous, asked Trump if he really meant he was going to deport the children of immigrants and their families. Trump repeated, "They have to go. They have to go." Quite obviously, they didn't.

NO, THEY DIDN'T TAKE YOUR JERB: ECONOMIC ILLITERATES GET TAKEN. AGAIN

A central tenet of Trump's nationalist populism is the rhetorical primacy of trade wars. He successfully convinced a chunk of the electorate that their economic problems came from the horde of job-stealing Mexicans and wily Chinese. Too bad none of it was true. The trade war Donald Trump launched in 2018 may have the support of his economically illiterate base, but the consequences to the American economy promise to be devastating.

Trump's dumb obsession with trade deals stretches back decades and reflects his own idiotic hubris at his own skills at the negotiation table. His promise to shred trade agreements like NAFTA and to renegotiate "stupid" trade deals reflects a common and utterly wrong view among his voters that international trade, the global supply chain, just-in-time delivery, and a rapidly expanding international economy in services are somehow a bad thing.

Trump's long-standing, notoriously dumb hatred of NAFTA was an echo of Ross Perot's 1992 complaints about the free trade agreement. That was what worried smart trade experts the most at first, but as with all things Trump, it can *always* get worse. After all, no one would be stupid enough to provoke a trade war with China and Asia, right?

As Trump slowly purged every commonsense, mainstream economist from his circle, he left the White House Goldman Guys, Republican free-traders (prior to Trump, the vast majority), and Wall Street suffering from their own case of ETTD. That left Peter Navarro, Larry

Kudlow, and Wilbur Ross still at the table, and those men share the Trump-Bannon view of trade, namely, that it is a sucker game and that America has been undercut both by the guile of devious furriners and by the perfidy of American trade negotiators who lack the Trumpian edge for the art of the deal.

It's not simply that Trump doesn't get it. This isn't a policy debate with two sides. Conservatives fought for free trade because markets matter. Conservatives fought against tariffs because tariffs are taxes. Trade is good; tariffs and isolation are bad. All nations seek advantage, and our global trade system is far from perfect, but the alternatives are spectacularly, existentially bad.

A drunk monkey can understand this, which is why it is an impenetrable mystery to this president. There is a monstrous, looming Mt. Everest of economic studies and real-world examples that the Trump trade war and tariffs path leads to economic disaster. The irony was lost on the MAGA crowd, of course, but they're the ones who will bear the costs and the burden of his blistering stupidity.

That cruel nostalgia about closed borders and high tariffs making the nation secure militarily and economically was a snare and a delusion. It was Steve Bannon and Peter Navarro circle-jerking themselves into an alternate economic universe where Americans would stand on an assembly line soldering chips to PCBs for $2 an hour. The so-called trade deficit in material goods ignored the fundamental reality of the new American economy: we *do* things, not just *build* things. I know the tangible end product of a widget assembly line may seem more real, but American services, intellectual property, and ideas matter as much now as do cars, pork bellies, and frozen concentrated orange juice.

Americans, more than most, benefit from the global web of trade in goods and services. A global regime of free trade has made us richer, more influential, and more secure. It has opened up markets for U.S. products and services around the world. As in any global system of multivariate inputs the upsides can be unevenly distributed, but closing down a multidecade system of trade freedoms would inevitably lead to less, not more prosperity.

What Trump didn't, wouldn't, or couldn't understand was that sometimes the vast global consensus of experts is right. He just had to touch the hot stove. Since the defenders of Trump's trade policy were thin on the ground, his supporters often fell back on Ronald Reagan as a policy backstop. They were, of course, embarrassingly wrong about the impact of trade policy under Reagan. Colin Grabow and Scott Lincicome of the Cato Institute wrote:

> The WTO—ironically a Reagan-era accomplishment today decried by President Trump!—provides a new and impressive venue for resolving trade disputes without, in almost all cases, the need for unilateral action. The United States has prevailed in 86 percent of the complaints that it has brought to the WTO—all without angering our trading partners, disrupting markets, or burdening American consumers.
>
> Trumpist intellectuals' frequent invocations of Reagan to defend President Trump's protectionism ignore ample historical context, actual policy results, and the evolution of the modern global trading system. Seen in the proper light, Reagan's legacy argues strongly in favor of free trade and multilateral engagement, rather than a return to a bygone era of trade-policy failure.[2]

Trump's unfortunate press secretary Sarah Huckabee Sanders made a statement at the launch of Trump's trade war that is sure to go down in the Famous Dumb Last Words Hall of Fame. "We may have a little bit of short-term pain, but we're going to have long-term success," she said, just before the stock market cooked off over 1,000 points in a week.[3]

But the game wasn't played on a one-way street. The Chinese got a vote in the battle, and vote they did. Within days, and with a precision that made me laugh, they launched their own new round of tariffs on things like corn, hogs, and soybeans.

Trump apparently couldn't see into the future far enough to know that China would immediately put tariffs on bourbon from Mitch Mc-Connell's home state of Kentucky and on the Harley-Davidson motorcycles made in Paul Ryan's backyard.

All of China's decisions targeted districts and states squarely in the heart of Trump country. If Iowans didn't know about the ETTD curse before the trade war, they certainly got the picture rather quickly after its opening skirmishes. Trump, indulging his economic ignorance, never considered that in a boxing match on trade that China could push back with sanctions that hurt folks who voted for him.

Like all technopeasants and economic boobs, Trump didn't understand the global economy or the imperfect but resilient web of commerce that has made the U.S. and China the ultimate economic frenemies. Yes, Americans no longer build certain things our Chinese slave factories deliver. On the other hand, we enjoy cheap consumer goods, an astounding quality of life, and an economy that is as much about ideas as it is about heavy manufacturing.

He failed to understand that the Chinese could crash the entire U.S. economy if they sat out just one T-Bill auction. The idea that Trump is a brilliant international business leader is deeply embedded in the minds of people who watch too much reality television. There's just one problem: he's not. In the first major trade skirmish of the 21st century, he proved it over and over.

THE MODERN PARANOID STYLE

Trump's base is the logical end point of both the anti-intellectualism and the oft-cited "paranoid style of American politics" predicted by the great historian and observer of American political life Richard Hofstadter in 1964. Their contempt for experience, knowledge, and qualifications was perfectly captured in Tom Nichols's *The Death of Expertise* just as the Trump movement began its descent into outright rejection of traditional Republican and conservative principles.[4]

After the election, almost unbelievably, that paranoia became even more pronounced.

The Republican Party's headfirst dive into breathless conspiratorial fantasies in defense of President Trump was a brand-defining moment for the party of Lincoln. The GOP spent 2017 and 2018 morphing into the party of LaRouche. Listening as members of Congress, the Fox News and talk-radio world, and the constellation of batshit-crazy people drawn to Esoteric Trumpism adopted increasingly baroque theories to protect The Donald wasn't just depressing, it was tragic.

The tools that radically democratized communication and broke the monopoly of a few corporate media titans on shaping the national media agenda formed a sluice into the Facebook feeds of millions of voters. These voters aren't looking for news or information. They're looking for confirmation of their beliefs and their biases and for ways to justify their rage.

The diseased slurry of fake news, post-truth Trumpism, and Russkie agitprop available at the click of a mouse is ludicrous, comically overdrawn, patently false, and depressingly common. It wasn't just the postmodern propaganda stylings of Russia's information warfare specialists; a cottage industry of fake news sites of varying longevity appeared in a Darwinian struggle to get lower-middle-class Americans to click "Share" on their latest story of "Hillary and Huma's Recipe for Roast Baby."

This Ebola of wild-eyed, MK-ULTRA paranoiac raving quickly spread to every organ of the Republican body politic through disease vectors no one could have foreseen. Suddenly Reddit wasn't just nerdy dudes talking gaming, tech, and Bitcoin. Suddenly it was Midwestern Trump-fanatic housewives following Reddit's /r/the_donald and, God-forbid, 4chan. Conspiracy theories from Pizzagate to Uranium One, from Seth Rich to QAnon ("They're *all* connected, man, and just *wait* till I tell you about the Jewwwwws and global banking") became more involved, more complex, and more contingent on a continued suspension of disbelief.

In the spring of 2018, a Trump fan sent me a long email connecting a project I had done in German politics in 2005 to the "fact" that Angela Merkel was Hitler's daughter produced by a secret artificial insemination program and claiming I was part of the Rothschild–Catholic Church–communist-Soros conspiracy that Trump was working his heart out to stop. This person wasn't an ordinary troll, just a Trump-lover who has slipped into the warm bath of conspiracy cray.

The depth of this dive into paranoia, propaganda, and alternate truth illustrates just how deeply Trump touched the psyche of his followers. Part of it is understandable human psychology. There must be *something* causing the cognitive dissonance between what they see and what they want, and the more crazypants the theory, the more they find comfort in it.

Trump himself is one of the most aggressive peddlers of conspiracy theories, which should surprise no one at this point. The conspiracies he pushes to his audience of 50 million social media followers range from infamous to inane, but no president before ever had a personal media channel into the minds of millions of Americans. Why does this matter?

First, there is an abundantly clear chain of evidence stretching back more than a decade before he ran for office that Trump was inclined to believe the world is governed by dark forces that simply don't exist. The world is dark and crappy enough without making up new conspiracy theories to add to the chaos. Roger Stone, a longtime Trump insider and confidante, has both monetized and weaponized conspiracy nonsense for a generation.

Second, it matters because his followers aren't, to be generous, all that brilliant about parsing fantasy from reality, confirmation bias from data, and truth from the most dramatic fictional perspectives. Alternate facts aren't facts. The leap from "I want to believe Hillary is bad on the issues" to "Hillary murdered Seth Rich with her bare hands before changing out of her bloodied pantsuit to head over to a cannibal pizza party" is a short one for these folks, particularly when they have characters like Sean Hannity the Lord Haw-Haw of Fox stoking the lunatic flames.

Third, it matters because he's now the president of the United States of America. A president makes decisions based, one hopes, on facts, and from those facts makes policies based on principles. Much of what Donald Trump believes is based on facts only in the most tangential way, and the election of 2016 didn't punish him for this. His continued visitations to the catalogue of Greatest Conspiracy Hits to rouse his base to anger and action are as corrosive as they are dangerous.

Let's review a few of the *Infowars* President's most treasured kookspiracy favorites, shall we?

The ludicrous theory that Barack Obama was a Kenyan sleeper agent and that his birth certificate was fake sits atop a golden pyramid of dumbassery. It was always absurd, easily debunked, and politically idiotic, so of course Trump (inspired by Roger Stone, you'll be shocked to hear) embraced it with gusto. If there was a single, long-lead warning that my party would eventually lose its goddamned mind and sink into the messy world of alternate facts, this was it.

Trump's promotion of birtherism spanned Twitter, Fox News, and a host of television interviews. In March 2008 he appeared on *The View* with Whoopi Goldberg and Barbara Walters, milking the birther game for all it was worth. "I want him to show his birth certificate! There's something on that birth certificate that he doesn't like," said Trump.[5] A few days later he told *Fox & Friends*, "He's spent millions of dollars trying to get away from this issue. Millions of dollars in legal fees trying to get away from this issue. And I'll tell you what, I brought it up, just routinely, and all of a sudden a lot of facts are emerging and I'm starting to wonder myself whether or not he was born in this country."[6]

As you'd expect, Trump's birtherism was a gumbo of racism and easily disproved conspiracy lunacy. It continued well after Obama released a copy of his birth certificate in June 2008:

When I was 18, people called me Donald Trump. When he was 18, @BarackObama was Barry Soweto. Weird.[7]

I want to see @BarackObama's college records to see how he listed his place of birth in the application.[8]

The capstone of the crazy, and a peak moment of Trump's birtherism, came when Loretta Fuddy, the head of Hawaii's Department of Health, was killed in a small plane crash. Fuddy had verified for the world that Barack Obama's birth certificate wasn't the product of some decades-old plot to hide his birth in Kenya but a perfectly routine matter. Of course, Trump put the most lurid spin on her death, tweeting, "How amazing, the State Health Director who verified copies of Obama's 'birth certificate' died in plane crash today. All others lived."[9]

As a side note, I was the among the first (if not the first) GOP consultant to call out the birther bullshit. It took my opposition researcher three phone calls in 2008 to confirm the existence of the birth certificate and the newspaper article announcing his birth. It was always a dumb conspiracy, and Trump was always its most aggressive and mulishly stubborn advocate.

THREE MILLION ZOMBIES

Once upon a time, our firm was hired by an advocacy group called True the Vote. It was a rising force in the conservative landscape during the late Obama era, including playing a starring role in the Obama-era IRS targeting of conservative groups. When my associate Ryan Wiggins and I came on board, we treated it like any other political public relations client and went to work learning the ropes of their advocacy needs and their operation.

The sole predicate of True the Vote was that millions upon millions of illegal votes are cast in every election and that voter fraud is a rampant problem across the nation, which gives Democrats, the architects of this broad and systemic problem, an unspeakable electoral advantage.

Just like lawyers fighting for their clients, Ryan and I were ready to swing for the fences for ours. I'm sure if you dug through my Twitter archive and press statements, you'd find us doing just that.

At least at first. You see, there was just one problem. As the leading voter fraud prevention group in the country, True the Vote couldn't provide enough data to make a convincing case even for *us*, far less to paint a picture of a massive conspiracy to push illegal voters to the polls.

Sure, they had some individual pissant cases they could point to, but nothing broader than some one-off local yokel stories. Voter fraud, like voter suppression, does exist, but not at scale. It's a onesie-twosie precinct-level problem, not a dark and sinister Soros-Hillary–gray alien plot to subvert democracy.

I tell you the story of my True the Vote experience because, of course, Donald Trump believes that his popular vote loss against Crooked Hillary couldn't be because he's a morally loathsome jack-hole. It *must* have been some kind of conspiracy against him to *steal* the votes he bigly deserved. Thus began the oft-repeated Trumpian lie of 3 million illegal voters. Before the election, Trump and his allies claimed that millions of illegal aliens, dead people, criminals, and other undesirables would be out in force, all marshaled by Hillary's chthonic allies.

Before the 2016 election, when the numbers, common sense, and political landscape all indicated a Clinton victory, Trump's drama-queen tweets looked like a combination of preloss martyrdom and raving paranoia:

> The election is absolutely being rigged by the dishonest and distorted media pushing Crooked Hillary—but also at many polling places—sad.[10]

> Of course there is large-scale voter fraud happening on and before election day. Why do Republican leaders deny what is going on? So naive![11]

Even after his victory, Trump continued to sell his followers the myth that the 3 million Americans who voted for Clinton were the political undead. Amazingly, his followers continued to buy the conspiracy wholesale, even as the voter fraud commission Trump established fell under its own weight.

TED'S DAD

I touched on this a bit earlier when I profiled how Ted Cruz was one of Donald Trump's most important enablers. The dumbest smart guy in the race, Cruz not only let Trump call his wife ugly but could barely muster a coherent response to an attack never before seen in American politics—a presidential candidate accusing another presidential candidate's father of having played a role in the assassination of another president.

In our "dogs and fleas" department, you won't be surprised to find the origin of this particular theory came from the fevered mind of Roger Stone, who had—by the merest coincidence, I'm sure—a book out around that time about the assassination of John F. Kennedy.

The influence of Roger Stone, Roy Cohn's Mini-me, on Trump over the decades is one explanation for Trump's embrace of conspiracy; rather than politics, Stone's product in the past two decades has been a string of books about the "Bush Crime Family" and how JFK was killed by LBJ and how the Clintons have left a string of dead bodies in their wake.

Trump's natural instinct for propaganda is coupled with his love of conspiracy; dark forces acting to stop him from fulfilling the promise of MAGA, be they in the FBI, the media, or the Bavarian Illuminati. Roger went from appearing on the cable networks rather frequently as a showy but entertaining political hack to appearing on *Infowars* wearing a black beret and engaging in spittle-flecked old-man rants about getting the Deep State off his lawn.

Conspiracy politics are engaging. They're a way to get to a unified truth for people uncomfortable with the chaos and messiness of the real world. They offer some hint of an esoteric truth to explain the mundane and to enlighten those without the discipline to learn more about the mechanical details of politics, economics, and society. The rise of highly discrete, self-reinforcing and -selecting social media platforms and channels makes it easier than ever to have ideas that are patently absurd become the defining truths and public character of political parties and movements.

As a rule, conspiracies are hard to sustain. The old adage that three people can keep a secret if two of them are dead is consistently true, and in politics, where the currency is information and gossip, even one might be too many. Conspiracies are even harder to manage when you're stupid, as the Trump team proves every day.

Since projection is the sincerest form of flattery in Trumplandia, the idea that the insidious Never Trump movement is constantly stirring hatred of the president is a constant. I wish. Believe me, I'd love it if the secret Never Trump meetings looked like the get-together in *Eyes Wide Shut*. Who doesn't love a good cloak-and-mask orgy in a New York mansion while you're manipulating the secret levers of power?

As I said at the beginning of this chapter, I know I'm not supposed to make fun of Trump's base voters, but between their cultish worship of Trump, their abandonment of conservative principles, and their headlong embrace of batshit conspiracies, they make it all too easy.

Inside the Oval Office

(A Comedy in Five Acts)

– ACT IV –

One by one, they're all gone. Spicer. Bannon. Gorka. The Mooch. Sure, Jared and Ivanka are still around, but most days they keep to themselves. You'd liked Tillerson and Price and Dearborn, and it had been cool meeting a real-life celebrity like Omarosa. The place just kept slowly emptying out. You'd been able to move up to a slightly larger closet.

The president, perhaps twice or even four times a week, would call or summon you to the Oval. Once, you heard Hope Hicks hiss into her phone, "He's talking to his pet again." Soon, she was gone too. You tried to give the president good advice, when he asked for it, but most of the time he didn't ask. He just talked. And talked. And talked.

It was in the spring of 2018 when you noticed something you'd tried to avoid for a long time: Donald Trump wasn't just a little off kilter. He wasn't just different. As much as you loved him and your job at the White House, it was frightening to see him up close; unfocused, agitated, and as much as you hated to admit it, delusional.

You didn't have the heart to tell him that the Wall wasn't "already over 3,000 miles long" or that Robert Mueller had never been a high priest in a satanic child cannibalism ring based in the Target store in Alexandria, Virgina. Maybe the GDP wasn't up 41 percent, as the president claimed.

Was it Mueller? Russia? Maybe. Was it Stormy Daniels? Almost certainly; he talked about her "bangability" with you time and again, counseling you to follow the old "Grab 'em" strategy he'd perfected over the decades. You didn't have time to get your dry cleaning, much less date. Finally, the grim day arrived. John Kelly resigned. Jim Mattis took a walk. Almost none of the original cabinet remained. Zinke's perp walk had shocked no one except POTUS. The corruption cases mounted, the domestic policy achievements fell flat, and 2019 looked bleak as hell.

The House fell in the Fall of 2018's electoral sweep by Democrats. The Senate was a tie. The idea of getting the president out on the stump for his reelection campaign kept being deferred, ostensibly because the president was so busy, but in reality because he was so broken and crazy.

The Mueller investigation ground on and on, with a broken White House now largely abandoned. The elections of the fall of 2018 made it clear there wouldn't be much more MAGA agenda.

Melania had been out on a permanent Be Best tour, and had been romantically linked to the head of her security detail. The president hardly seemed to care, or even remember her. All he could talk about was Mueller.

Then, abruptly, the president looked up and said, "Fartknocker, I don't think you're cut out for this job. I asked you to save America, and all you've done is betray me."

You don't know where it came from. You thought everything was fine. You'd done your best to clean up the messes the old members of the cabinet and executive branch appointees had left behind. You realize something right then; he's loyal to nothing, and to no one.

8

LIMITED GOVERNMENT

AS A YOUNGER CONSERVATIVE, I TRIED MANY TIMES TO unwind some college liberal for conflating conservatism with fascism. "Conservatives aren't fascists," I'd say in slow, nonthreatening tones as I reached for a rock. "Fascists believe in government control of the state and of the economy. We believe in limiting the power of government and in free markets, individual liberty, and the rule of law."

On the other side of the equation, our libertarian friends used to basically pretend we could burn the entire enterprise of government to the ground and let a jolly wave of pure, cleansing anarchocapitalist fire set things right.

Of course, neither extreme was correct about mainstream limited-government conservatism, but we were largely in the sweet spot. We didn't want the government getting much bigger, but we didn't want grannies wrestling rats in the street for scraps of food, either.

Looking back on Republican presidents since Nixon, we see one hallmark in their campaign rhetoric and in their governance: a caution over the size, scope, cost, and power of government. None of them was perfect at restraining its growth (the Department of Homeland Security and George W. Bush's Medicare expansion stand as two particularly painful examples), but fans of an expanded state would be hard-pressed to see Reagan, George H. W. Bush, or George W. Bush embracing massive expansions in federal power without compelling reasons. After a beat-down in the 1994 elections, even Bill Clinton famously said, "The era of big government is over."

The defining ethos of limited-government conservatism still recognized the legitimate role of government and the powers of the state. The broad conservative consensus was that while the government is generally inefficient, slow, clumsy, dumb, overly intrusive, chock-full of layabouts, and has god-awful design sensibilities, there are areas for which the family, churches, social institutions, the market, and local government simply can't scale. No one expects Topeka, Kansas, to field a nuclear deterrent or Rhode Island to administer its own postal system.

So much for *that* argument in the era of Trump.

Generations of Republican candidates for House, Senate, governor, and local offices argued that government's size, power, and impact on everyday Americans was a pernicious danger to the Republic. Donald Trump erased that from the Republican vocabulary in a matter of months. Those in office who still believe government can be too big keep silent when President Statist pushes for a bigger, more intrusive state.

The GOP is now the party of big government, and it's all Trump's fault.

Like so many would-be and actual autocrats, Trump believes in an expanded state and putting the power of an expanded federal government to work for his political ends. He's also been surrounded at various times by a group of remoras that includes Steve Bannon, Michael Anton, Peter Navarro, Wilbur Ross, Larry Kudlow, and Stephen Miller, all of whom seem perfectly delighted to expand government power, as long as they're using it to carry out their nationalist-populist agenda.

In his first State of the Union speech, Trump called for a massive infrastructure bill, an affordable child care plan, trade restrictions, a border wall, and allowing governors "flexibility" to expand Medicare. If that last sounds familiar, it's what Obamacare did most effectively: gave states enormous tranches of money to spend like drunken sailors on shore leave.

"Compassionate conservatives" sought to turn the power of government to accomplish conservative ends while shrinking its numerous deleterious side effects. The thought that we could use government to aid the truly needy while moving people toward laudable goals like improved education outcomes, homeownership, and community service may not have been libertarian perfection, but it was at least a middle ground in the political space in which we really live, not Randian, not Fabian. The Troll Party of Trump has no hesitation in using the power of government to bring their fantasy economic and social policies to life. Trump has done more to destroy limited-government conservatism than George Soros could have accomplished in a thousand years.

This is where Trump's rhetorical hypnosis went to work. The message was no longer "Conservatives like me will restrain the power and scale of government." Now the message was "I'm going to expand government to fuck over the people you hate." This was the underlying Bannon-Anton-Miller Axis of Assholes' nationalism in its true form: "We're going to put the all-powerful state to work punishing those who have caused your grievances."

For all their objections to the "administrative state," it turns out that Trump's merry band of arsonists are perfectly happy to use the power of government to punish their enemies and to appease their base. If government is, as Ronald Reagan put it, "the enemy of liberty," then Trump's base has turned that idea on its head; now the government is the enemy of whoever the base hates most.

Reagan also spoke to generations of Republicans and conservatives when he said in 1986, "The nine most terrifying words in the English language are, 'I'm from the government and I'm here to help.'" For the Trump team, the new message is "I'm from the government, and I'm here to punish the people you hate."

WE HATE BIG GOVERNMENT, EXCEPT WHEN IT'S GETTIN' THE MESSICANS

In the 2008 presidential election, Barack Obama said in a July 2 speech something that set Republicans howling in paranoia and fury: "We cannot rely only on our military in order to achieve the national security objectives we've set. We've got to have a civilian national security force that's just as powerful, just as strong, just as well-funded." The quote was, of course, taken wildly out of context, but it didn't stop talk-radio hosts from losing their damn minds over it for days, and it didn't take long for members of Congress to follow suit.

Representative Paul Broun, a Republican from Georgia, spoke for many on the conservative side when he said, "That's exactly what Hitler did in Nazi Germany and it's exactly what the Soviet Union did. When he's proposing to have a national security force that's answering to him, that is as strong as the U.S. military, he's showing me signs of being Marxist."[1]

Contrast this with the Republican-cheering of Trump's national deportation force. A favorite trope of the 2016 campaign, Trump declared war on immigrants from his first speech as a candidate, and his promises to deport 11 to 14 million illegal immigrants was a singular hit with his base. As opposed to Obama's imagined—and never implemented—civilian national security force, Trump's team moved quickly to deliver on his promise to put the power of the state to work to Make America Less Hispanic.

Trump immediately signed Executive Order 13767 to kick off the immigration and deportation crackdown he repeatedly, tiresomely promised his base.[2] Almost immediately the party of small government was pushing to vastly expand the size of the Customs and Border Patrol, Immigration and Customs Enforcement, and the Department of Homeland Security.

It was also all-in on expanding private prison contracts to house those arrested in the deportation effort and bellowed about how soon Trump would build his border wall.[3] These not so subtle efforts were a signal to his alt-right and less savory supporters that he was going to prevent the one future that makes Mark Krikorian, Mickey Kaus, and Ann Coulter wake up in a cold sweat, the infamous "browning of America."[4] By the spring of 2018, however, Trump's promises to build the Wall had flopped like a branded Trump Tower in some third-world craptocracy. Time and again he'd tweet about the Wall, only to blow it when Congress presented spending bills in which a smarter, more canny president might have made a deal and delivered on his signature promise in the first year. Sad!

Trump had to do something to relieve the pressure. For a hot minute, he tried to fund the Wall through the Department of Defense budget, only to be schooled on the appropriations process. He then ordered 4,000 national guard troops to the border. This move was a lot less than it seemed; Presidents Bush and Obama both had deployed U.S. forces to support ICE and Customs. His followers, though, including the odious Ann Coulter, hoped that American troops would soon be shooting Mexican migrants as they crossed into the United States. On the Lars Larson radio program, Coulter said, "If you shoot one to encourage the others, maybe they'll learn."[5]

FISCAL CONSERVATISM GOES BELLY UP

Trump's budgets and spending plans are, as you might imagine, reflective of a man who has lived on credit his entire life, never balanced the books, and never cared if his debts were paid. The party that screamed its lungs out that Barack Obama was bankrupting America during his eight-year term is suddenly just fine on record debts, deficit spending, easy money flooding Wall Street from the Fed, and every other form of economic heresy of the erstwhile Republican philosophy of fiscal probity. Trump's proposals of a trillion here and a trillion there in new federal spending are reflective not only of his own lifetime addiction to greater-fool-theory credit but also of an utter lack of even a passing regard for fiscal sanity.

Trump's first budgets were wonders of rosy scenarios, mathematical legerdemain that opens up entirely new fields of number theory, phantom budget cuts, and mythical savings from that old favorite "Ending fraud, waste, and abuse." His first budget was received even by many of Trump's fans in Congress with the same delight as one might experience on finding a turd in a punchbowl.

Even the Heritage Foundation's Stephen Moore, a Trump supporter and sometime advisor, was displeased. "It is a big spending budget," he said. "And that's not what, you know, conservatives want to see. Whether Republicans are hypocritical—I mean, I think right now you could say they are because they certainly criticized Obama for running up big deficits, which he did. But now we're seeing that happen under a Republican administration. . . . This is a very unusual Republican budget."[6]

And about that whole "smaller government" promise? Not so much. The Trump budget projects a 55% rise in federal spending between 2017 and 2028. For those of you playing our game at home, 55% is rather a goddamn lot.

Trump gave the GOP what it obviously had always wanted. Instead of the fiscal discipline we pledged and campaigned on for generations and that is objectively necessary for the nation's long-term fiscal health, we adopted the economics of Donald Trump's life. Borrow. Spend. Crash. Go bankrupt. Find greater-fool lenders for the next round of borrowing, spending, crashing, and bankruptcy.

Our reputation for fiscal conservatism always had a whiff of bullshit about it, even in eras when we had control of the House, Senate, and White House. We talked a big game on entitlement reform, lowering the burdens on middle-class taxpayers, and ending the kind of government lard voters roundly pretend to hate until it gets spent in their districts or states. In the age of Trump, we largely stopped pretending. I've made a hundred ads for candidates and written as many speeches in which they promise on the lives of their children that they're going to be the one who finally gets to Washington and cuts the wasteful spending at the Department of Wasteful Spending. They're going to be the one who finally gets control of government spending, cuts regulations, and bitchslaps that deficit so hard it never shows its face in This Town again.

Yeah. At least Trump let my party stop pretending. Eat, spend, and be merry, for tomorrow we may die broke.

Oh, there are still a few tattered, dodgy fig leaves covering our fiscal junk. With the passage of the tax bill, Paul Ryan and Mitch McConnell created a new super-extra-special Budget Committee to finally, really, pinkie-swear-for-real finally get America's fiscal house in order. Wink emoji. Love ya. Mean it.

Budget expert and economist Stan Collender nailed it when he said, "This new select committee on the budget isn't just utter nonsense, it's an insult to our intelligence. We're being told not to look at the big deficit hikes that were just enacted but to pay attention instead to yet another attempt to prevent it from happening again."[7]

INFRASTRUCTURE

Ah, infrastructure. The policy unicorn that everyone loves in theory, that Congress and lobbyists dine out on for their constituents and clients, and that always flops on execution. In the Trump era, Republicans threw aside their objections to massive, top-down federal stimulus programs. And let's face it, that's all "infrastructure" plans are, really. Everyone loves cutting the ribbons and having a bridge named after them, but most of these programs fall far short of their promised economic benefits. Or at least that's what conservatives used to believe.

Trump's $1.5 trillion infrastructure plan was a back-of-the-envelope political creation of Commerce Secretary Wilbur Ross, trade warrior Peter Navarro, and Steve Bannon. Their interests were a combination of oligarchic self-interest, economic nationalism, and raw populism, and the plan reflected just that. The Kellyanned version of it went like this: "We are going to fix our inner cities and rebuild our highways, bridges, tunnels, airports, schools, hospitals. We're going to rebuild our infrastructure, which will become, by the way, second to none. And we will put millions of our people to work as we rebuild it."[8]

A few conservative economists, such as the Competitive Enterprise Institute's Marc Scribner, expressed their skepticism over the plan. Scribner wrote, "Contrary to the dominant political narrative from members of both parties, which is parroted uncritically by most of the press, there is little evidence that these public works projects promote long-run economic growth."[9]

Trump's $1.5 trillion infrastructure plan included $200 billion in federal spending and a whole lot of "public-private partnership" magical thinking and never got much further than being mocked each time it was brought up as the theme of the week.

MORE BOOM-BOOM FOR SUPREME GENERALISSIMO TRUMP

Here's an irony: I spent part of my early career trying to save the defense budget when I worked in Dick Cheney's Pentagon at the end of the cold war. We were going to have a "peace dividend" if it killed us. In terms of our defense budgets, it almost did.

In the years that followed I helped corporate defense contractor clients fight for DOD contracts to build a variety of things that either spy on the bad guys or leave a smoking crater where the bad guys were just before we decided their bunker, desert tent, drug lab, or condo needed to go boom. While it's not all for North Korean–style missile parades, Trump's defense spending plans aren't tethered to a revised international defense strategy, but rather to a mere bigger-is-better preference. Donald Trump's record-breaking defense spending plan hit the $716 billion mark in 2018, leaving even Mick Mulvaney, Trump's relentlessly upbeat budget chief, shaking his head. In the anodyne language of the *Washington Post*, it was "a major increase that signals a shift away from concerns about [the] rising deficit" and was "a setback for deficit hawks."[10]

By "setback" they meant "Sweet Jesus, that's a lot of money. At least it's for Mattis."

FAMILY LEAVE

Another of Trump's proposals that dragged conservatives down a path of policy apostasy came in the form of Ivanka Trump's family leave proposals. Giving parents paid leave so they can care for newborn kids is a puppies-and-kittens plan. Who wouldn't love that? In 1993 Congress passed and President Bill Clinton signed the Family and Medical Leave Act, which provides up to 12 weeks of unpaid leave for family medical needs or childbirth.[11] The catch, of course, is the whole "unpaid" part.

Long a tentpole argument of the Democrats, paid family leave is the standard everywhere else in the world. Republicans had forever rolled their eyes over this, with an ironic sigh, and said, "Yes, we get it. Norway is awesome. How ya gonna pay for it?" The idea had its Republican adherents, including my friend Marco Rubio. You can see why it's broadly popular.

At least until the topic of, you know, paying for the damn thing comes front and center. Republicans struggled for ages on how to provide paid leave without breaking the bank.

Looking for a way to get suburban mommies to think the GOP isn't a party of rotund, ass-slapping old white dudes? Well, hello, ladies. Meet the Ivanka Trump Family Leave Plan.[12]

Sounds great, right? The Devil in the details was the price tag. The plan championed by Ivanka Trump used—wait for it—Social Security to pay for it. Already reeling from an unsustainable financial model and staggering under costs driven by a steep growth curve on its disability benefits, Social Security wasn't a logical pool of money for this proposal, which almost any rational political figure could have suggested to Team Trump on day one.

The Democrats' proposal for paid family leave has long been centered on a new federal payroll tax, which in a moment of stark political irony makes their position more conservative than the Trump plan. Yes, they want a gazillion-dollar new nanny state entitlement. But at least they weren't engaged in magical thinking on how to get there.

ENTITLEMENT REFORM AND THE GOP ARE NEVER NEVER NEVER GETTING BACK TOGETHER

When it comes to reforming Social Security, Medicare, and Medicaid, Trump knows his audience; he's not touching the three entitlement programs that drive the vast bulk of federal spending. Those folks rely on federal largesse, despite their avowed desire to get gubmint on a fiscal diet. Despite the acknowledged coming insolvency of all of them, Trump said from the start that he'd leave them as is.

Paul Ryan, an otherwise passionate champion of entitlement reform, first said that without entitlement reform he couldn't bring the budget in balance and pay for Trump's defense spending spree. Later, Ryan appeared to give Trump a pass, because frankly, that's become Ryan's only option. Instead of accepting Trump's Shermanesque statement on entitlement reform, Ryan did a back flip worthy of a Bulgarian gymnast by claiming entitlement reform would affect "people near retirement age."

Ryan has been consistently right about the need to fix these programs, but he keeps missing the emotional problem with cutting even a dime from Medicare, Medicaid, and Social Security. They are wired deeply into the American culture of soft socialism, and the GOP never truly had the appetite to fix them, despite the Tea Party's endless bloviating on the subject.

Despite Ryan's desires, Trump read the hypocrisy of the GOP base like the experienced con man he is. He knows his support skews older, poorer, and whiter. Particularly in the red-state target markets where Esoteric Trumpism was greeted with whoops that would shake the mold off a trailer's walls, those social programs—and increasingly the disability program of Social Security—aren't considered big government. They are an economic mainstay.

A much-mocked trope from the peak of the Tea Party era occurred at a town hall meeting held by Representative Robert Inglis of South Carolina. A man stood up and angrily demanded of Inglis,

"Keep your government hands off my Medicare." Now take that moment and inject it with a massive bolus of meth, Oxycontin, resentment, and simmering white working class anger, and Donald Trump was never, ever going to go there.

Decades of fell warnings of the entitlement program doom that was coming to us are now in the memory hole. Paul Ryan can't even broach his favorite topic of entitlement reform in 2018, given midterm elections are coming and most of America views the GOP with the same warmth and regard as they do genital warts. Whoever replaces Ryan as Speaker won't do it in 2020, because Donald Trump will be running for reelection. The fiscal time bombs of Medicare, Medicaid, and Social Security are still ticking.

Trump will likely be dead of a KFC-induced heart attack before we face up to them.

"COAL" IS TRUMP FOR "SOLYNDRA"

Donald Trump's economic nostalgia is a powerful force, both for him and for his followers. Nothing, though, seems to ring his Proustian bell for the industrial era like coal.

Ah, coal. The shittiest, most miserable, most polluting, most dangerous energy source in our portfolio. The industry had been dying a deserved slow death at the hands of natural gas and solar until Donald Trump decided to try to revive it with a suite of executive orders and the leadership of Scott Pruitt at the Environmental Protection Agency.

Barack Obama's early plans to encourage a green-energy sector in the U.S. included loan guarantees for companies like the solar-energy vaporware firm Solyndra. When Solyndra was granted a $535 million loan guarantee in March 2009, Republicans lost their minds in anger. The phrase "picking winners and losers" was one of the GOP's central talking points in opposition to Obama's stimulus and its emphasis on green energy.

Representative Paul Ryan didn't like it much then, and made it clear on *Fox News Sunday* after Solyndra met its inevitable demise.

"There are billions more of this exact kind of spending that came out of the stimulus that will produce these results we fear. This is industrial policy and crony capitalism at its worst. It's exhibit A for how this kind of economic policy doesn't work. We shouldn't be picking winners or losers in Washington. We should be setting the conditions for economic growth so that the private sector can create jobs. Washington is not good at picking winners and losers, so we shouldn't try."[13]

Trump consigliere and walking time machine Steve Bannon once said of his plans, "I'm the guy pushing a trillion-dollar infrastructure plan. With negative interest rates throughout the world, it's the greatest opportunity to rebuild everything. Shipyards, ironworks, get them all jacked up. We're just going to throw it up against the wall and see if it sticks. It will be as exciting as the 1930s, greater than the Reagan revolution—conservatives, plus populists, in an economic nationalist movement."[14]

Coal? Ironworks? Why not America's long-lost buggy whip industry? Isn't it time we revived our vital town crier market sector as well?

Trump's own tactics attempting to shame companies who threatened to outsource jobs played out both on the campaign trail and in the early days of his presidency, and reflect Trump's authoritarian streak as the National Bully.

These were American companies competing in a global marketplace. Trump's threats to punish them with the power of his tweets, his bully pulpit, and his government sent a shock through the corporate world.

Trump's early experiments with trying to browbeat private companies into submission were like chapters out of the Junior Authoritarians Activity Guide. Ford, Carrier, GM, and Boeing were early examples of Trump's attempting to use his Twitter pulpit. He scared firms into announcements they would be bringing jobs back from overseas, or canceling foreign manufacturing deals in order to placate Mad King Don's online rages: "General Motors is sending Mexican made model of Chevy Cruze to U.S. car dealers—tax free across border. Make in U.S.A. or pay big border tax!"[15]

LESS GOVERNMENT . . . BUT
IS THAT WEED I SMELL?

The nation made up its mind on marijuana a long, long time ago. We're okay with it. Personally, I haven't smoked it since 1985, but you do you. In what represents almost a perfect test case of conservative hypocrisy in the age of Trump, suddenly the great and terrible powers of the federal government have been activated in Drug War Version 9.0.

For all the blathering by conservatives about respecting the states, adhering to the 10th Amendment, and fighting for individual choices and freedom, the Trump Party looked at the ballot initiatives and laws passed in the states to reform the draconian sentencing and possession guidelines for marijuana and said, "Whoa there! The Devil's Weed must be stopped!" in the righteous tones of a southern tent preacher.

Massive majorities in both major political parties favor legalizing medical marijuana and the decriminalization of possession. Majorities favor legalization of marijuana for personal use. In states that have decriminalized and legalized, regulated, tax-paying markets have emerged, providing jobs and revenue to the states and stopped the prison pipeline where (primarily) young black men have languished for possession of as little as one ounce of marijuana.

In the event you've been living under a rock, the war on drugs has failed spectacularly. All wars on drugs fail spectacularly. Republicans used to believe this. Libertarian Republicans used to hold this as a central article of faith.

No longer.

Trump's payback to antidrug hard-liner Sheldon Adelson played directly into the skill set of Jeff Sessions, a Republican senator turned attorney general, turned scourge of the 420 crowd. Sessions saw the states exercising their power to manage their own affairs, set their own sentences, and decide what recreational chemicals their citizens could consume after a long day and turned the DOJ into a wrecking ball.

Reversing an Obama-era policy of minimal federal regulation of

state marijuana laws, Reefer Madness Sessions went to work destroying a multibillion-dollar sector of the emerging economy.

When Obama's administration used Operation Choke Point to
cut off access to banking, credit card processing, and other financial
services to thousands of legal, licensed firearms dealers, many Republicans (myself most certainly included) went apoplectic at the vast
federal overreach. Sessions has turned exactly those same tools on
the marijuana industry, with only muttering from the GOP in return.

Individual choices? The 10th Amendment? Getting Washington
out of the business of the states?

Not in the age of Trump.

LIVE BY THE EO, DIE BY THE EO

The problem with unlimited government is that it keeps getting bigger, metastasizing into more and more forms that its creators never
envisioned. Departments and their missions creep over wider and
wider swaths of American life, expanding into territory their creators
never intended.

Many Republicans looking for ways to justify their embrace of
Trump fall back on one particular node of reasoning that I find completely insufficient: claiming that Trump is using executive orders and
regulations to "get things done."

They keep insisting that Trump's governance by executive order
and by policy changes is a true accomplishment for conservatism.
They're wrong, of course, both in substance and in the procedural
nature of how a conservative can and should govern.

By their own words from just a few years ago, Obama was a law-
less tyrant for using executive orders. The headlines from the conservative press were breathless and hyperbolic:

EXECUTIVE ORDER TYRANNY—OBAMA PLANS
TO RULE AMERICA WITH PEN, PHONE[16]

OBAMA'S CHIEF OF STAFF ADMITS THEY WANT TYRANNY[17]

THREE WAYS OBAMA'S EXECUTIVE ORDERS
ARE THE WORST OF ANY PRESIDENT[18]

OBAMA THE TYRANT: A PRESIDENTIAL OVERREACH
THAT UNDERMINES THE MOST IMPORTANT FOUNDATION
OF THE WESTERN POLITICAL TRADITION[19]

I was no fan of it myself, but if governing by executive order was wrong when Obama did it, why not when Trump does it? Is it just one more hypocritical knot in this skein of excuses Republicans will make for Trump? The likely explanation is the paucity of other accomplishments; executive orders and regulatory tweaking are almost all they've got to show for a president who kills most of the legislation he touches.

Executive orders are by their very nature ephemeral, intangible, and easily subject to the whim and whimsy of the next president, be they Democrat or Republican. When executive orders are reversed, as Trump reversed many of Obama's, we end up reposing more and more power in the hands of the executive branch. It gives Congress less and less motivation to act.

Executive orders and bureaucratic tweaking have almost no impact compared to the passage of a law. Will you get every single thing you might like in a sweeping executive order compared to a messy legislative fight? No, of course not.

I know it's old-fashioned, but it takes us back to the pesky intent of the Founders, as always. They envisioned this kind of problem and built the dynamics of compromise into our Constitution and our system of government precisely because they knew competing states and districts would have competing interests and ideals. They understood that Congress would be responsive to different cues than the executive. The goal was to pass laws and govern, and not merely by executive fiat. There are areas where executive orders are appropriate, necessary, and beneficial. Day-to-day governance is not one of those areas.

Conservatives taking victory laps over Trump's reversal of rules on coal, oil drilling, climate change, abortion, and other issues important to the cause are overlooking the fact that they haven't truly achieved anything more than a momentary victory. They've given future Democratic presidents the justification not only to undo what Trump has done but to impose new executive orders of their own and continue to diminish the role of Congress in setting the laws that govern this nation.

Inside the Oval Office

A Comedy in Five Acts

– ACT V –

You look around your office one last time. The uniformed-division Secret Service officer is standing behind you. There's not much to take, really.

A small framed photo of you and POTUS, the president grinning and shooting the thumbs-up. Your phone. A handkerchief Ivanka had dropped coquettishly near your door. The copy of "The 879th Turning: An Examination of History and Power Through the Story of Locusts" Steve Bannon had given you.

You realize you're a microcosm of the entire administration. You had no business being here, and once you were, you didn't know what your real job was from one moment to the next. You'd been surrounded by people who were similarly in the dark about their real missions, and about who had power and authority in the process. No one was loyal to anyone else in the building. It wasn't a team of rivals; it was a raw Hobbesean nest of vipers.

Like everyone else, you'd bought in to the image of Trump as a decisive leader, but after so many months up close, you discovered he was anything but. This moment of self-awareness stretches for a long, long time, until the officer politely clears his throat.

As you walk down the White House drive, you think about home, and how you'll tell your family the president fired you. Then you realize it.

Being fired by this president may have been the best thing that could have come out of this experience. You head for a bar near the White House. It's on the edge of the George Washington University campus, about a block away. It's dim and quiet and there's a gorgeous woman at the bar, sipping a tequila. It's the First Lady. Her detail is nearby, but they recognize you.

She beckons you over and smiles.

You croak out, "He fired me. And God help me, I'm happy."

"Don't vorry," she whispers, "Ze Donald divorces everyone in ze end. In meantime, tequila. Is good. Be best."

9

THE GROWN-UPS
ALL DIE TOO

BY APRIL 2018, DONALD TRUMP'S ADMINISTRATION HAD lost more Cabinet members and senior staff than any administration in the past 150 years. Even the mature, experienced people who came to serve the president with the best of intentions left with their dignity strip-mined away by Trump's circus act. Reputations and political futures have been shattered. Decades of good deeds and honorable service have been stained. The burn rate of the moral, intellectual, and political capital of the people who joined Team Trump is spectacular by any standard.

THE TERRIBLE TRAGEDY
OF JOHN KELLY

After the departure of the hapless, luckless Reince Priebus at the end of July 2017, the White House needed a break. The chaos field around Trump was intense, and the news hits coming against his presidency made it seem as if the White House was lurching from one crisis to the next. In the brief interregnum between naming a new chief of staff, America watched the antics of Anthony Scaramucci, a man with the affect of a person deeply familiar with the edgy joys of Bolivian

Marching Powder. Scaramucci's rise as the court jester of the Trump White House soon came to a screeching halt.

The warring factions inside Trump World that had pushed Reince off the cliff needed a steady hand. They needed a grown-up. They needed adult supervision. They needed John Francis Kelly. Kelly, a 45-year Marine Corps veteran, had served honorably and well, rising through the Corps with a reputation as a man who got things done. In the long-running war on terror, he also made a sacrifice few in the highest reaches of government do in this age; his son, 1st Lt. Robert Michael Kelly, USMC, died in combat in Sangin, Afghanistan, in 2010.

In Kelly each faction thought they'd be getting something they needed. For the Bannonites, Stephen Miller, and their ilk, Kelly would be an administrative accelerator for their plans to purge America of the brown people. For Jared and Ivanka, it was a way to discipline Daddy and keep their sinecures intact. For Team Crony and the Gold-man Guys, it was a moment to relish—finally, a strong professional who could tamp down Trump's worst impulses, end the tweeting, and focus the White House on what mattered: their tax cut plan. A nervous Washington expected Kelly would finally discipline Trump, cut off the flood of crazy articles thrown on his desk, and end the tweeting.

Gen. John Kelly is a man out of central casting for the job of White House turnaround executive. He was already vetted and was serving as secretary of homeland security when he was named chief of staff. He was perfect on paper, a disciplined, accomplished military leader with deep experience in managing complex, multivariate problems and or-ganizations. Kelly is bluff and straight-talking, finally the grown-up that Trumper Room needed to settle the boisterous children down for a nap.

Kelly has qualities Trump himself lacks: discipline, focus, and di-plomacy. Like every other military general who pins on that fourth star, Kelly had been through the military's charm school and he can work with discretion and determination.

He would also begin to lose all of those characteristics the mo-ment he took the job as chief of staff.

He had some wins on the front end. If there was a polar opposite to John Kelly for seriousness, it was the aforementioned hypercaffeinated White House leprechaun Anthony Scaramucci. Within hours of Scaramucci's announcing he reported directly to the president and didn't have to work through the chief of staff, Kelly dropped the hammer on the Mooch. Trump gave Kelly the latitude to do it, and DC saw the firing of Scaramucci from his role as White House communications director as a Good Thing. After a twilight struggle with Steve Bannon, Kelly sent Bannon off to spend more time with his gout.

In a reality-TV show moment worthy of an Emmy, Kelly fired Trump's longtime sister-from-another-mother reality-TV frenemy Omarosa Manigault. Omarosa had been identified as one of the people around Trump who would stoke his already lavish sense of entitlement, his rampant paranoia, and his juvenile desire to scrap with people. Lachlan Markay and Asawin Suebsaeng of the *Daily Beast* called her "'Patient Zero' for unfettered access to the Boss."[1] She played Trump's ego, vanity, and rages like a fiddle, and Kelly needed exactly the opposite.

On the day she was dragged from the White House grounds, it was said she tried without success to enter the Residence.[2] It's remarkable she's alive. Someday, the video will leak. Omarosa, honey, the cameras were rolling, but not the ones you're used to on *The Apprentice* and *Big Brother*.

It went downhill from there. By the spring of 2018, Kelly's transformation as an effective counter to Trump's impulsivity and indiscipline had fallen apart. Like the rest of the White House and the rest of America, he was just along for the ride. Kelly might make the paper flow move smoothly, but he can't stop the president from digging himself into deeper political and legal holes and from giving the perverse imp on his shoulder free rein.

After the death of U.S. Army Sgt. La David Johnson, a Green Beret killed on a mission in Nigeria, the president called his grieving widow. It didn't go well. Trump is alleged to have told her that Johnson "knew what he signed up for" and that the president struggled to remember her husband's name.[3]

Their conversation took place in the presence of Congresswoman Frederica Wilson, an African American Democrat from Florida who backed up the wife's account. A few days later, Kelly tried to challenge Wilson's account by claiming Frederica Wilson had lied and exaggerated at an event he'd attended during his tenure with U.S. Southern Command. It turned out Kelly's account was itself a lie.[4] It wasn't a good look.

Then Kelly raised eyebrows in October 2017 when he wandered into the swamp of defending Robert E. Lee's honor.[5] In a White House that had nearly been destroyed by its long flirtation with the alt-right and its disastrous handling of the racist hate march organized by white supremacist and Nazi fanboy Richard Spencer. After Charlottesville, Kelly might have been a wee bit more mindful when it comes to celebrating Confederate generals.

Kelly had originally been placed in the Department of Homeland Security because he was perceived to have two things Trump loves: a military background and a hard-line position on immigration. Kelly was there during the notoriously botched rollout of Trump's Muslim ban and had been a stalwart defender of the ban and of the rest of Trump's vocal anti-immigrant rhetoric. It should have been a tell that some of the values our military holds dear today—inclusion, teamwork, the sense that America really is an ideal, not just a race—got lost somewhere along the way in the belly of the Trump beast.

Days before what would become a defining moment in the progression of Kelly's terminal death from ETTD, he stepped into a verbal bear trap. When asked if the president would extend the deadline for deporting the American-raised children of illegal immigrants covered under the DACA program, he responded, "There are 690,000 official DACA recipients and the president sent over what amounts to be two and a half times that number, to 1.8 million. The difference between 690 and 1.8 million were the people that some would say were too afraid to sign up, others would say were too lazy to get off their asses, but they didn't sign up."[6]

"Too afraid or too lazy" was a sign Kelly was growing quite comfortable with the Trump White House's style of racial dog-whistling. DACA is an issue the rational few in the White House understand is a double-edged sword. On the one hand, the Make America White Again demo at the heart of Trump's base wants everyone with a vowel at the end of their surname deported on the next train down Mexico way. On the other hand, they understand how utterly catastrophic the politics of ripping apart law-abiding immigrant families looks. As DC struggled to resolve DACA, Trump's chief of staff's gaffe tore another hole in Kelly's position as an honest broker.

For all Kelly's missteps and failure to rein in Trump's behavior, it was Rob Porter who permanently broke John Kelly's reputation. The story of Rob Porter would be unexceptional in most cases, but Kelly's handling of it shows in many ways just how deeply compromised he'd become by spending time in the moral vacuum of Trump's personal orbit.

Porter was serving in one of those faceless, anonymous, and utterly vital White House jobs you've never heard of: staff secretary and personal assistant to the president. The person holding this job has some of the most frequent and intimate contacts with the president and chief of staff. It was Porter's role to help John Kelly keep the paper flowing to the president, and by all accounts his was a rising star in Trump World.

There was just one problem. Porter's ex-wives and friends told the FBI he had been physically violent and emotionally abusive in the course of their relationships. Porter, a man handling some of the most sensitive and consequential documents placed before the president, was unable to be cleared by the FBI for a Top Secret/SCI clearance the job required. Hell, with a reputation like that, Porter wouldn't pass the background check at a Waffle House.

This was a widespread problem in the Trump White House, given that many of the people willing to work there were either dragged away from the bus station with promises of a fifth of Olde Ocelot bourbon and a hot meal, or were of the problem-child sort of DC fourth-stringers.

The problem for Kelly wasn't simply that he defended Porter even after the revelations were public. It was that Kelly knew of Porter's difficulties in getting a clearance six months earlier. White House Counsel Don McGahn was also aware of Porter's background as an alleged domestic abuser for more than a year by the time the story broke.[7]

Kelly made it worse by initially issuing a ringing defense of Porter's character, partly engineered by Porter's then-girlfriend Hope Hicks, who took over as the White House Communications director after Scaramucci was booted. "Rob Porter is a man of true integrity and honor," Kelly vouched, "and I can't say enough good things about him. He is a friend, a confidant and a trusted professional. I am proud to serve alongside him."[8]

Kelly was forced to issue an awkward backfill statement to try to undo the mess he'd created for himself.

Days later, Kelly was forced to dismiss another White House staffer for domestic abuse. In a period when the MeToo movement was reviving a frankly moribund class of political feminism, Kelly's actions would have hurt any chief of staff. Hovering over Kelly's failures in judgment, however, was President Pussy Grabber's reputation as a serial and self-admitted sexual harasser.[9]

From the now-ubiquitous adult-film actress and object of Trump's temporary affections Stormy Daniels to a cast of 19 women who came forward to tell their stories of Trump's sexual misconduct, harassment, and sleaze, Trump's attitude toward women is a matter of public infamy. Even though Trump was later reported to have said Porter was "sick," he continued to defend his former aide as Kelly twisted in the wind.[10] Trump's views toward women clearly infected his White House at some level, John Kelly included.

Everything Trump touches dies, and in this White House, John Kelly's reputation and honor were no exception. Watching Kelly's stature dissolve in the acidic slurry of amorality, stupidity, and moral blindness of the Trump White House was a slow-motion tragedy that made his former military comrades shake their heads and made Washington ask itself a painful question: "If this guy can't get him under control, who or what can?"

REX TILLERSON'S YEAR IN HELL

Rex Tillerson was a letter-perfect pick for a Trump secretary of state; the wealthy corporate titan is the former CEO of Exxon, Russia-philic, tall, and equipped with a sweeping head of silver hair. He looks the part, which is important for Shallow Don, and he is a big-swinging-dick corporate type Trump only dreams of being.

While Tillerson hadn't been his first choice, a number of people close to Tillerson put his name on Trump's radar screen as the president was trying to decide between Mitt Romney, Rudy Giuliani, and Shakes the Clown.[11] His first reaction to the Exxon CEO bordered on gushing enthusiasm combined with his usual reality-TV salesmanship.

Trump jumped in as Tillerson's hype man, teasing Tillerson's name for secretary, and from December 2016 to February 2017 it was all sunshine and praise. Reading these tweets a year and a half later and knowing how far Tillerson would fall is redolent with irony:

> Whether I choose him or not for "State"—Rex Tillerson, the Chairman & CEO of ExxonMobil, is a world class player and dealmaker. Stay tuned![12]

> I have chosen one of the truly great business leaders of the world, Rex Tillerson, Chairman and CEO of ExxonMobil, to be Secretary of State.[13] The thing I like best about Rex Tillerson is that he has vast experience at dealing successfully with all types of foreign governments.[14]

> Congratulations to Rex Tillerson on being sworn in as our new Secretary of State. He will be a star![15]

Trump's coming hatred of Tillerson should have been obvious from the start. Tillerson's decades of international business experience involved more than licensing skyscraper projects and cheap ties. He knew people abroad and where many of the levers of power were located, particularly in the Middle East and Russia. While Donald Trump was hustling real estate branding deals, crappy steaks, and a strip-mall "university," Rex Tillerson was running the largest public corporation in the world. While Donald Trump was eyeballing beauty pageant contestants in their dressing rooms, Rex Tillerson was expanding Exxon's global reach as the world's energy giant.

Tillerson was confirmed with a sigh of relief from Republicans and Democrats in the Senate. He was one of the Axis of Adults, a man who spoke their language and who wasn't one of the outliers or edge cases inside the already restive White House.

His marching orders at the State Department represented some of the worst instincts of the nationalist populist mafia at the White House and Trump's own vast overestimation of his ability to negotiate with foreign leaders and powers. The long-running cliché of the State Department as a branch of government on its own, impervious to reform and to reorganization, wasn't far from the truth, but its unique, vital, oddball set of needs and roles in the world meant that no president of either party burned it to the ground.

The arsonist cadre around Trump had other ideas. The soft power of the State Department represented a role for America in the world they simply can't abide: multipolar, internationalist, global in reach and perspective. The neo-isolationist, Build the Wall and Stop the Brown People crowd around Miller, Gorka, Bannon, et al., viewed State as an enemy of their vision of an America with a smaller footprint around the globe. Also, Hillary Clinton had been secretary of state under Obama, so the only rational solution was to nuke Foggy Bottom from orbit.

Tillerson's first actions were to ensure his frenemies at the White House would let him get on with the work at hand, so the firings in Foggy Bottom began. It was, as the *New York Times* reported, "a parade of dismissals and early retirements that decimated the State Department's senior ranks." As happened in other departments under other secretaries, Tillerson either never had the authority to fill State's politically appointed positions or lacked the inclination to do so.[16]

Applying all the dumbest management clichés from the corporate sector, Tillerson clearly had been told that shredding the institution was the order of the day, and he got to work doing just that. One former diplomat wrote:

> Tillerson has canceled the incoming class of foreign service officers. This is as if the Navy told all of its incoming Naval Academy officers they weren't needed. Senior officers have been unceremoniously pushed out. Many saw the writing on the wall and just retired, and many others are now awaiting buyout offers. He has dismissed State's equivalent of an officer reserve—retired FSOs [foreign service officers], who are often called upon to fill State's many short-term staffing gaps, have been sent home despite no one to replace them. Office managers are now told three people must depart before they can make one hire.[17]

No matter how much Tillerson was initially willing to endure of Trump's erratic nature, pissy sniping, and the chaos in the administration, by the summer of 2017 the honeymoon was over. Tensions arising from Trump's shoot-from-the-lip style, and particularly his hideous showboating at the National Scout Jamboree, put Rex on edge. It was a July 20, 2017, meeting that led Tillerson to finally snap and commit a Kinsley gaffe, which is Washingtonese for a verbal misstep that states an undeniable truth.

One of the most secure rooms in the country is located in the Pentagon. It's called the Tank, and it's the conference room of the chairmen of the Joint Chiefs of Staff. It's less imposing than you might think. Unless they've remodeled since my days at the Pentagon, it looks like a pretty standard government conference room. On that

July night, it was crowded with Trump, Bannon, Priebus, Prince Jared, and senior military leaders desperate to get Trump to focus for five minutes on the trivial things, like America's national security challenges in a changing world.

This attempt rapidly went off the rails. As Trump and his senior staff were briefed on America's defense and nuclear posture, Trump insisted on a tenfold increase in our nuclear arsenal. This, of course, would be globally destabilizing, abrogate a number of treaty obligations, and require somewhere in the neighborhood of $15 trillion, which even by Washington standards is real money. At the end of this train wreck of a meeting, and presumably once Trump had left the room, his military leaders sat slack-jawed and stunned and Rex Tillerson said what was on all their minds, "The president is a fucking moron."[18]

Well, duh.

Tillerson's star fell at that point, though even Trump wasn't stupid enough to lose three Cabinet officials at once. Tillerson for a time was part of the famed Mattis-Tillerson-Mnuchin Suicide Squad, wherein a tacit agreement reportedly existed to quit en masse if one of them was to be fired in some fit of Trumpian caprice.[19]

With Vice President Mike Pence in as conciliator, Trump and Tillerson papered over their differences for a time, but as with all things Trump, his simmering, juvenile resentments and obsessions meant Tillerson would be sidelined over and over again.

The breaking point came in March 2018. Trump had been rooked by the crafty North Korean despot Kim Jong Un into a face-to-face summit meeting, a goal that the DPRK's government had been desperate to achieve for decades. It would elevate Kim, solidify his power inside the Hermit Kingdom, and defer further American military action. It was a consequential decision by Trump to agree to the terms of the wee Korean dictator, but agree he did. He did not, however, inform his secretary of state.

The tension was so thick you could cut it with a knife, but Til-

EVERYTHING TRUMP TOUCHES DIES   153

lerson soldiered on until, during an official visit to Africa, he made a fateful error. It had to do, you'll be shocked to learn, with Russia.

On March 4, 2018, a former Russian GRU officer named Sergei Skripal and his daughter Yulia Skripal were poisoned by a rare Russian nerve agent. Skripal had spied for the British, been caught and imprisoned by Russia, then was traded in a spy swap years later. He'd been living a quiet life in Salisbury, about 90 miles from London. Vladimir Putin, being Vladimir Putin, and feeling empowered by a U.S. president clearly willing to let him run amok, decided to whack Skripal. This did not sit well with the Brits, and Secretary of State Tillerson spoke out in support of our oldest and most important international ally:

> We have full confidence in the UK's investigation and its assessment that Russia was likely responsible for the nerve agent attack that took place in Salisbury last week.
>
> There is never a justification for this type of attack—the attempted murder of a private citizen on the soil of a sovereign nation—and we are outraged that Russia appears to have again engaged in such behavior. From Ukraine to Syria—and now the UK—Russia continues to be an irresponsible force of instability in the world, acting with open disregard for the sovereignty of other states and the life of their citizens.
>
> We agree that those responsible—both those who committed the crime and those who ordered it—must face appropriately serious consequences. We stand in solidarity with our Allies in the United Kingdom and will continue to coordinate closely our responses.[20]

When you read it, it has the cadences, signifiers, and seriousness of the secretary of state of a serious nation talking about a serious issue. It's not a tweet, a Breitbart headline, or some professional wrestling kayfabe. It was Tillerson's last official act.

To most people with a pulse it was pretty obvious the Home Office in Moscow called with some management critiques of Tillerson
shortly after his support for the Brits, because Trump fired him within
hours of the statement's release. Contrary to the White House's assertion, Tillerson had not been fired days before, but instead learned of it
from President Passive-Aggressive's tweet. The connection between a
clear-cut critique of Russia in defense of an ally and Tillerson's firing
did not go unnoticed.

His transformation from the CEO of Exxon to a victim of Donald Trump's foot-stomping outrages and bizarre defenses of Putin and
Russia in the space of a little over a year must have left Tillerson dis-
oriented. Whatever his other characteristics may have been, he was a
serious person in an administration staffed to the walls with clowns,
jokers, borderline personalities, and Trumpalike man-children. You
don't run Exxon for over a decade without a suite of interpersonal,
management, and decision-making skills, but in the end those skills
were insufficient to protect Rex Tillerson from the curse of Trump.

Tillerson's departure came during a week of extraordinary chaos,
even by Trump standards, but served as a very clear warning shot for
other professionals considering service in the Trump White House or
administration. If a man like Tillerson could be humiliated, his good
name disparaged, his reputation wrecked, and be booted out the door
with a tweet, what could lesser mortals expect?

MATTIS SAVE US

The coalition of adults around Trump is small, fragile, and not nearly
in control enough. As of May of 2018, Jim Mattis is the only one who
still matters.

Presidents traditionally name strong cabinet members, appoint
competent people to execute their agendas out in the agencies, and
select ambassadors to be the face of the United States abroad. Trump
essentially rounded up people from behind the bus station and hoped
for the best. With a handful of exceptions—Jim Mattis being at the top

of the list—Trump has named the weakest, most ineffective cabinet in generations. At the time of this writing, he has been going through his cabinet like an industrial wood chipper, firing and moving the deck chairs on the *Trumptanic* with abandon. The singular pillar of sanity, competence, stability, and integrity in the Trump administration is Jim Mattis. As secretary of defense, Mattis is the unique anchor in Trump's world who seems immune from firing, humiliation, and Trump's tantrums.

For the good of the nation, let's hope it stays that way.

Joel Searby, Bill Kristol, and I met secretly with Mattis in the spring of 2016, making a last, desperate bid to find someone—anyone—with the stones and the record to leap into the presidential race, pull an Eisenhower, and save the country from Trump.

Why Mattis? Why would we chase a former general who had no incentive at all to suffer the slings and arrows of a short-term independent presidential run? Because if you went into a lab and said "Build me a clone army of kick-ass American warriors," they'd fire up the CRISPR and build Jim Mattis. His service, his character, his intellect, and his no-bullshit affect seemed like the perfect remedy for a time when we were facing a test of America's faith in itself every day.

It was a last-ditch play, but it made sense. A profound faith in mediating institutions helped bind the American dream, but in dozens of polls and focus groups, nearly every American institution—both parties and their leaders, banks, the business world, organized religion, academia, and beyond—is distrusted by the American people. One institution, however, remains at the very top of public ratings of trust and confidence: the military.

In the political world, Eisenhower wasn't the inevitable or expected choice for 1952, but his positioning against both Robert Taft and Adlai Stevenson based on the universal confidence in his military accomplishments and integrity solidified his candidacy. In a restive postwar moment, Ike didn't want the job, but he accepted the mission because the country's future was at stake.

Mattis didn't want to run for president, but to save the country he took a role in this administration. Today he represents the most vital stabilizing force in that administration, the de facto leader of American foreign and military policy outside the lanes of Trump's White House cadre. Trump leaves him to his own devices, and we should sleep more soundly for it. He's the single person in Trump's administration I hope the curse misses.

Mattis has kept well clear of the White House vortex, determined to face the challenges of Russia, Syria, ISIS, Iran, North Korea, and the rest of the portfolio of dangers with his usual Marine froideur.

The physical comparisons couldn't be more glaring. Softbelly Donald Trump versus Mattis's lean, hangdog frame is a comparison of one man who spent a lifetime shoveling Kentucky Fried Chicken and Filet-O-Fish sandwiches down his maw, and one so abstemious he eats two meals a day and rises before dawn to put in five miles of road work. One man answered his nation's call for four decades of decorated service in the Marine Corps, and one spent his life fighting the battle of Pussy Grabber Ridge. One man has read deeply in strategy, history, military affairs, economics, and the classics; the other can barely grunt out the words on his teleprompter and serves as America's least intellectually curious and least-read president since Andrew Jackson. (Note to Trump lovers: that's not a compliment.)

PART THREE

SURROUNDED
BY VILLAINS

The following transcript was provided
by Wikileaks in the Fall of 2024.

– INTERCEPT 1 –

The following transcript represents the collection of sensitive discussions among senior military and civilian leadership of Russia. Audio quality is variable, as it was collected using a drone-based directional recording system hovering over Mr. Putin's Black Sea dacha at Krasnodar Krai.

[BEGIN TRANSCRIPT]

[MACHINE AND HUMAN TRANSLATED]

[SPRITFIRE VOICE MATCH .996 CERTAINTY Vladimir Vladimirovich Putin]

PUTIN: . . . can't be real. You're fucking with me.

[SPRITFIRE VOICE MATCH .803 CERTAINTY Igor Valentinovich KOROBOV, Director of the Russian Main Intelligence Directorate (GRU)]

KOROBOV: Vola, you won't fucking believe these guys. And how easy it was.

PUTIN: He really uses an insecure cell phone? All the time? *Fuck your mother.* (Translation note: Mr. Putin is using a common Russian expletive, and not directing KOROBOV to fuck his own mother.)

KOROBOV: (laughter) Such luck. An old Android phone. A seventeen-year-old from Donetsk cracked it. We've been listening since before he was elected.

PUTIN: Play it again.

[ROOM SOUND. AUDIO BEGINS]

OPERATOR: Please hold for the president.

TRUMP: Hey.

HANNITY: S'up?

TRUMP: Blowing off homework.

HANNITY: That stupid summit? Just wing it. You can cheat off Xi.

TRUMP: Yeah, it's boring anyway. And Kelly keeps trying to make me read the President's Daily Brief. Eff that. That's my *Fox & Friends* time.

HANNITY: Damn right, Mr. President. The Friendly Friends at *Fox & Friends* have your back.

TRUMP: So, what's up with Tucker? I feel like he doesn't love me as much as you love me.

HANNITY: No one loves you as much as me, Mr. President. In a very straight way that would never bother Mike Pence at all.

TRUMP: (softly) You know, there was only one time at Studio 54 . . .

HANNITY: Sir . . .

TRUMP: Never mind.

HANNITY: Sir, I'm going on the air in thirty seconds.

TRUMP: I'm watching. I'm always watching.

[DRONE OUT OF RANGE. TRANSCRIPT ENDS.]

10

WELCOME TO HELL

THE NEW TRUMP ESTABLISHMENT AND THE LEGION OF Trump fans hate one thing more than Hillary Clinton, more than Barack Hussein Obama, Nancy Pelosi, George Soros, or Zombie Ted Kennedy—and that hatred burns with a passion hotter than a supernova. It's a hatred cleaner, sharper, and more immediate than they have for any real or imagined demon on the left.

By now, unless you've been living in an underground bunker, you know the thing they hate beyond words and reason is conservatives who won't bow and take a knee before Trump. For them, the Never Trump movement represents history's greatest monsters.

They hate us because we've done things and know things. Expertise is their Kryptonite. They hate us because we stuck to our guns. They blame us for every loss and forget our roles in the thousand victories that led to Republican and conservative majorities in the House, Senate, and state legislatures. They project their treachery to the cause with our determination to preserve it.

Their sweetest fantasy was that Trump's New Establishment would overthrow and exile all the Old Establishment and purge the experts, the smart guys, and the operators from the hated Ancien Régime that tried to stop The Donald and save the Republic.

Those of us who had served in prior administrations legitimately hoped for the best, feared for the worst, and stocked up for Schadenfreudeapalooza. We were amply rewarded for our preparations. The spectacular body count in the Trump White House includes firings, disgraces, dismissals, witchcraft trials, panicked flights from the building, and Trump PTSD victims with a dead-eyed stare that chills the soul. In all, 34% of the White House staff was gone in the first year, a number unprecedented in an any country that isn't run by pirates, drug lords, or cannibal dictators.[1] And yes, it gave us more than a bit of pleasure to say we told you so.

From Masters of the Trump Universe to disgraced, unemployed, and unemployable laughingstock is a bad look on anyone, but the personnel meat-grinder of this White House has those of us on the outside looking at them with a weapons-grade case of schadenfreude. Revenge, being best served cold with a nice charcuterie platter and a good Barolo, is delicious.

Let's indulge, shall we?

Let's get the firings of people who were trouble for Trump out of the way first. These folks aren't technically victims of the ETTD curse, but in each case they were a threat to his Trumpcentric kleptocracy and his dreamed of royal court of lackeys, lickspittles, jesters, spittoon holders, and minstrels.

Every administration purges the most senior, most political types from the prior era. The president has every right to name a Cabinet and appoint senior government officials, but because of the Trump team's flaming ineptitude and inexperience, their early wave of firings was handled with all the subtle delicacy of a monster truck show.

Their purges were, as expected, politically moronic and legally dubious. Trump's firing of FBI director James Comey is the jewel in the stupid crown of his disastrous, tone-deaf, extralegal approach to government. He didn't just fire his FBI director in a flagrant effort to obstruct justice; he bragged about it to both Lester Holt of NBC News, and to—you might want to sit down for a moment—the Russian ambassador in a private meeting in the Oval Office. This decision would be the single most consequential moment in his early presidency, if only because it was so predictably going to lead to an epic political shitshow, launch the Mueller investigation, and haunt his every waking hour.

His choice to fire other officers, including Deputy Attorney General Sally Yates, Ethics Advisor Walt Shaub, U.S. Attorney Preet Bharara, and FBI Deputy Director Andrew McCabe, created media and political martyrs, guaranteeing them a role in the constellation of critics who were liberated and vocal.

Capo of *l'affaire russe* MAGA crew Mike Flynn, a disgraced former army general, was so outrageously in bed with the Russians that even Trump was forced to fire him. A predecessor to Flynn as the Defense Intelligence Agency director once told me the Russophilic anti-Muslim general was "the most dangerous asshole ever to head a three-letter."[2]

The fastest route to being fired in the first six months of Trump's regime was to have any record of working in Washington with actual adults. They should have known better, but Reince Priebus, Katie Walsh, Mike Dubke, Sean Spicer, Rick Dearborn, and other DC pros fell victim to Donald Trump's unmanaged and unmanageable personality. They didn't understand that Trump's character would render their experience moot, their efforts for naught, and their reputation in tatters.

Congressman Tom Price, an affable back-bencher from Georgia, was perfectly comfortable in Congress, but he made a critical mistake; Donald Trump liked him, and Price accepted the position of secretary of health and human services. Like many of Trump's appointees, Price suddenly looked at the federal budget as his plaything, taking private jet flights instead of flying commercial. He was the first to be fired, but he wouldn't even be close to the last.

It wasn't that Price was a particularly bad actor, in the great scheme of things. It was that the environment of the Trump White House made that kind of behavior normal. EPA head Scott Pruitt demanded first-class and private jet travel because—I kid you not—people said mean things about him on social media. Housing and Urban Development Secretary Ben Carson was caught up in a scandal over a $31,000 dining room table for his office. It was all so tragic because it was all so petty. As of May 2018, Pruitt, Carson, and others under the clouds of scandal that seems to darken the days of almost every Trump cabinet official are still clinging to power.

DOWN THE CHAIN

At the beginning of the Trump presidency, official Washington still held out hope that Trump would bring in a professional team and that he would listen to counsel, allow a strong chief of staff to fulfill that vital role, and tap into some well of discipline, focus, and resolve heretofore unseen. They convinced themselves he would act and look and operate like a president and that the majesty of the office would bring his staff along into that same dignified frame.

That didn't quite work out. The Misfit Toys at the top, and the clowns, rejects, human refuse, ne'er-do-wells, and wild-eyed ideological edge-case drifters who populate the administration prove the Emerson rule is always right: an institution is the lengthened shadow of one man. As hire Bs and Bs hire Cs, and Trump hires people you could find sleeping on a subway grate or planning their basement abattoirs.

Their greatest joy seems to come not from taking power in DC and executing the amorphous but passionate Trump agenda, but from attacking, insulting, and punishing those who did the actual work in the field for the Conservative Revolution. Nothing outrages this president or his minions more than the slightest resistance to his madcap urges and the stunningly terrible policy ideas that spring from his Fox-addled brain.

In the long arc of American political history, a job in the White House—any White House—is considered one of the greatest career opportunities in the world. Serving the president of the United States is a singular honor and a privilege, a role for the best of the best, those driven and skilled enough to sacrifice four years of their personal lives for the 24/7 job of a White House aide.

If you're valuable to the president of the United States, corporate America is ready to snatch you up the moment you walk out those gates for the last time. A White House bump on one's résumé has never been a Bad Thing, regardless of party, the politics of the day, or the success or failure of the administration. Not so in Trump's White House; these jobs are a curse, and just as his death touch affects everyone he encounters, its effects linger.

In early March 2018, the White House was suffering from a wave of scandals, departures, setbacks, crop failures, and political own-goals. Suddenly, many of the Masters of the Trump Universe were looking for jobs.

You could hear the sound of the nanoscale violins of the reviled Old Guard and Never Trump crowd as résumés started hitting email inboxes from Trump White House and administration staffers looking for a quick exit from the disaster area. Their desperation was palpable: "The longer I stay, the more likely it is that I'm going to get Muellered," said one when pitching a colleague of mine for a job.

BuzzFeed reported that White House staffers were "not necessarily getting the kinds of high-paying offers in the corporate world [that] former aides usually do." One White House aide said, "I've talked to several people in the last week trying to find a way out, but they can't get out because no one is really hiring people with Trump White House experience. Not a fun time to say the least."[3]

Trump's Island of Misfit Toys is chock-full of people who possess only the barest competencies one would expect from a White House staff, including little things like professionalism, a sense of personal honor, dignity, and the understanding that the White House is not a palace for a king, and that 1600 Pennsylvania isn't a royal court.

As policymakers go, none of them will likely leave a mark because all policy emerges—and I hope you'll pardon this term of legislative art—from Trump's ass. There was little to recommend them to start

with, and nothing upon their exits. Those who left in scandal and due
to the purges run by Chief of Staff John Kelly in some ways have a better story to tell than those who fled because the stress of working for
our version of Mad King Ludwig broke their will to live.

Those who leave soon discover there are only so many slots for
contributors at Fox News. Washington's lobbying firms and think
tanks are looking for people with abilities beyond boot-licking, knob-
polishing, and obsequious ass-kissing of the Umber Overlord. Those
skills may be sine qua non in Trump World but are, to put it mildly,
less valuable elsewhere. Other Trump Team skills, like dog-whistling
the alt-right, stoking ethnic and racial tensions, and fighting for the
return of 19th-century trade and industrial policies, are also in low demand on K Street, Wall Street, Silicon Valley, and the civilized world.

Some senior White House staffers will wander into the new ecosystem of Trump cheer squads, media outlets, and ScamPACs as long
as The Donald is still around. Future administrations won't beat a path
to their doors or consider them voices of counsel and consequence in
the long run. No Wise Men will emerge from this debacle.

It's the lower-level appointees who will suffer longest, even those
who came on board for the good of the country in hopes of moderat-
ing and managing Trump's catalogue of pathologies and obsessions.
They're stained. They'll spend their lives explaining why they elected
to serve a president destined for disgrace, and if that fails, a barista
position at Starbucks or selling blood plasma are good options.

Are you surprised they're about to be unemployed and unemployable? Don't be. Everything Trump touches dies.

ROT FROM THE BOTTOM UP

Donald Trump hasn't drained the swamp or changed Washington in
part because the only people he could find to join his government are
human train wrecks.

Setting aside the clown show of the inner White House team,
Trump's administration combines all the things you'd expect: venal-

ity, incompetence, a stunning lack of policy knowledge, and a slurry of people dragged from Trump's business world who couldn't manage a Waffle House.

Trump doesn't have staff; he has acolytes. He doesn't have experts; he has enthusiasts.

In every administration, the true power of a president comes from staffing the government with his people. Every president picks appointees who represent his values and policies and who—to use a technical term—get shit done. Within weeks of Trump's inauguration it was clear: things weren't going well, and never would. CNN reported Trump's administration still had over 1,900 vacancies in March 2017.

Even allies like *National Review*'s John Fund wrote, "The Administration needs to pick up the pace of hiring. . . . If nothing is done, the problem will only get worse. At the current rate of nominating individuals to positions, we could see the Trump administration's first or even second anniversary before it would actually be filled with Trump people."[4]

In every prior modern administration, the thousands of jobs each government must fill were a matter of transition discussions long before election day. Leaders have allies, friends, subject matter experts, and policymakers they start talking to well before election day. Personnel, famously, is policy.

Trump staffed his administration so slowly and so poorly that the federal bureaucracy couldn't believe their luck. Far from draining Washington's swampy bureaucratic precincts, the Trump administration—when they bothered to staff them at all—put in place appointees without the skills, experience, or judgment you might find in the staff of a particularly badly run K-mart in some small Midwestern town.

The handful of Trump appointees who made it into appointed positions were soon made aware that making America great again would depend on Donald Trump shutting the hell up from time to time. They barely made it through the day, waiting for their impulsive commander in chief, the tweeter of the free world, to go off the rails.

This president's skill isn't the art of the deal but the art of setting his own ass on fire and causing the world around him to panic.

Not every person in the Trump administration is a low-rent, mouth-breathing doofus who couldn't get hired at a car wash. Many serving in Cabinet, sub-Cabinet and White House roles joined Team Trump in good faith, believing they could help steady the ship, smooth the rough edges, and, just maybe, put some conservative policy wins up on the board.

All of them understood that President Trump's undisciplined style was risky but hoped his distractions would give them cover to work steadily and quietly on the administration's legislative priorities.

A few were of the Bannonite taint, with a history of overtly racist douchebaggery, like Carl Higbie and Sam Clovis. Some of them even bought into the 'merica First new nationalism. Many quietly assured friends in Washington that Trump would settle into his job. After all, he *did* reassure Americans, "I can be the most presidential person ever."

Uh-huh.

They figured Trump would turn his political capital, social media power, and deal-making acumen into big, popular Republican legislative wins, and that his lack of interest in policy details would let them and their allies, former bosses, and friends in Congress set the agenda.

Feeding Trump's ego came with the territory, but why not let him take a victory lap after every success? Then reality set in. The tax bill being the notable exception, 2017 and 2018 were legislative disasters, and the tax cut survived only because Ryan and McConnell kept Trump a million miles away from the process.

The president botched Trumpcare 1.0 and contributed little as Speaker Paul Ryan managed to ram the public relations nightmare, Trumpcare 2.0, through the House at the cost of much political blood and treasure, only to see it fail in the Senate. Policy wins beyond that? Not much, unless you count executive orders.

Instead, Trump's fumbles in 2017 left many members of Congress ducking town hall meetings like they were in the witness protection program. By the end of the year most of Trump's agenda was deader and more pungent than six-day-old fish. Then, almost unbelievably, 2018 was worse.

Most Trump appointees were treading water, not really doing much except playing defense and wondering which of their colleagues was leaking to the *Washington Post*, *Axios*, and the *New York Times*.

Trump's appointees learned quickly that failure in Washington rolls downhill and that the bureaucracy was going nowhere. No swamps were getting drained, no Walls were getting built, and their chances for leadership and achievement in their agencies were next to zero. They discovered that their job wasn't actually to serve the nation, manage an agency, or do their job on the White House org chart. In reality, they spent most of their time fluffing Trump's delicate ego and worrying about rivals shanking them.

Those ordained to appear on television as administration surrogates learned that for the most part their job wasn't to advocate for their agency or issue but to lavish the president with praise. Only Kellyanne Conway and Soulless Steve Miller seemed to relish the job truly. After Sean Spicer's inglorious heave-ho, Sarah Huckabee Sanders took to the podium with a daily dyspeptic glare.

The Trump curse meant this White House was in turmoil from the very first day. Unmanaged and unmanageable, this president governs by ragetweet and paranoia. Most White Houses have an 18-month shakeup, during which the president decides what works and what doesn't. With a president unable and unprepared for the job and surrounded by a circle of incompetents, toadies, family, reality-TV flotsam, and corporate vassals, the first reset stories hit within days.

A February 5, 2017, *New York Times* piece by Maggie Haberman and Glenn Thrush gave us a prescient look at the way the White House under Trump was a chaotic shitshow from the jump. Its first moves were a disaster: "The bungled rollout of his executive order barring immigrants from seven predominantly Muslim countries, a flurry of other miscues and embarrassments, and an approval rating lower than that of any comparable first-term president in the history of polling have Mr. Trump and his top staff rethinking an improvisational approach to governing that mirrors his chaotic presidential campaign."[5]

Trump's war on James Comey and the FBI—and even his own hand-picked attorney general—sent chills through prospective appointees. In most administrations, people are beating down the doors to get these positions.

In the era of Trump, people with experience, competence, and judgment were fleeing from the Five-Finger Quivering Palm Death Touch: "Republicans say they are turning down job offers to work for a chief executive whose volatile temperament makes them nervous. They are asking headhunters if their reputations could suffer permanent damage, according to 27 people the *Washington Post* interviewed to assess what is becoming a debilitating factor in recruiting political appointees. The hiring challenge complicates the already slow pace at which Trump is filling senior leadership jobs across government."[6]

Every day a couple hundred Trump appointees wake up in their homes in the DC suburbs, slide into their Trump-stickered SUVs (and if they're high-ranking or wealthy enough, exchange a few polite words with their driver), and check Twitter.

Whatever they feel each day, it sure isn't Morning in America. Aside from the tiny handful of true, crazed dead-enders, they know this is what it must feel like in some faraway kleptocracy where the center hasn't held, the airfield and radio station have fallen to the rebels, and the Maximum Leader is holed up in his secret bunker, waiting for the other shoe to drop.

By the fall of 2017, they knew they couldn't save Trump because he never wanted to be saved. White House and administration staffers were determined to escape. Without even the traditional year under their belts, 23 White House staffers had been fired or resigned by that point and were "talking to headhunters about positions as in-house government affairs experts at major companies, or as executives at trade associations, universities, or consulting firms."[7]

Morale was at what they thought then to be rock bottom. Most had determined by that point that a different, better version of Trump would emerge from its cocoon like some portly, gold-plated butterfly. But it never, ever got better.

The scandals and legal troubles in the White House—not simply Russia, though that's one of the most fearful ones—rumble on the horizon like a summer thunderstorm, drawing nearer. Many wake up wondering, "Is today the day I need to lawyer up?"

When regimes collapse, dead-enders are the most fun to watch—the ones who end up with the profitable concessions and sought-after mistresses. When this regime falls, the most interesting part of the show will be watching those who say "Not me. I'm out" and those who want to go out like a Baath Party generalissimo.

Sticking with Trump to the bitter end and pretending the unfolding chaos is just "fake news" won't save anyone's reputation as the walls close in. It won't ease the judgment of history. It won't do anything to polish up their future Wikipedia entries. Some of the most absurd—Conway, Sanders, Miller—will be the punchlines of the future histories of this strange time.

Others—the midlevel appointees, the campaign kids who took a spin in government—will be asked in future job interviews, "So I see a four-year gap in your résumé. Weren't you in the Trump administration as a deputy assistant to the deputy undersecretary for praising the president at the Department of MAGA?"

That former Trump loyalist will squirm and mutter something about prison or how he ran a brothel in Berlin, or spent that time curating his My Little Pony plushie collection, or how those four years were spent on the run from Interpol.

– INTERCEPT 2 –

TOP SECRET//SI//ORCON//REL USA, FVEY

[BEGIN TRANSCRIPT]

[CALL BEGINS IN PROGRESS]

TRUMP: . . . and two Filet-O-Fish, extra sauce. Sorry, that was Ryan.

HANNITY: Gross. What does he want?

TRUMP: Who cares? He's weak. No stamina.

[CALL WAITING TONE]

HANNITY: Is that you or me?

TRUMP: You. Who is it?

HANNITY: Michael Cohen.

TRUMP: Again? Are you gonna take it?

HANNITY: Nah. He thinks you're mad at him.

TRUMP: I told him I'd pardon him. I just didn't say when.

HANNITY: I'm surprised he didn't flip for Mueller and testify.

TRUMP: He's loyal. Like-a-dog loyal.

HANNITY: He's loyal, but fifteen years is a long stretch for a guy like Michael.

[CALL WAITING TONE]

HANNITY: Jesus, this guy is persistent.

TRUMP: God, I know, right? Hey, Sean . . . how did Cohen smuggle a cell phone into a Federal prison?

HANNITY: You don't want to know. You really, really don't want to know, but it starts with stretching your . . .

[SIGNAL LOST]

11

THE TRUMP FAMILY SYNDICATE

TRUMP'S DYNASTIC ASPIRATIONS WERE CLEAR FROM THE moment his White House started to take shape. Far more inclined to view themselves as a royal family than any other presidential clan in history, including the Kennedy lot, Trump pushed to have his family embedded in the core of government. His daughter Ivanka and son-in-law Jared Kushner would take central roles in his court.

In the minds of his fanatics, the Trumps *are* a royal family, with everything but titles of nobility, and I have to imagine he thought at least once about having White House Counsel Don McGahn look hard at Article I, Section 9 of the Constitution. Last time I checked, Clause 8, which bars titles of nobility, doesn't have a Trump exception, but honestly, we're so far past normal that nothing is out of the range of the possible.

A popular meme in the early going of the Trump era was a projected Trump presidency timeline: Donald 2016–2024, Ivanka 2024–2032, Donald Jr. 2032–2040, Eric 2040–2048, and Barron 2048–2056.

I know what you're thinking: this kind of idea is errant silliness, a mere trifle some Trump fanboy dreamed up. Perhaps, but it speaks to a larger point about the fanaticism and intensity of his followers. Even the Kennedy clan at least pretended their raw ambition was at some level about public service. The argument that these gimcrack royals represent the future of American politics would be laughable if it wasn't 2018. Sure, the whole thing seems absurd, but this is the kind of ludicrous idea that gets stuck in the heads of people who believe Donald Trump was a titan of business based on reality television, and the intensity of loyalty to Trump has become something decoupled from what was a small-d democratic through-line in our political culture since the founding of the Republic.

Let's set aside the future of a country where Donald the Unready is succeeded by the Shoe Queen, Donald the Oily, Eric the Unready, and Boy King Barron. It would end with Habsburg jaw and misery. The current Trump family enterprise will almost certainly fall of its own weight, but in the meantime, the ethically dubious practices, incompetence, and moral and political failings of the Trump family disprove Donald Trump's assertion that he has the best genes, believe me.

The degree to which this president has monetized the presidency for the direct benefit of himself, his soft-jawed offspring, and his far-flung empire of bullshit makes the Teapot Dome scandal look like a warm-up act in the Corruption Olympics. Unlike every president in modern history, Trump didn't place his assets in a blind trust.

He's used his position as president as a marketing tool for his hotels and country clubs in Mar-a-Lago, Bedminster, and Doral, Florida. He's made his downtown DC hotel a go-to place for foreign and domestic lobbyists to rent suites of rooms at ludicrously jacked-up prices and to rent ballrooms for events. It's not just that it's corrupt; it's shabby and low corruption. If you're going to sell your influence as president, it needs to have a "b," not an "m," in front of the -illions.

JARED AND IVANKA

Trump's desire to have Ivanka close at hand in Washington is creepy but explicable. She's the least slow-witted of his adult children, she looks the part of Trump Princess, and he likes her. A lot. Just ask any of his various porn star, model, actress, escort girlfriends; Trump's pattern of using the worst pickup line of all time—"You remind me of my daughter Ivanka"—was a consistent theme in his pillow talk. After writing that sentence, I spent a few minutes watching puppy videos just to clear my mental palate.

Like the rest of the Trump enterprise, Ivanka's claim to fame was a reflection of Daddy's celebrity. Her "business" was a clothing and accessory line with delusions of fashion grandeur manufactured by Asian sweatshop labor. Sold first at Nordstrom, then in midpriced stores in dying shopping malls, it seemed destined for QVC even before the election. She was a triumph of branding and bullshit, and in that regard was a perfect fruit dropping from the Trump tree. She was the smart, accomplished, polished Trump scion. For a hot minute in 2016 we even had a brief flurry of pieces on "the Ivanka Voter."

> The Ivanka Voter is not the stereotypical Trump voter. She doesn't have a Trump sign in her yard, either because it would get egged or she doesn't want to fight with the neighbors. She knows all about Ivanka's clothing line and brand, and thinks she would be great in the White House, because she's classy and sophisticated, polished and well-spoken, all the things her father is not. She's very clear that there are things that Trump says that she doesn't agree with. She does not think of herself as racist. She describes herself as "socially moderate."[1]

It was one more triumph of branding, wishful thinking, and willful suspension of disgust. Whether Ivanka was a secret weapon for her odious father with suburban women is still a matter of deeper political analysis, but there was clearly an explicit message from Jared and Ivanka to their Manhattan friends: they would temper the infamously mercurial Trump.[2] They would be the Don Whisperers, walking him back from that grunting, vulgarian populism that for their friends on the Upper West Side was so repellent to people who sent their kids to Dalton and attended the Met Ball.

It seemed like nothing but upsides for the ambitious couple. Jared would be the master of the universe; Ivanka would be a smoother, more palatable Trump, extending and expanding the brand, and the Trump empire while she was at it.

But the curse of her father struck Jared and Ivanka before they'd even crossed the Beltway.

In a different world, the adult daughter of a sane, human president would be in a position to make a difference in policy, politics, and the unseen but vital Washington social scene. Before you make a "This Town" joke, there's a deep, generational truth here: outsiders don't understand how to run the government and navigate the demimonde of connections, power brokers, insiders, smart guys, money men and women, and inside players of Washington.

You don't have to like that this world exists; it does, and denying it's real is like denying fish swim and birds fly. Sometimes it's petty, absurd, and full of high school drama, only with security details and drivers, but it's also the secret ad-hocracy outsiders glimpse and revile but simply don't understand. A million pissy jokes about "Washington cocktail parties" never get old for the people who actually hold and attend Washington cocktail parties. (And no, doing Jell-O shots at the Breitbart Embassy doesn't count.)

It went without saying that Washington was cautious about the Trump family from the beginning, but there was an early, eager bubble of speculation that Jared and Ivanka were the keys to cracking the Establishment wide open. But even though Jared and Ivanka (I *refuse* to use the common portmanteau of their names) scanned differently than many of the "burn down DC" crowd in Trump's orbit, they failed to make it in Washington.

If Ivanka had been under the wing of a Sally Quinn, Juleanna Glover, or Tammy Haddad, or, in another era, a Muffie Brandon or Evangeline Bruce, her introduction to Washington society would have been altogether smoother. Instead, the golden children of Trump got the receiving end of a NQOC whisper and were sent into the darkness. They could have learned that the numinous cloud of Washington's secret life wasn't there just to keep people out; it was there to connect people within. Not understanding Washington was allowed; not *trying* to understand it was dumb.

Henry Kissinger had seen this play out before: "This fortress mentality, which was to have such a corrosive effect on the entire [Nixon] Administration, showed itself in many ways. The team was temperamentally unable, for instance, to exploit the opportunities of Washington's social life for oiling the wheels of national politics. . . . There is no need to expend effort to crash this charmed circle; membership— or at least its availability—is nearly automatic; but so is the ultimate exclusion."[3]

Instead, she and Jared went from the putative DC power couple of the Trump Dynasty to an afterthought. As Margaret Carlson put it, "Jared Kushner and Ivanka Trump came to Washington seeking power and glamour. They'll leave with neither."[4] Her few forays into policy, including a family leave plan with a blockbuster price tag, had a snowball's chance in hell of passing.

Jared was another matter.

Looking more like a court eunuch than a crown prince, everything about Jared appears and sounds soft, feminine, bereft of ideas or edges. He looks as if he was grown in a laboratory to deliberately not give offense. It took months before he spoke aloud to reporters in front of cameras, and his whisper-soft delivery didn't scream competence and strength, which was ironic since Trump had named Jared Minister with All the Portfolios.

It was screamingly obvious from day one that Jared Kushner needed three things in this life: a way to get out from underneath the monstrous debt load of his family's white elephant property on 666 Fifth Avenue, some tangible accomplishment in his life to push him into a tier of Manhattan and national business prominence, and, finally, an exit strategy from the Trump orbit.

It was an early tell for Washington observers that the Trump White House was going to turn into a five-alarm shitshow when Jared's portfolio went from being First Son-in-Law to, well, everything.

Kushner was placed in charge of so many White House domains it was hard to imagine a platoon of world-class executives even making a dent in them.

Jared was going to fix the Middle East peace process, which has gone about as swimmingly as you might expect. The stalemate is as intractable as ever, and Jared's tricky play to help the Saudis' shenanigans with Qatar brought up endless questions about his side hustle of begging Middle Eastern petro-billionaires for bridge loans to save 666 Fifth Avenue.

He was given the thankless task of reviving diplomatic relations with Mexico (you know, the people paying for the Wall), all while his father-in-law continued to rave on an almost daily basis about the dire threats of Mexicans coming to the United States to work and threatening to end the North American Free Trade Agreement.

He was inexplicably given the China portfolio, which delighted the Chinese almost beyond words. Kushner started taking meetings with the Chinese ambassador to the United States without staff, intelligence briefers, or China specialists. A brutal *New Yorker* piece by Adam Entous and Evan Osnos captured one of the many problems with Jared that led to his downfall as a White House power player:

> Kushner often excluded the government's top China specialists from his meetings with Cui, a slight that rankled and unnerved the bureaucracy. "He went in utterly unflanked by anyone who could find Beijing on a map," a former member of the National Security Council said. Some officials who were not invited to Kushner's sessions or briefed on the outcomes resorted to scouring American intelligence reports to see how Chinese diplomats described their dealings with Kushner. Other U.S. officials spoke to Cui directly about the meetings. Kushner was "their lucky charm," the former N.S.C. member said. "It was a dream come true. They couldn't believe he was so compliant."[5]

Of course, in one of the biggest domestic challenges facing America, Trump charged Jared with ending the opioid crisis. Luckily, no one's getting black-market fentanyl, so that's good. Oh. Wait.

And what veteran suffering from long treatment delays, PTSD, and injuries from our wars abroad didn't feel a surge of optimism when Donald Trump put Jared, veteran of the Manhattan Real Estate Wars and the Battle of Turtle Bay, in charge of fixing the Veterans Administration?

He also ran the Office of American Innovation, charged with reinventing government and making it (to use Washington's usual, trite cliché) run like a business. This office is rebooted every administration, and Jared was probably no more or less disastrous than any of its prior leaders. If Jared ever does decide to clean up government magically, one hopes he knows enough not to model the reformed U.S. government on a *Trump* business.

Ironically, Trump also tasked Jared with reforming the criminal justice system, an area where he should pay very, very close attention given his alleged use of his government office and requesting classified intelligence to help seek loans for his family business.[6] Jared will not thrive in the Big House, and I'm guessing he'll be traded for cigarettes the first day unless he shows some previously undetected skill with a shiv.

Whether it was Kushner taking on jobs and issues he lacked the knowledge, bandwidth, and competence to execute, or Trump simply picking a family member out of loyalty, Kushner's role as an advisor to the president was marked by a chain of inept decisions that led the White House deeper and deeper into a mire of their own making.

Jared and Ivanka couldn't win; the Washington political and social elites *wanted* to help them. They saw them as a pair of reasonable, centrist, New York sophisticates who could moderate and polish Donald Trump. The rest of the White House, Trump's outside advisors, and the Trump-right media saw them as traitors to the cause almost from the start. Jared didn't help his case by giving Trump one piece of bad advice after another.

"Jared is the worst political adviser in the White House in modern history," longtime Trump advisor and full-time lunatic Sam Nunberg said. "I'm only saying publicly what everyone says behind the scenes at Fox News, in conservative media, and the Senate and Congress."

Imagine that. How could two cossetted, elite children of wealth who had lived their entire beautiful lives at Manhattan's pinnacle misread the situation in Washington, DC, involving intelligence, the Justice Department, legal jeopardy, and Russian influence? Their judgment about absolutely everything was comically terrible from the very start.

Among the most controversial elements of Jared's Lord of Misrule period at the White House was the firing of James Comey, the FBI director and bête noire of Donald Trump in the early days of the administration. By all accounts, it was Jared Kushner, the Metternich of Barneys, who came up with the genius plan of firing Comey. "Let's just fire the beloved, longtime FBI director whom everyone in Washington views as an ethical stalwart and a man of pure integrity! What could go wrong, Mr. President?"

Comey's firing was both the peak of Jared and Ivanka's power and the most cataclysmically stupid political move they could have made. Their strategic vision stretched for about the next five minutes, and they had no idea how the Comey firing would reverberate through Washington, the Justice Department, and the FBI.

Jared also found himself in a constant state of embarrassment when he was forced to revise his government security and financial disclosure forms not once, not twice, but dozens of times. Nothing says "I'm clean as a whistle" like forgetting to disclose millions in assets and dozens of banking relationships. He was sued over it, naturally.[7]

When news broke that Jared, along with Don Jr., was a participant in the infamous Trump Tower meeting where Team Trump was offered the dirt on Hillary Clinton, Jared became a more visible target of Robert Mueller. Of course, the clown-car conspiracy of the Trump team left a deep electronic and paper trail when meeting with Russian lawyers, former intelligence officers, and fixers. This was in addition to Kushner's meetings with Russian bankers ("Have I told you about this fabulous investment opportunity in my family's building at 666 Fifth Avenue?") and the Russian ambassador and his connections to the Trump campaign's Russia-juiced social media campaign and Cambridge Analytica.

If he wasn't the president's son-in-law, he'd never get even a Secret clearance, much less be read in to the President's Daily Brief, the holiest of holies in the intelligence world. Hell, if he wasn't the president's son-in-law, he'd be happily back in the comforts of Manhattan, swimming in a sea of red ink and fellow travelers in the world of real estate.

Steve Bannon, a man who is as grizzled as Kushner is fastidious, had no compunction against burning Jared and Ivanka from the moment they walked into the White House. Bannon leaked story after story of Jared's incompetent decision making and his role as resident globalist cuck shill. (Y'all, that's Steve saying Jared is a J-e-w, if you didn't guess.)

Bannon turned his flying monkey minions at Trumpbart against Kushner early, with headline after headline blasting Kushner in all the usual Breitbartian code words. Although Kushner survived Bannon, the damage was done.[8] Headlines and stories called the couple "West Wing dems" and painting them as anathema to the Trump base on issues like immigration and gay rights. Bannon kept shoving the knife in, directing his writers to produce headlines like "Five Times Ivanka Trump and Jared Kushner Vacationed During a Crisis" and "Ivanka Trump Helped Push Steve Bannon Out of the White House" to their usual impact on the Trump-right echo chamber: panic, fury, and jacked-up outrage.

Perhaps Jared's most persistent nemesis was the notorious loon Roger Stone. A fixture of the Trump universe since Jared was visiting his father in prison, Stone had drifted in and out of Trump's orbit over the years and within a few weeks of Trump's taking office was hammering Jared in public. On *Infowars*, Roger Stone and Alex Jones tore into Kushner with abandon not long after the Mueller probe was announced: "Jared Kushner, perhaps the one presidential aide who cannot be fired, is now in regular text message communications with Joe Scarborough. Many of the anti–Steve Bannon stories that you see, the themes that you see on *Morning Joe*, are being dictated by Kushner. And while Mr. Kushner's plate is very full with Middle Eastern peace and the China visit, and so on, in this case I think he is dis-serving the president."[9]

It was classic Roger Stone ratfuckery, playing to Trump's paranoia, his hatred of Joe Scarborough, and his monstrous vanity. Stone worked to protect his alt-right ally Bannon while also working to burn Kushner, whom he blames in part for his diminished access to and influence over the president.

The one moment I loved about Kushner was when he shanked Chris Christie for a role in the administration. Christie, who served as Trump's errand boy and bottom bitch in the campaign, was desperate to serve as attorney general of the United States. Kushner slipped the daggers in over and over, slowly bleeding Governor Shinebox out.

By the end of the first year, Jared and Ivanka were, in the words of *Vanity Fair*, in a world of shit.[10] Failures in their official capacity, both Jared and Ivanka continued to play their roles, but as the Mueller probe continued to rise in intensity, Jared was under monstrous financial pressure from his investment in 666 Fifth Avenue, which by then was teetering on insolvency.

Kushner had flailed for cash to keep the deal alive, and by 2018 the pressure was almost unimaginable. He may have believed the White House position would lead foreign investors to send money flooding his way, but 666 Fifth was a curse he couldn't shake.[11]

When John Kelly came on board as White House chief of staff, he immediately recognized Jared as a type he'd seen in his military service: the rich kid from a powerful family in way over his head. Kelly was quick to limit the scope of Kushner's portfolio, and Jared seemed to largely fade from view until he and Ivanka made a play to oust Kelly over the Rob Porter matter.[12] This Night of the Long Sporks move flopped, and though Kelly is not the savior most hoped he might become, he had enough juice to survive their last big attack.

As the writing process of this book comes to a close, Jared and Ivanka have had their wings clipped firmly by John Kelly. While Kelly's lost power, he tried to take them down with him during the bloody White House purges in which Trump went rogue and decided he didn't need professional guidance, management, or counsel.

As with everyone who joins the Trump administration, Jared and Ivanka came with an agenda of their own, plans to execute it, and almost none of the skills needed to pull off the caper. In the end, nowhere was safe. Even *Vogue* turned on Ivanka, a cut that sent a signal that any hopes of returning to Manhattan social life or her former business of selling shoes and costume jewelry might not go smoothly.[13]

UDAY AND QUSAY

Don Jr. and Eric prove the fruit falls very close to the tree in the Trump family. Hair slicked back as if they were 1980s cosplayers, spread-collar shirts, and the entire gold-leaf-and-pinky-ring Trump affects scream that these scions of privilege most likely won't ever display even a hint of noblesse oblige, taste, or dignity. Like copies of a copy of a copy, Eric and Don Jr. now run Trump's business empire, though not very well. Oddly enough, outside of the narrow audience of Washington lobbyists using his hotel and his country clubs to gain access to the president, the Trump brand has turned to shit. Partners are pulling out of deals, removing the gold Trump logo from buildings, and adopting a "Donald who?" attitude.

If at the end of this Eric and Don Jr. aren't holed up in a wrecked house, surrounded by U.S. troops, I'll be shocked. The Uday and Qusay of the Trump clan combine their father's skeezy pomposity with an air of *je ne sais dumbass* that won't quit.

Donald Trump Jr.'s Comedy of Traitors

The most infamous moment in Don Jr.'s role in the campaign was a carefully guarded secret until brought to light by the Mueller probe.

It turned out that the campaign that had absolutely no business with, contact from, knowledge of, or even the vaguest connection to Russia had held meetings with representatives of the Russian government, and Don Jr.'s handling of the news dragged his father and the administration deep into the weeds of obstruction of justice. Team Trump doesn't comprise the most gifted liars in the business, even if they are some of the most persistent.

The statement written by the president and Hope Hicks on *Air Force One* to provide the meeting with a cover story was laughable and reflected just how little the Trump team understands that bullshitting through a Manhattan real estate deal is vastly different from trying to bullshit Robert Mueller.

Even Steve Bannon knew this was a disaster for the president. He is recounted in Michael Wolff's *Fire and Fury* as saying that Mueller would "crack Don Jr. like an egg."[14]

Don Jr. also enjoys a special place in the game of alt-right footsie the Trumps seem to love. You can count on him to retweet the bottom-feeders of the MAGA pool. On Gab, the alt-right's home after their inevitable Twitter bans hit, Don Jr. is a hero. He's also a frequent retweeter of Trump-friendly edge-case sites like the Gateway Pundit.

A friend once observed, "Don Jr. is truly an asshole's asshole. If there were an *Asshole Aficionado* magazine, he would be the cover boy."

MELANIA

I have a scintilla of sympathy for Melania. It's barely detectable even with the most sophisticated scientific instruments, but it's there. Occasionally. She's gorgeous, in that perfectly polished, price-is-no-object Manhattan way. Her Botox froideur is magnificent. Stylish in the way only a former almost-supermodel trophy wife married to an air-quotes billionaire accidental president can be, Melania is a mystery in the heart of Trump World.

In the story of Trump, Melania proves the ETTD theory in spades; you can see how dead her soul is with every appearance. Every moment looks like a hostage video, her tense, dark eyes looking for a break in the security cordon, damn the prenup.

Obviously miserable even before her role as a prisoner in 1600 Pennsylvania Avenue, stories in Michael Wolff's *Fire and Fury* and elsewhere reported her shock and dismay at Trump's victory. Her real role in Trump's world, like owning a private jet or a personally branded golf course, is to signify Trump's virility to the little people, "I have obtained the unobtainable Hot. Banged the unbangable."

While trapped in Trump Tower, she at least still had a little freedom to slip outside the gravity well of The Donald. After all, he was busily banging a constellation of adult-film stars, *Playboy* models, and other victims of his pussy-grabbing charm.

Once in the White House, her caged-bird situation was obviously, visibly painful. She is equipped with a magnificent resting bitch face in good times and bad, and her smile collapsing into a poker face whenever he turns away from her at White House events is the political equivalent of a fake orgasm, a performance for an audience of one, hoping to rush things along so she can get back to her Peloton.

When news that Trump had engaged in an affair with porn star Stormy Daniels—Who are we kidding with the anodyne term "affair"? He fucked her, and she spanked him with a *Forbes* magazine—the trouble in Slovenian trophy bride paradise was evident. Melania mysteriously dropped out of a trip to Davos shortly after the news broke, and the Trumps' anniversary photograph in 2017 looks like it should have been attached to a list of ISIS hostage demands.

For all my dislike of Trump, Melania seems like the kind of girl who needs a few tequila shots in a bar where no one knows her, the music is loud, and no one pronounces the letter "h" as the letter "y." That prenup must be a monster.

– INTERCEPT 3 –

TOP SECRET//SI//ORCON//NOFORN

[BEGIN TRANSCRIPT]

[CALL BEGINS]

OPERATOR: Please hold for the president.

BANNON: Go for the B-Man.

TRUMP: Steve-O!

BANNON: Big T! Making America great?

TRUMP: Always, my man. I was calling to thank you for that book. It was really good.

(Analyst note: Human-source intel indicates the book Trump refers to is *Authoritarian Nationalism—An Illustrated Pop-Up Guide to Destroying Democracy*)

BANNON: Cool. I'm sending you my new *Evola for Kids* coloring book this week.

TRUMP: Thanks, Steve. Hey, have you talked to Gorka lately?

BANNON: Yeah, saw him last week at Scores. Usual table in the Champagne Room. It was me, Gorka, Stephen Miller, and Pence. We missed you.

TRUMP: Wait . . . *PENCE*?

BANNON: (laughs) I'm fucking with you. There's one weird thing about that night, though. You know that dancer I like? Destinee Raynebow? She was giving Miller a lap dance and they went back to a private booth. Now she's gone missing. Weird.

TRUMP: You know how he gets . . . (wistful) I miss being able to tear it up.

BANNON: Pussy. You should come out. Who's gonna stop you? That globalist cuck Kelly? I don't think so.

TRUMP: Nah, you know. *Her.*

BANNON: Melania?

TRUMP: Worse.

BANNON: The Hucklebeast?

TRUMP: Worse. Kellyanne. Shit. That's her now. Gotta go.

[CALL TERMINATED]

12

TEAM CRONY

FROM THE MOMENT HE WAS ELECTED, TRUMP WAS SUR-
rounded by Goldman Sachs and other Wall Street alumni who behaved just as they always do: with weapons-grade venality, an abiding
love of crony capitalism, and Master of the Dick Universe affects.

They were there for the tax bill. Only the tax bill. Nothing else ever
mattered to any of them.

From the tone-deaf, determinedly out-of-touch treasury secretary Steve Mnuchin and his wife, sometime actress and LARPing
supervillainess Louise Linton, to Wilbur Ross and Gary Cohn, Team
Crony was in the White House to make the market happy, to ensure
the Goldman Guys were at the helm no matter what kind of yahooism
Bannon was cooking up in his laboratory in the White House basement. One by one, these men fell by the wayside as Trump's trade-war
fetishism, economic ignorance, and rampant corruption became the
central features of the administration's economic posture.

Trump's administration also has been a hotbed of remarkably obvious pay-to-play and crony capitalist game-playing. How obvious?
Think 1970s Times Square hooker on the corner obvious. Think, finding your wife in bed with her personal trainer obvious. You'd have to
be spectacularly indifferent to reality to not observe the endemic corruption in this White House. From the petty rip-off artistry of Trump's
DC hotel to the big policy changes and executive orders, it was clear
from the start that Trump had the "For Sale" sign out.

THE TAX BILL AND ITS DISCONTENTS

I'm a Republican with broad libertarian leanings. I think taxes are a necessary evil, and so as a general rule I like things that reduce the burden borne by American citizens to feed a largely ravenous and wasteful federal government. Yes, yes, I know. Starving orphans, fragile grannies poised on the edge of the cliff, etc.

The 2017 tax bill, though, was a whole different creature. Surprisingly slanted to—wait for it if you can't guess ahead of time—Wall Street hedge funds, the banking industry, real estate developers, and the very peak of the economic pyramid, the tax bill was a whale of a payday for the sectors of the economy that already receive a pretty consistent dollop of federal largesse when they periodically crash the economy.

Republicans are supposed to love tax cuts, right? They're universally good, central to a booming economy, and should finally, at long last, provide relief for struggling middle-class families in the forgotten heartla—

Oh. Sorry. I fell asleep there, recounting the same phony line we repeated for a generation on taxes. The reality of the Trump-Ryan tax cut is that it is a spectacular, budget-busting payday for Wall Street. Full stop. It provided rounding-error benefits for Middle America, and even those benefits sunset in a few years. The corporate tax rate was permanently dropped to 21%. Sounds great, right?

The tax bill knocked a $1.5 trillion-with-a-t hole in the federal budget. No amount of supply-side mojo is going to bring that into alignment with fiscal reality. The stock market had *already* priced the tax cut into its already spectacular rise. We can debate the political effort to market "Trump bonuses" as a third-order effect of the tax bill, but the rounding-error-level increases in paychecks are a drop in the fiscal bucket for most Americans, particularly in an era when inflationary pressures in health care, college tuition, energy, and other sectors are squeezing people even in a *good* economy.

For all of my party's yammering about the evils of wealth redistribution, we've done a *spectacular* job of it with this tax bill; the corporate benefits are forever, but the Tax Policy Center predicts that just ten years from now Americans making under $100,000 a year will pay much *more* in taxes given the provisions of the Trump tax bill.

Wall Street, the unofficial home of American state capitalism, was protected not only from their own cupidity and errors by taxpayer-funded bailouts but now is rewarded with a suite of tax benefits that would be risible in other circumstances. You know, after a decade of quantitative easing (that's "free money" to us rubes in the hinterlands) and record growth, Wall Street bankers, investment houses, and hedge fund bros were just suffering *terribly*. The slings and arrows of outrageous fortune included having to decide between the G650 and the Falcon jet or what color Lambo to choose at bonus time.

The saddest, dumbest part of this tax bill isn't that it stinks to high heaven of Trump-era fiscal indiscipline. It isn't that it's a budget-buster. It's that the GOP convinced itself that, like Trump, they could play the "Fake it till you make it" game and genuinely believed two things that show how badly out of whack their political GPS is. First, they bought into the idea that voters would be robustly cheering the tax bill's impacts come Election Day 2018. Second, in their panic to pass something—anything!—in 2017, they bought the donor-sector political pressure hook, line, and special-interest sinker.

The bill does nothing to reduce the complexity, expense, opacity, and general brain-frying shittiness of the tax code for ordinary Americans. So much for our "Do your taxes on a postcard!" rhetoric. The tax code, baroque and ludicrously convoluted before, is now even more baffling unless you can afford a fleet of corporate tax attorneys and consultants.

A prominent tax lobbyist I know wrote, "This is almost too easy. Even I feel dirty." This person literally sat in the majority leader's office crafting parts of the tax bill, laughing all the way to the bank. The members of the House and Senate who voted for this 479-page bill had only a few hours to consider it. I asked this lobbyist at the time what the job-creation effect would be from the corporate tax cut, and he replied, "How the fuck do I know? Something? Maybe?" This wasn't just lobbyist shit-talking. His goal, for which he was richly compensated, was to ensure a set of his corporate clients could use the tax cut to buy back their stock.

If you think I sound like a Democrat, you're mistaken. I sound like a fiscal conservative who believes in a tax system that is broad and simple and treats every American equally. That's certainly not what we got in this mess.

WINNERS AND LOSERS, COAL EDITION

In Washington lore, payoffs are subtle, suitably laundered, discreetly referred to through a veil of elliptical terms and subtle glances. "I took care of that thing with the guy we spoke about. By the way, how's that other thing in Appropriations going?" is the kind of formulation all too familiar to Washington denizens.

When it comes to Trump, subtle isn't in the mix, and one of the most obvious, egregious examples of the new era of pay-to-play crony capitalism is related to the coal industry.

Coal mining's employment heyday was in the 1920s, when 785,000 Americans worked in the industry. The number stands at just under 50,000 today. The coal industry, though, has continued to be a dirty, destructive, and profitable business. The heroic image of the coal miner is part of the Appalachian iconography of working-class West Virginia, Ohio, Kentucky, and Pennsylvania. Those workers, though, have increasingly been swept aside by market forces—the declining price of natural gas, primarily—and by the declining cost of renewables. Those miners have also been replaced by machines and by the practice of mountaintop-removal mining. If you're wondering if it's an environmental nightmare, it is.

With the election of Donald Trump, the coal industry had a friend in the White House. As much as Bannon and Trump loved the image of the gritty, salt-of-the-earth workin' man that coal miners represent, it didn't hurt the cause of coal that coal company CEOs were stroking checks faster than you can say "black lung."

When Trump signed his executive order reversing the Obama era's restrictions on coal, one of the coal executives flanking him was Joseph Craft of Alliance Resource Partners, one of the nation's largest coal mining conglomerates.

Just after Trump's election, Craft donated a cool $1 million to the Inaugural Committee, so his presence there was no accident.[1] As a bonus, Trump nominated Craft's wife, Kelly Knight Craft, to be our ambassador to Canada, or as Trump calls it, "Snow Mexico."

Another winner in the Coal Crony Capitalism Olympics is Robert Murray. Murray plays the role of comic-opera coal baron to the hilt: rotund, blustery, and ready to bellow out marching orders to the Trump administration. His $1 million donations to the Trump America First PAC and $300,000 to the Trump Inaugural Committee opened doors as wide as he opened his wallet.

Murray wasn't subtle in his ask; he presented the administration with a five-page memo that reads like an environmental villain's wish list.[2] Most of the changes Murray sought from the Trump White House were directly about protecting and expanding Murray Energy's bottom line. For the bargain price of $1.3 million, Murray wanted a few minor tweaks: withdraw the U.S. from the Paris Climate Accord, cut the Environmental Protection Agency by 50%, and shrink the Mine Safety Administration down to a size where its inspectors could fit around a six-person booth at Denny's. Did I mention he also wanted to do away with a host of other pollution control and worker-safety regulations, and virtually anything else that made coal mining cleaner or safer?

Importantly, he wanted to have Trump's executive order reverse Obama's Clean Power Plan so that the coal-fired power plants that burned Murray's coal would remain open.

You know, the little stuff.

Murray also went straight at it in the most brazen request possible: force people to buy his product. In asking for a direct federal subsidy on top of the regulatory tweaks he dreamed of, Murray's big-government capitalism was on full display. In the words of the *Economist*, "Subsidizing coal production is a really bad idea. In the fierce competition for the federal government's worst policy, this is a contender."[3]

Murray, Craft, and others represent one of the Trump-era paradoxes of the conservative movement. When Obama "picked winners and losers" in the market and subsidized clean energy companies, the collective GOP hissy-fit was incandescent. Members of Congress and the Senate railed like street-corner preachers. Free-market think tanks churned out reams of studies decrying his executive overreach into the energy sector. Now, as Trump uses his regulatory powers to prop up an industry that can't stand on its own in the marketplace, they're suddenly enthusiasts for the government saving coal from its dirty, deadly self.

The illusory "war on coal" is over, but Trump's promise to restore the industry has failed. By mid-2018 the number of coal plants closing down exceeded that of the Obama era.[4] Dirty, expensive, and with enormous downstream costs to both lives and the environment, coal is losing out to clean natural gas and increasingly cheap renewables. It is a stark reminder that markets matter, and that everything Trump touches dies.

– INTERCEPT 4 –

[BEGIN TRANSCRIPT]

[CALL BEGINS]

OPERATOR: Please hold for the president.

TRUMP: Is she on?

OPERATOR: Not yet, Mr. President.

TRUMP: Hope? Are you there?

HICKS: Mr. President.

TRUMP: Hope, I miss you.

HICKS: Mr. President . . .

TRUMP: I told you to call me your Donnie.

HICKS: Mr. President, we can't . . .

TRUMP: Hope, I'm just a boy, standing in front of a girl . . .

HICKS: That's from *Notting Hill*.

TRUMP: When you realize you want to spend the rest of your life with
somebody, you want the rest of your life to start as soon as possible.

HICKS: *When Harry Met Sally.*

TRUMP: I want you. I want all of you, forever. You and me, every day.

HICKS: Donnie, I love *The Notebook* as much as anyone, but . . .

TRUMP: You said you couldn't be with someone who didn't believe in you. Well, I believed in you. I just didn't believe in me. I love you, always.

HICKS: *Pretty in Pink.* My mom loved that movie.

TRUMP: You make me want to be a better man.

HICKS: Mr. President, did someone give you a list of romantic movie quotes to read to me?

TRUMP: You complete me.

HICKS: *Jerry McGuire.* Mr. President, I have to go.

TRUMP: Wait, I have more.

[CALL ENDS]

13

CLOWN PRINCES OF THE TRUMP MEDIA

YOU CAN'T HAVE EVEN A WANNABE DESPOT WITHOUT toadies ready to sing the Leader's praises. You can't have a strongman without sycophants fawning and scraping. You can't have a caudillo without women swanning around in gold lamé evening gowns as the city burns around you. If the thought of Ann Coulter reclining on a chaise lounge and throwing Donald Trump a come-hither leer just popped into your mind, I apologize.

All of the people we'll discuss in this chapter have had their profiles elevated by their lust to please Donald Trump in spite of the realities of his profoundly flawed leadership and character. These are the outliers, the Trump dead-enders, the Donald über alles folks who even their clickservative brethren don't pretend not to look down on.

FOX NEWS, THE FOURTH
BRANCH OF GOVERNMENT

Trump may not read his daily intelligence briefings, but he is America's number one *Fox & Friends* Superfan. Every morning, he sits in front of a wall of television sets, nursing his long grudges against Chuck Todd, Joe and Mika, and, well, everyone at CNN. As his minions carefully spoon out his morning porridge into his spill-proof bowl, Trump's beady eyes flick from screen to screen, watching for any slight, any deviation from worship. Rage tweets at the ready, it's a constant contest to see who will draw the ire of Grandpa Ranty.

One channel, though, is different. One morning show sets America's national agenda more completely than anything else on TV and any political force in Washington. That show is *Fox & Friends*, and their power is without measure. Trump's morning tweets have been demonstrated time and again to be summaries of whatever morning story lines are driving the perky, peppy hosts of the number one morning show. "Are Muslims trying to impose sharia law in *your* dentist's office?" "Can President Trump's bathwater really cure psoriasis?" "Have we won the war on Christmas, or does ISIS still want to destroy us?"

The waves of adulation and validation *Fox & Friends* provides is a mutually reinforcing dynamic that shapes Trump's entire day. Among the people who noticed the causal relationship between Fox's morning hit show and Trump's tweets was Dan Snow, a graduate student at the University of Chicago, who posted a brilliant infographic showing the vivid hot spot of Trump's tweets to the *Fox & Friends* broadcast window.[1]

Trump, ever sensitive to any assertion that he isn't sui generis in every respect or that anyone, anywhere could have some influence over his "thought" processes, got his back up when asked about his obsessive television viewing habits. "I know they like to say—people that don't know me—they like to say I watch television. People with fake sources. You know, fake reporters, fake sources. But I don't get to watch much television, primarily because of documents. I'm reading documents a lot."[2]

Uh-huh. Documents. Sure, Don.

As the great Andrew Marantz wrote of Trump, " 'Reading documents a lot' is high on the list of activities it's nearly impossible to imagine Trump doing, along with foraging, Pilates, and introspection."[3]

With all things Trump, the vaguely ludicrous proposition that the president of the United States is watching a morning talk show with the intellectual weight and policy depth of a Katy Perry video would be risible if it wasn't so damn terrifying.

It's not all the rude grunting of lowest-common-denominator outlets like Breitbart. A new species of DC conservative sprang out of the Trump waste pile like some kind of hypocritical mushrooms.

Meet the clickservatives—conservative media types more interested in web traffic and ad revenue than ideology—who have embraced Esoteric Trumpism at the low, low price of their integrity. It's a deal with the Devil, and far too many in the conservative intellectual class and the commentariat couldn't wait to sign. "Eternal damnation later for making libtard snowflakes cry now and raking in those hot clicks? Bargain!" Defending the principles of limited government, personal liberty, and strict adherence to the Constitution is old and busted. The new hotness? "Nationalism is the new black." So many of them dropped their panties and put out on the first date because Big Donnie talks dirty to the media.

After Trump's win in November 2016, it was particularly painful to watch principled conservatives (a term now said with ironic air quotes and that hits the ETTD rule squarely) become advocates for Donald Trump on a scale that ranged from grudging to toadying for a singular reason that seemed to overwhelm all other factors: Trump attacks the press.

They seem perfectly happy to embrace tactics they'd rage about if a liberal president deployed them, and that they'd condemn in the hands of any foreign strongman or authoritarian.

After all their talk of fundamentally returning the country to its Constitutional roots, reducing the power of the state, demanding America be a nation of laws, they sold themselves to a vulgar authoritarian statist because he tweets mean things about reporters.

All it took to break the spirit of far too many in the conservative class was for Trump to leaven his deranged, autocratic rantings with "fake news" and "duh librul media" bait. People who think of themselves as being smarter than the average sack of hair still seem to miss that they're either the latest victims of the Trump Con or willing patsies. Neither is a good look in the war of ideas.

We now routinely see a formulation something like this: "Well, Trump isn't perfect, but at least he's attacking the media." I wrote in the *Daily Beast*, "This outsourcing of media aggression is the haute-bourgeois pleasure of watching someone else to do your dueling."[4]

Now, even elite intellectual conservative writers who tore the bark off Barack Obama since 2008 for "picking winners and losers"—conservative shorthand for clumsy government intervention in the marketplace—are delighted by Trump for doing the same and largely silent on pie-in-the-sky blowout budgets with massive new debt and deficit spending. They direct a large fraction of their ire to mainstream media outlets scrambling to find a way to process the election and governance of Trump.[5]

Rather than examine his daily assaults on conservative values, common sense, and that little thing we used to value called "the truth," they look politely away, at best, and at worst strap on their kneepads and grab their pom-poms. "Conservatives" who have for decades sung the praises of free trade, low tariffs, and multilateral trade agreements now mutely nod at the brute stupidity of Trumpian economic populism, largely because he yells at Maggie Haberman and batters CNN, the *New York Times*, and *BuzzFeed*.

Of course, intellectual conservatism is a rather small pool in the great scheme of things. What really mattered then and matters now is that a half-dozen gatekeepers in the conservative movement decided Trump would be lucrative fodder for their audience. They monetized the transition from promoting conservative ideals to selling the umber con man with the same vigor with which they pitch reverse mortgages, catheters, survival food, and gold.

This constellation of media players could have slammed the brakes on Trump and Trumpism during the 2016 election, and could do so now. At any moment, Rupert or the sons could have told Roger Ailes, "Okay, that's enough, Roger."

They and others actively elected to elide Trump's endless catalogue of ideological sins, thinly veiled racism, moral shortcomings, mob ties, Russian money men, personal weirdness, endemic cheating, trophy wives, serial bankruptcies, persistent tax shenanigans, low-grade intellect, conspiracy email–forwarding kooky grandpa affect and disregard for American values and standards.

The "populist movement" explanation for 2016 isn't entirely wrong, but it took conservative sellout media enablers to promote Trump as the singular remedy for the alleged moral, economic, and political collapse they decried each day for their credulous readers, viewers, and listeners to make that "movement" happen. Tune in Fox today, and it meets every clichéd liberal critique of the past twenty years: counterfactual conspiracy nonsense, yahoo-ism, least-common-denominator jingoism, deep and overt bias in story selection, and out-of-context smears.

It turns out some Republicans didn't want fair and balanced after all; they wanted an insular, partisan media environment biased toward the lunatic fringe and that delivered 24/7 Trump adoration. The all-in crew of Fox, Breitbart, social media, and talk radio built an ecosystem for Trump voters where all the news was good news, where the beet harvest always exceeds the Five-Year Plan, and where Donald Trump is a singular, uncontested voice.

Attacks on the media have become the definitional characteristic of this administration and today's Republican Party. In terms of today's discourse, the endless whining about the media isn't just something they do; it's essentially *all* they do. From Trump himself to his minions, the press is the Main Enemy, and the reporting of Trump's problems *is* the problem.

Although Donald Trump swore to uphold the Constitution in the most solemn political oath in the American system of government, he is notoriously not good at abiding by agreements. Every oath Trump has ever sworn, every promise he's made in business, or his personal life is contingent on his moods, personal beefs, incoherent rages, bizarre conspiracy theories, poor impulse control, horndog nature, and raging venality. Thus, it shouldn't come as a shock that Trump's view of the First Amendment and the protection it affords a free press is somewhere between dismissive and Saddam Hussein.

I wish this was just a game played by a president more suited to the World Wrestling Federation than to the Oval Office, but it's not. This constant attack on a central pillar of our liberties isn't good politics for Trump; it's his only politics. Of all the norms Trump has shattered, of all the damage he's done to the Republic, the war on the press is the deepest affront to our traditions, values, and freedoms.

I wonder where the same conservatives will be on the day when some leftist statist in the Oval Office decides to try to shut down Fox or Limbaugh or moves in even more sweeping directions to regulate, control, or suppress conservative voices online. If conservatives don't see the downsides of this future, they're working with a set of mental predicates that assume there will never be a tough election ahead, and never be a moment when the jackboot is on the other foot.

The media's flaws are our flaws. The media's shortcomings are our own. The members of the press may not all look like and vote like Middle-American conservative evangelicals in red Trumper hats, and that's okay. It's not a secret. The frictionless media world we live in today makes it easier than ever to fact-check, argue, debate, and contest biased coverage on all sides. The way to move past bad or biased media is to produce better media, not to engage in state threats.

The press is never perfect, and will never please all sides, but the idea of the leader of the free world revving up his mob to intimidate reporters or to use the awesome power of his office to shut down media outlets would have been repugnant to the Founders.

Trumpism now demands its votaries believe that conservative values and conservative policies are better served by government intimidation, bullying, and restrictions on the rights guaranteed under the Constitution than by the Constitution itself. It's a sign of how fallen, compromised, and sick the conservative movement has become under this man's spell. Free speech is still too rare in the world. Having the president of the United States as an implacable enemy of that freedom is a grotesque example for the rest of the world. Trump's ideal media looks like the press in places like Iran, Turkey, Egypt, Venezuela, and North Korea. In those nations, the liberal media know their place and print only what their respective Dear Leaders find pleasing.

When independent journalism is allowed at all, censorship, spying, and demands that media outlets follow state propaganda templates make it nearly impossible for informed public discourse. Print and broadcast outlets are strictly licensed and controlled, and often are owned by the families of leading government officials. Online reporting is subject to intense government monitoring. Harassment, violence, and physical intimidation are routine features of the lives of reporters in nations lacking the fundamental press freedoms our Founders wrote into the operating system of the United States.

In those nations, censorship and state control of the media are features of their political landscape. "I can't believe the media is allowed to write anything they want" is the language of despots and tyrants. In many ways, this attack on the press and the roaring approval by Republicans illustrates the real divide in American conservatism today. It isn't simply about Trumpism versus conservatism. It is about statism versus constitutional freedom. Republicans are failing the test of our time, and slipping into the warm bath of totalitarian language, practice, and politics.

The conservative critique of oppressive states once centered on the suppression of speech and on the use of state power to silence dissent. Today, conservatives are rushing to embrace Trump's attacks on NBC, CNN, the *Washington Post*, the *New York Times*, and any other media outlet refusing to bend the knee.

The reasons the clickservatives flood the zone for Trump isn't because they embrace the same nationalist hooey as Breitbart or Gateway Pundit. They know better. For many, it's a shtick, playing the rubes for clicks and ad revenue. For all that conservative websites, writers, and blogs mocked the *BuzzFeed* model of AI-driven listicle storytelling, they've become what they loathed. "Five Reasons Robert Mueller

Is Satan" is the clickservative equivalent of "You won't believe these cute puppies playing on Kim Kardashian's bed!" or "Take this quiz to learn what Disney Princess you'd be in Medieval France!"

Some see the Trump culture of endless media confrontation as a felicitous moment to write clickbaity, hair-pulling essays about "the Left" and "the media" being infinitely worse than a man who fails every standard of conservatism. I had this old-fashioned notion that standards were part of what made conservatives what they are. The "But the liberal media" excuse feels increasingly thin as Trump's failings are increasingly obvious.

SEAN HANNITY

Sean Hannity plays a singular role in Team Trump's media cheer squad. The biggest name on the biggest cable network, Hannity also hosts the number two–rated radio talk show in the country. He is a bright, bright star in the newly defined conservative firmament, because all that matters now is constant, endless, fawning praise of Trump and endless vitriol for his opponents. Already successful, Hannity rose to new heights during the era of Trump.

All it took was cashing in all his conservative priors. As with so many other on-air "conservatives," Sean Hannity bailed on the tenets of conservative orthodoxy he claimed to advocate on his rise to influence them. Hannity smelled something in the wind as Trump rose in the polls in 2015 and switched into overdrive. Without missing a beat he's become the loudest voice on Fox—and therefore in the one media silo that matters to Trump—as the proselytizer and enforcer of Trump juche. He even spends his evenings on the phone with the president.[6] I can't help imagining them like a pair of teenage girls on their Princess phones: "You hang up first." No, you hang up first." "Love you." "Love you more."

It's paid off for Hannity in spades. His evening Fox show is the highest rated on cable news. His radio show draws in 13.5 million listeners.[7] Sean Hannity's combined daily reach is more than 13 million

Americans, and these days they're there for one thing and one thing only: unconditional love for The Donald and Sean's daily Two Minutes of Hate for anyone and anything not on board with Trump.

Sure, Hannity's populist woke workin' man shtick rings a bit hollow now that he lives in a multimillion-dollar mansion and owns a private jet, but the man is a profit-making machine for Fox and for Premiere Radio Networks.

Republicans have long engaged in hissy-fits over the relations between Democratic elected officials and the news media. Hell, there's a cottage industry of books blaming this bias for every failing of the conservative movement for the past 60 years, and plenty of grist for the mill, though the case is often rather wildly overstated.

In my 30 years in political consulting I've pushed back on hundreds of stories that I believed were biased, sloppy, or based on dumb predicates. I also praised good reporting, even from folks in the media I knew were wildly to my left, and maintained good relations with reporters and editors because I went at the facts, worked the details, and pushed back like a professional.

Making the rookie media mistake of confusing correlation for causation is sine qua non for Republican media critics. Early in 2015, I realized that Republicans were using the media bias angle not to get their side of an argument into the media ecosystem but to create a hermetic bullshit bubble of confirmation bias. I looked back at some writing I'd done in the past couple years about the media and found I'd been falling into that same trap.

Many times critics of the press have been right to note the cultural and social connections and affinities between the elite media and liberal politicians. Cozy relationships between the powerful and those who report on them have been an obsession for conservatives since Ben Bradlee and John F. Kennedy chased tail and drank too much in Washington. The marriage and family relationships of Obama administration officials to reporters covering the White House were the subject of much conservative hyperventilation.

Sean Hannity is the frenzied end point of this particular flavor of conservative hypocrisy. The role he plays for Trump would launch a thousand screaming Media Research Center and Breitbart articles if the partisan brogue was on the other foot.

Imagine for a moment the Republican meltdown that would have come to pass if—hypothetically—Joe Scarborough had spent weeks advising Barack Obama on how to respond to the Benghazi investigation, or if Jake Tapper had counseled Hillary Clinton on her email server scandal. The incandescent, ass-on-fire meltdown would have been one for the ages.

Oddly, conservatives saw absolutely nothing wrong when Hannity's role as a Trump campaign advisor leaked out in the midst of the 2016 campaign.[8] Hannity spent every night grunting out a relentlessly pro-Trump message on television, while also serving as an advisor to the campaign. As an entrepreneurial power play it was the marriage of a reality-TV show candidate to a talk show host. Trump loved it because Hannity never shaded his coverage in any direction but full-on Trumpisma. Hannity loved it because it was a ratings bonanza, and Trump was whispering about a post-Fox Trump TV project.

"I'm not hiding the fact that I want Donald Trump to be the next president of the United States," Hannity told the *New York Times*. "I never claimed to be a journalist."[9]

Oh, we understood that part, Sean. Trust me.

The *New York Times* reported the Fox host "peppered Mr. Trump, his family members and advisers with suggestions on strategy and messaging."[10] Hannity's massive platforms delivered the Trump message to the GOP primary audience, undercutting many of the formerly rising stars of the party whom Sean had highlighted for years. In Hannityland, Ted Cruz, Rand Paul, Marco Rubio, and the rest were reduced to afterthoughts at best, targets at worst. Fox favorites like Ben Carson also disappeared from the network's most watched hour of television.

When the election shifted to the general, Hannity went into overdrive. He peddled some of the most batshit crazy theories about Hillary Clinton's health, echoing the lunatic trolling of lispy lunatic Mike

Cernovich and others. The moment the Hannity-Trump marriage was sealed, though, was in the Trump campaign's darkest hour.

When the world was falling down around Donald Trump's head in the wake of the *Access Hollywood* "pussy grabber" revelations, it was Sean Hannity, almost alone in the top ranks of the conservative media, who sprang to Trump's defense. He turned the story—at least for the tribal base of Trump's GOP cohort—into a tale of the perfidy of Bill and Hillary Clinton. His full-throated defense of Trump's "locker room" talk told Trump that Hannity would never abandon him for anything as trifling as the truth, or morals.

It was one thing for conservative keepers of America's media mores to look away from Hannity's direct involvement in the campaign of Donald Trump. It was quite another that they saw nothing wrong with the president of the United States of America, the head of the world's longest-running and most successful experiment in constitutional democracy, taking marching orders from a blowhard talk show host.

Hannity's role as a political enforcer for Trump was clear within weeks of the election. Lest any Republican voice even the slightest hint of concern over Trump's policies, statements, or tweeting, they could count on Sean Hannity to hammer them, and for Hannity's audience to turn their Facebook and Twitter feeds into a nightmare of grammatically challenged but passionate MAGAgasms. One member told me that the one-two punch of a Trump tweet against him followed by Hannity's follow-on attack made him consider shutting down his social media accounts.

The irony of Hannity going after conservatives like Ben Sasse, Mitch McConnell, Bob Corker, and John McCain was rich. Trump, a man with no ideological moorings, was being held up by Hannity as a paragon of conservative virtue. Watching him rage against Republican critics of Trump reminded me of a quote by a noted specialist in the semiotics, hermeneutics, and metaphysics of Trump and Trumpism, Jacobim Mugatu: "I feel like I'm taking crazy pills."

Noted nuclear weapons expert, Middle East policy guru, and fluent Farsi speaker Sean Hannity also advised Donald Trump on how to handle the continuation of the nuclear weapons deal President Barack Obama struck with Iran.[11] I mean, it's only one of the most consequential decisions a president can make about the future political, diplomatic, and military landscape of the Middle East, so why not consult a talk show host with a high school education? Why not ask for advice from a man who makes even the most superficial talking-head policy lightweights seem like a combination of Metternich, John Foster Dulles, and Henry Kissinger?

A media low point in the Hannity experience came in the wake of the death of Democratic National Committee staffer Seth Rich. Rich, who was killed by muggers in Washington, was the subject of some of the most baroque, cruel, and downright insane conspiracy theories ever to hit the Clintons, who are a magnet for this kind of cray to begin with. Hannity jumped in feet first.

Hannity tried to outflank Alex Jones, leading his own network to retract the story that launched this particularly embarrassing line of conspiratorial nuttery. The nut of the claim was that Seth Rich was murdered for leaking the DNC emails to Wikileaks. It was widely, thoroughly, exhaustively debunked well before Hannity took up the story again in May 2017. Think of it as Pizzagate, only even more tendentiously stupid, wrong, and cruel to the parents of Rich, who called the garbage theory "something promoted by disgusting sociopaths."[12]

David French, writing in *National Review*, made what I think was a perfect indictment of Hannity's role in this shameful mess:

> It's a dramatic and lurid misdirection, one that even the writers of *House of Cards* would find far-fetched, and it has the benefit of tricking gullible Trump supporters into further mistrusting the media. After all, the real story is over at Gateway Pundit or at Breitbart or Drudge, or on Fox News at 10:00 pm. The true facts are known only to those who can perceive the pure evil of the Clintons, the deep state, and the rest of the establishment media.[13]

None of it stopped Hannity, who enlisted a clown college of Fox contributors like Newt Gingrich and Geraldo Rivera to echo the theory that the Clinton Enterprise had Seth Rich murdered, even reviving the ludicrous 1990s "Clinton Body Count" conspiracy theories.

The market did to Hannity what any innate sense of decency could not; as his advertisers started to abandon his show, reality set in. Even Fox News, an organization with a Roy-Cohnesque "never apologize, never defend, never give an inch, punch back twice as hard" PR approach, was forced to apologize and withdraw the story.[14] Hannity briefly also became a line of defense for Trump and Bannon's candidate in the Alabama Senate race, teen-curious and creepy Judge Roy Moore. It was a sign that the moral rot in the conservative media didn't skip Sean when it came to defending a pedophile. More advertisers bailed, and Roy Moore's problems were beyond even Sean's ability to ignore.

Hannity's role as a Trump advisor and enforcer never varied, and by the end of Trump's first year in office, the "Fox Feedback Loop," as coined by *Vanity Fair*'s Gabriel Sherman, was complete. Sherman, describing the cycle, put it like this: "Fox may be Trump's safe space, but Trump is Fox's safe space, too. It's a circular feedback loop."[15] The expulsion and subsequent death of Roger Ailes, a man with a true gift for creating television, meant the network was unmoored. It still had producers and air talent who could play from the songbook Roger left behind, but it lacked a real conductor from that moment forward. Following the Trump wave was its only real option, and one that still made the network over $1.5 billion in 2016.[16]

Understanding the centrality of Fox News, and Hannity in particular, in the way Donald Trump shapes his message, strategy, and national policy is vital to understanding how deeply broken his presidency was from the start. The institutions of media and government were, in the eyes of the Founders, separate. Even in our darkest hours, our nation has been cautious about the power of state propaganda, as we have been cautious about state-run media. (No, libertarians, Big Bird and NPR don't count.)

Fox and Hannity have upended that. If you're a conservative who sees this as a good outcome merely because Fox is nominally conservative, you might want to examine your priors. The president of the United States is addicted to an endless stream of praise from a shallow, dangerously stupid man. That same dangerous, stupid man feeds America's president a constant flow of conspiracy nonsense, uncritical praise, and uninformed opinion. It's a disaster in every way but the ratings.

ANN COULTER

Ann Coulter, tales of whom are whispered in dark rooms to frighten children, went from being a snarky, in-your-face hyperconservative to a tiresomely relentless Trump cheerleader based on his promise to deport 13 million people and build the infamous Wall. If there's one person who displays the ETTD agony of being on a constant roller-coaster ride of Trump adoration to condemnation, it's Coulter. Her arc, like that of so many Trump backers from the conservative media, could only ever end in one way: hot, angry tears and a morning-after binge of chain-smoking Marlboro Reds, hammering back indifferent box-wine Chardonnay, and devouring the souls of orphans.

Frank Bruni perfectly framed Coulter's unique position in the Trump media ecosystem: "So Coulter was Trump's muse. She was also his oracle, predicting his nomination and election back when most others still dismissed him as a joke. And she's a barometer of, and tribune for, some of his core supporters, including her good friend Matt Drudge."[17]

Watching Ann's on-again, off-again relationship with Trump rise and fall with his positions on immigration has been a genuine pleasure. I can hear her, à la *Fatal Attraction*, whispering into the phone, "DON, I won't BE ignored." It was the definitional issue for Coulter and a handful of other paleo-cons, and the subject of her obsessive, bunny-boiling rages. It showed us just how little the rest of the conservative portfolio mattered to her when she tweeted, "I don't care if @realDonaldTrump wants to perform abortions in the White House after this immigration policy paper."[18]

The recursive irony was that she'd helped write the immigration policy paper she described as "the greatest political document since the Magna Carta."[19] At the direction of Steve Bannon, Coulter and Stephen Miller had crafted the white-nationalist immigration plan she was praising.

Donald Trump, the king of the political pump-and-dump, would betray Coulter, and she would return the favor. By early 2018, the author of *E. Pluribus Awesome: In Trump We Trust* was in full-on psycho ex-girlfriend mode. After a year of prevarications, lies, and typical Trumpian bullshit over immigration, Coulter's patience was exhausted.

Her own ragetweets started, and their relationship deteriorated to the point of an obscenity-filled Oval Office screaming match. By Coulter's account, she was greeted by Trump as "the great betrayer" and Trump mumbling, "But Gorsuch."[20] By the time Trump signed the 2018 Omnibus spending bill, the romance was strained to the breaking point.

In a bitter, testy appearance at Columbia, Coulter would say of Trump, "I knew he was a shallow, lazy ignoramus, and I didn't care."[21] Oh, Ann. You really *are* in touch with the Trump mind-set.

TRUMPBART

If you're looking for weaponized, white-hot, immigrant-hating trailer-trash postconservative nationalist populism, look no further than Donald Trump's loudest screaming section, Breitbart "News."

How could Breitbart News have risen faster or fallen harder? After Andrew Breitbart's death in 2012, Steve Bannon became the new capo of the enterprise, marked it with his own special ichor, and went all-in on what became the main operating principle of the new-right media: provocation over reporting, instigation over analysis, and jackassery over all. They were outsider media for an outsider president.

Not everyone inside Breitbart was happy about it at first. McKay Coppins in his 2017 book *The Wilderness* reported, "According to four sources with knowledge of the situation, editors and writers at the outlet have privately complained since at least last year that the company's top management was allowing Trump to turn Breitbart into his own fan website—using it to hype his political prospects and attack his enemies."[22]

For a time, it looked as if Bannon's twin bets on the alt-right and Donald Trump would pay off big. As candidate and president, Trump was often presented with glowing Breitbart headlines, which would leave him giggling and smiling like a D student being told he's brilliant and accomplished. Their turn to Trump was sharply clear in mid-2015, to the point I tore Breitbart's editor in chief, Alex Marlow, a new one on CNN, telling him that Breitbart was "Trump's *Pravda*." It hit a nerve.

But Breitbart also fell victim to the Trump curse. They were the id of the right wing of American politics from the beginning of Bannon's tenure and worked hard to play the "Trigger the lib snowflake tears" game to its hilt. When Breitbart was just Bannon's troll site, headlines like "Birth Control Makes Women Crazy and Unattractive" might have been laughed off, but as the brand became permanently stained by their close association with the alt-right, anti-immigrant agitprop, and as Donald Trump's media mouthpiece, trouble appeared on the horizon.

Their self-reinforcing vicious cycle meant it wasn't enough to be edgy; edgy wasn't going to feed the lunatic comments section folks. Chasing the clickbait dragon meant the headlines got louder, the stories got wilder, and the politics got closer and closer to the fringe:

BILL KRISTOL: REPUBLICAN SPOILER, RENEGADE JEW[23]

HOIST IT HIGH AND PROUD: THE CONFEDERATE
FLAG PROCLAIMS A GLORIOUS HERITAGE[24]

WOULD YOU RATHER YOUR CHILD HAD
FEMINISM OR CANCER? [25]

Breitbart had long relied on three revenue drivers: programmatic ad placements by large digital ad agencies, sweet, sweet chunks of quan from Robert Mercer, and Facebook traffic. Breitbart bragged in its public affairs materials about traffic, Facebook engagement, and a whole spectrum of other indicators. One thing they never mentioned? Revenue and profit.

There was always a mystery about just how much cash Mercer dumped into the Bannon version of the House Andrew Built. It was enough that Breitbart's ad sales and development team were always an afterthought, but not enough to where they could forgo advertising. Those automatically placed ads from digital agencies didn't look at *where* the ads were placed; they merely looked at the demographics of the sites and their traffic. It was the power of automated, digital markets operating on autopilot.

Then came Sleeping Giants and their countercampaign. The *Chicago Tribune* called them "the mysterious group that wants to kill Breitbart's ad revenue, one tweet at a time."[26] When advertisers a million miles from Breitbart's political values were notified that they were supporting Trump and the alt-right, the social pressure led to their blacklisting Breitbart. It wasn't a "free speech" question, as Breitbart's executives squealed like pigs. It was a market question. Who wants to be associated with a media outlet tied at the hip to the Pepe Brigade and the least popular president in history? No one, that's who.

By late 2017 it was clear that Robert Mercer had reached his limits with Bannon, Breitbart, and the collection of trash people around its orbit. From deep-pocketed sugar daddy to "I barely know him" was a sign of just how far Bannon's fortunes had fallen. It's hard to imagine a sharper rebuke of Bannon than this from his former patron:

> The press has also intimated that my politics marches in lockstep with Steve Bannon's. I have great respect for Mr. Bannon, and from time to time I do discuss politics with him. However, I make my own decisions with respect to whom I support politically. Those decisions do not always align with Mr. Bannon's.

> For personal reasons, I have also decided to sell my stake
> in Breitbart News to my daughter.

"Advertisers have rapidly and steadily fled Breitbart News this year as the site's reputation is increasingly tied to the alt-right. So far, more than 2,500 companies have jumped ship," said the Sleeping Giants team.[27] It wasn't about left and right. It was about markets in action. As MediaRadar reported, "Six months ago, Breitbart was riding the wave of the election, plotting an international expansion to provide a platform to spread far-right, populist views in Europe. But today, Breitbart is facing traffic declines, advertiser blacklists, campaigns for marketers to steer clear and even a petition within Amazon for it to stop providing ad services."[28]

Isn't capitalism grand?

Facebook changed its algorithm in the spring of 2018 to reduce the prevalence of fake news sites driving clickbait edge-case lunacy. You'll be shocked to learn Breitbart's traffic numbers took a sharp dive when Facebook upped their quality filter.

The curse touched the edge-case "reporters" who kept pushing the brand deeper into the weeds. We'll cover Milo Yiannopoulos in a separate section. Katie McHugh, a vicious little racist even by Breitbart's standards, was an overt alt-righter who was fired after a series of tweets that were—and ride with me here—too racist for Breitbart.[29]

McHugh's tweets have included: "There would be no deadly terror attacks in the U.K. if Muslims didn't live there"; "The only way to strike a balance begtween vigilance, discrimination, (& terror) is to end Muslim immigration"; and "British settlers built the U.S.A. 'Slaves' built the country much as cows 'built' McDonald's. Amateur . . ."

Lee Stranahan was forced out because he was too lunatic even for Breitbart and now is reduced to reporting for the Russian government propaganda agency Sputnik. At least he's cut out the middleman.

Pudgy virgin Matt Boyle, the site's lead political reporter, is an unkempt little beachball, full of fury at the Establishment, unalloyed praise for Donald Trump, and endless Tinder rejections. He thought he'd end up as Breitbart's Ben Bradlee but is increasingly marginalized in the wave of mainstream reporting that truly gets inside the doings of the Trump White House.

I'm sure you can hear the sound of my tiny violin playing right now as I close this section, because if there was a single alt-right, pro-Trump media outlet that went all-in and expected to change the game of conservative media, it was Breitbart. It was the bet of all bets, and Bannon's leadership there ensured they were permanently bound to the rising and falling fortunes of Donald Trump. In late March 2018, the online metrics firm ComScore reported that Breitbart's traffic numbers had fallen as sharply as their advertising revenue.

Between January 2017 and January 2018, Breitbart's traffic dropped 51%, from 240th to 273rd of U.S. websites.[30] Engagement of Breitbart's traffic on Facebook and other social media platforms vanished. If there's one media ETTD story that shows the entire arc of how dangerous tying one's fortunes to Trump can be, it's the Breitbart story.

RISING TRUMP STARS, CRASHING TO EARTH

As the age of Trump dawned, a cluster of rising new-right, alt-right, and Trump-right media stars blossomed. Just as Trump and his followers believed they represented a new era in politics, these folks believed they were the future of conservative journalism. Their contempt for actual conservative ideas and policy was vivid; they saw themselves as part of the new, hot nationalist wave. This list is by no means complete, but represents a few of the more prominent and colorful types who presumed they were destined for Trump era greatness . . . until the curse hit.

Milo

What can be said of Milo Yiannopoulos that won't feed the singularity of ego need and attention-seeking that defines his entire character? A narcissist who rivals even Donald Trump, he was in some ways the perfect monster at the perfect moment. As one of the satellites orbiting Trump's world, Milo looked as if he was about to become a media star for the Trump era. He was one of the cool kids of the alt-right: blond, flamboyant, provocative. Milo was just the kind of pretty provocateur Bannon wanted to inflame the desires of his growing alt-right fan base.

He was fond of referring to Trump as "Daddy" and built a fan base off of his post-Gamergate move to Breitbart, where he produced a series of inflammatory juvenilia and alt-right agitprop. The arc of Milo's career and popularity rose fast, with a national tour of college campuses, all in an effort to generate viral buzz over his liberal-triggering antics.

There was a moment when Milo was almost interesting, a kind of political stunt character, a comments-section troll made into a real boy, but then came the endless series of crashes. Karaoke in a bar full of white supremacists featuring Nazi salutes, a defense of pedophilia, and a botched book deal all hit Milo hard.

Then, during the height of Bannondammerung, Robert Mercer tossed Milo to the wolves at the same moment he was disposing of the disgraced White House advisor. Milo's "Dangerous Faggot" tour of college campuses had been a provocation of the sort in which Bannon and Milo reveled. Campus riots were a part of their imagined culture war.

For his corporate sponsor, it wasn't as appealing. Mercer's public note was a slap across Milo's sneering face:

> Without individuals thinking for themselves, society as a whole will struggle to distinguish the signal of truth from the correlated noise of conformity. I supported Milo Yiannopou-

los in the hope and expectation that his expression of views contrary to the social mainstream and his spotlighting of the hypocrisy of those who would close down free speech in the name of political correctness would promote the type of open debate and freedom of thought that is being throttled on many American college campuses today. But in my opinion, actions of and statements by Mr. Yiannopoulos have caused pain and divisiveness undermining the open and productive discourse that I had hoped to facilitate. I was mistaken to have supported him, and for several weeks have been in the process of severing all ties with him.[31]

Milo helped spread the alt-right's poison into the American political system, but for him, it wasn't ideological. Milo's sole needs set is about Milo. His famewhoring over Trump tied neatly into the rise of the alt-right, and his flirtation with them was about associating his own brand with controversy rather than some ideological alignment. Milo's love of the transgressive isn't political; he's drawn to the gleaming eye of the camera, not by something deeper or more meaningful.

His 15 minutes were firmly up even before the end of Trump's first year in office. Abandoned by Mercer, dumped by Breitbart, his tours impossible without a sugar daddy to support them, he was left doing nothing but a cam show from his Miami home.

In a sad piece on the decline and decline of the former alt-right poster child, Tanya Gold of the *Spectator* quoted the fading star as saying:

> "People love me everywhere. It was a tumultuous 2017 but everyone who put Trump in the White House got punished somehow. It's what happens after elections."
>
> We speak again a few weeks ago. He has a new strategy, he says, because new media wants to destroy him: "We made a mistake handing over our distribution to people who want to exterminate us. Personalities like me are being strangled

to death by Facebook and YouTube and Google and Twitter. I have millions of fans worldwide. But they can't get my stuff."[32]

Don't weep for Milo, though; when I last spotted him, he was hawking vitamins and the 30 Day Liver Cleanse on an *Infowars* webcast. Who says the universe doesn't have a sense of humor?

Alex Jones

The dog's breakfast of conspiracy-driven, industrial-scale kook media in Trump's orbit has nothing on Alex Jones, the red-faced, hyperventilating host of the *Infowars* "network." Jones makes Breitbart look as measured and considered as the *New Yorker* in William Shawn's day.

Of course, in the Trump era, no conspiracy is complete without an appearance by Roger Stone. Clad sometimes in a black T-shirt and beret, Stone frequently appears on *Infowars*, looking like a member of the Gray Panthers' Viagra Liberation Front and sounding as if he's mainlining Red Bull, steroids, and the ghostly ectoplasm of Lyndon LaRouche. Stone and Jones are perhaps the most vocal promoters of the Deep State theory, in which America's intelligence agencies, the military industrial complex, and other dark forces, including the Federal Reserve, the secret Zionist World Government, the dudes from *Eyes Wide Shut*, and the lizard people manipulate the economy, the media, the justice system, and the fluoride in your water.

Jones was an early, enthusiastic supporter of the oft-mentioned Pizzagate theory, in which Hillary Clinton is part of a global child kidnapping and cannibalism ring, and promoted the Seth Rich conspiracy. In both cases, Jones ran into a legal buzzsaw, hitting the skids in the spring of 2018. No longer allowed even in the farthest orbits of Trump world, he continued to support the president in his inimitably lunatic style. Like many other outlets on the fringes drawn into the political mix, *Infowars* started to run afoul of social media platforms.

As with neo-Nazis, at some point the private companies like

YouTube and Facebook Jones used to spread his batshittery realized his brand is consumer poison. Fearing YouTube and others would demonetize his videos, Jones was in a box. Feed the monster, or save the cash flow? The surge from interviews with Trump helped normalize *Infowars* with the kook set, but after its peak in November 2016, Jones was back to his usual sweaty screamfest farrago of UFO theories, amateur demonology, lurid conspiracy talk about the Bilderbergers, the Illuminati, the Gray Aliens, fluoride, chemtrails, Bigfoot, Jade Helm, Agenda 21, and the fish people. (If you're ever looking for the perfect video clip to explain him, just search "Alex Jones Fish People." It's worth it.)

Tomi Lahren

A moment, if I may, about Alt-Right Barbie Tomi Lahren. You've heard of her. Of course you've heard of her. She's a nonstop presence in the lives and minds of Trump World. The subject of a thousand fanfic moments in the heads of pudge-gutted Trump trucker-hat-wearing MAGAites, Tomi rocks an Aryan teen-queen mane of blonde extensions, a bilious attitude, an acidic tongue, and a withered, blackened crust of a soul when it comes to anyone of the wrong race, religion, or national origin.

Tomi is young. Tomi is quite pretty-ish, in a kind of Middle America trashy-hot fake-Instagram-model way. She's learned to read a teleprompter well and emotes the oppositional-defiant-disorder style of contemporary Trumpian Republicanism with a certain livid verve. Tomi understands the way to the Trump demo's heart is pure, hot, constant hate.

Tomi and I appeared on *Real Time with Bill Maher* on February 3, 2017. Even before the show, she seemed less confident than I would have expected for someone who at the time was a commentator for the new conservative One America News Network and a rising star in the Trump media firmament. (As an aside, OANN is a Dumpster fire of sparkly-eagle-animated, flag-wavin' warnings about the Muslim-

Mexican conspiracy to bring sharia-compliant illegal immigrants to America, and truly a brain-melting experience.)

She rolled into the show with a few well-prepared talking points about the then-frisky protests against the egregious Milo Yiannopoulos. They say live television shows who people really are, and that night, as Tomi lost the Trumpian narrative thread and started speaking from the heart, I saw the future of "conservative" media up close. She was Ann Coulter without the pungent smell of cat litter, Marlboro Reds, and despair.

Bill Maher asked Tomi a question that would have worked perfectly for her on Fox or OANN: "Two-thirds of Republicans agree that discrimination against whites has become as big a problem as discrimination against minorities. Do you agree with that?"

After a little prevarication, Tomi stuck her head in the proverbial noose: "As we sit here today, I do think that there is an element of racism against whites," she whinged.

Given my low tolerance for bullshit, I wasn't going to put up with it, and replied, "Since I'm a conservative, and not a Trump person, let me say this. That's absurd. That's fucking crazy." The reaction across social media was not, to put it mildly, kind to Tomi.

She didn't spend a lot of time at the after-party.

Tomi has a massive social media presence and a gig with Trump's SuperPAC as its spokesbot and is in regular rotation on Fox. She is also an utterly spoiled little trashfire of a human being, and thus a perfect exemplar of Trump's media enablers.

*The following transcript was provided
by Wikileaks in the Fall of 2024.*

– INTERCEPT 5 –

TOP SECRET//SI//ORCON//NOFORN

MUELLER: Mr. President, thank you for sitting down with us today.

TRUMP: President? Am I President?

MUELLER: You are, sir.

TRUMP: I like television. I like to watch.

MUELLER: Mr. President, I'd like to begin by discussing the June 9, 2016, Trump Tower meeting with representatives of the Russian government. . . .

TRUMP: My name is Forrest Gump. People call me Forrest Gump.

MUELLER: Very well. I'd like to discuss payments to your campaign chairman Paul Manafort by . . .

TRUMP: I'm an excellent driver. Wapner.

MUELLER: Let's move on to . . .

TRUMP: I like lamp.

MUELLER: On the date of . . .

TRUMP: Stamina. Wall. MAGA. Incredible.

MUELLER: . . . June ninth, 2016, did you discuss . . .

TRUMP: Hey, you wanna hear the most annoying sound in the world? EEEEEEEHHHHHHHHH!

MUELLER: I'd like to discuss the Letter of Agreement you signed regarding Trump Tower Moscow in the summer of 2016 . . . Here's the prospectus and an artist's rendering of the tower.

TRUMP: What is this? A tower for *ants?*

[SOUND OF TABLE FLIPPING]

[[TRANSCRIPT ENDS]

14

TRUMP'S ISLAND
OF MISFIT TOYS

DONALD TRUMP'S ADMINISTRATION REFLECTS HIM PER-
fectly. Corrupt, angry, dumb, weird, ignorant of the world, venal as
hell, and totally over their heads. Americans were shocked by some
of Trump's early hires, then stunned as they were chewed up and spat
out either by resignations or firings. It shouldn't have shocked anyone
that Trump ground people to dust in the White House.

Of course, Trump spins it differently; on March 6, 2018, days
after firing Rex Tillerson, his secretary of state, via tweet (naturally),
he protested, "The new Fake News narrative is that there is chaos in
the White House. Wrong! People will always come & go, and I want
strong dialogue before making a final decision. I still have some people
that I want to change (always seeking perfection). There is no Chaos,
only great Energy!"[1]

I mentioned the Emerson Rule earlier, and in a lifetime of politics,
I've seen that play out over and over again. Trump's administration is
no different.

As a younger man, fresh off the 1988 campaign trail, I had the
honor to work as an appointee in the administration of George Her-
bert Walker Bush. Our 41st president led by example, expecting all
of his appointees, from Cabinet secretaries down to the lowest-level
staffer, to reflect the values of patriotism, modesty, judgment, humanity, and service that had shaped his career. Moral examples work.

When I worked for Rudy Giuliani in New York's City Hall, the team culture was a combination of two-fisted, hands-on management and *The Sopranos*. We were high-speed, balls-out all the time, filled with a sense of mission to restore and protect the greatest city in the world. We were also swaggering assholes, with a heyfuckthatfucking-guy attitude. (My *God* that was fun.)

Nixon's paranoia and inferiority complex were ramified and re-flected in his administration. Clinton's lack of personal and profes-sional discipline led to a talented but chaotic wreck of a White House. Obama's technocrats, reflecting their boss almost perfectly, believed that if they could just set up the right regulatory nudges, paradise awaited.

Usually American presidents of both parties have had *some* virtu-ous streak in their character that allowed the Emerson rule to apply. No longer.

We've gone from the best and the brightest to the dumb and the dangerous in 50 short years. In the few weeks before I turned this in to my editors, the White House was firing people at a breakneck pace.

Bad hirings and opera buffa firings are a hallmark of Trump's ad-ministration, and by the time you read this he will have fired, driven out, or caused over 50% of his staff to commit either real or meta-phorical seppuku. The staggering turnover rate is the highest in mod-ern history, rivaling only medieval royal courts in which advisors to mad kings were poisoned, stabbed, thrown into wells, immured inside walls, eaten by wolves, carried off by plague, or killed by highwaymen.[2]

In the history of American politics, no campaign and no adminis-tration can rival the sideshow cast of characters who compose Trump World. Instead of smart, dignified men and women striving to serve the nation in the People's House, they more closely resemble a casting call for the set of *Real Housewives of Vulgaria*. Team Trump is the dross in the American political melting pot, combining raging crony capitalism, conflicts of interest, ideological dead ends, industrial-scale ass-kissing, and the worst instincts and beliefs scraped from the dark-est corners of our national shame closet.

It's an administration that combines astounding incompetence and consistent failure with a pungent combination of arrogance, bullish stupidity, and a relentless, juvenile desire to run a government dedicated not to service but to offense. The collection of miscreants, nutcases, extremists, and dead-enders around Trump is an extended middle finger to American values, institutions, and anyone, anywhere not sufficiently awed by and obeisant to this president.

Let's have a look at the cast of Trump's reality-TV government, campaign hangers-on, oddball allies, creepy fans, and long-term troublemakers, shall we?

STEVE BANNON

The brightest, hottest, weirdest, shittiest star in the Trump constellation from the moment of The Donald's unexpected electoral victory was Steve Bannon. If you're looking for the white-hot center of Esoteric Trumpism, Bannon is its intellectual architect, once you get past the homeless-drifter-with-a-hitchhiker's-head-in-his-backpack affect.

Bannon, a man who looks like the spokesmodel for a new line of gout medication, is known for his oddball sartorial choices; the multiple shirts, the tactical "operator" pants, and the Barbour jacket are all hallmarks of his bus-shelter-chic style. Persistently rumpled, persistently grizzled, and persistently looking like he's been dragged over 30 miles of bad road, Bannon was no one's idea of the White House's dull but professional suit-and-tie culture. His rheumy-eyed stare and an odd constellation of facial moles, warts, scrofula, weeping sores, and grizzled beard patches make him look vaguely piratical.

A devotee of the alt-right's favorite writers ("You haven't read Julius Evola in the original Italian? You're missing it *all*") and shoddy pop-history like *The Fourth Turning*, Bannon is one of the two types of DC intellectuals: the first type are nerds who have read everything and can't sell anything; the second are Bannon types who want you to *think* they've read everything and are out to sell themselves.

Bannon's confidence he is the smartest guy in the room isn't misplaced in Trump World, and certainly not in the presence of Trump. Famous nonreader Donald Trump, scanner of headlines, ignorer of summaries, writer of nothing longer than a tweet, has by many accounts never read much of anything and appears to have absolutely no interior intellectual life. He was a perfect mark for Bannon's blustery, whiskey-infused showmanship. Bannon would make a yeoman's effort to gentrify and polish Trumpism into nationalist populism. He would build not just a campaign but a national movement around the idea, using Trump as its avatar, symbol, and martyr.

Breitbart was famously scrappy, famously inflammatory, and a rising force on the right before Bannon. As head of Breitbart News, Bannon turned the site into a self-described "voice of the alt-right" and weaponized it to attack anyone he felt varied from the new, narrow confines of what he defined as conservatism.

In the 2016 cycle, Bannon's suicide-bomber version of the House Andrew Built would be turned into a blowtorch against every other Republican candidate in the primary field. His minions were particularly hard on Marco Rubio and Jeb Bush, for whom Bannon's personal animus dripped from virtually every story.

Bannon discovered immigration was the killer app in the Breitbart news mix, and it allowed him to shape the primary battlefield to Trump's advantage. For Trump, a man who craves favorable headlines like a meth junkie, Breitbart rewarded his impulsive behavior and extreme mood swings with better and better headlines. Trump then would then use Breitbart as a driver for more of his own messages and policies, such as they were. The cycle fed on itself.

Before Trump, it was an article of faith that Bannon and Breitbart would be all-in for Ted Cruz, as Breitbart's sponsors Robert and Rebekah Mercer had stroked a series of eye-popping SuperPAC checks and made no secret of their love of the Texas Senator. Bannon brokered their betrayal of Cruz in favor of Trump, and Trump for a time was taken by Bannon's shtick.

Bannon's tenure in the Trump White House went about as well

as expected; he's a sloppy thinker, largely disorganized, and given to impulses that run him into political and ideological box canyons. He's also a man who loves to have enemies. He needs enemies—real and imagined—to function. In the Trump White House, his enemy was everyone. Everywhere. All the time. Bannon fought with Ivanka and Jared. Bannon fought with Priebus. Bannon fought with Pence. Bannon famously fought with Gary Cohn and the other "globalists" among Trump's plutocratic economic advisors. ("Globalist" is Bannonese for "Jew," y'all. Just letting you know, in case you've been living under a rock.) Bannon fought and fought and fought himself out of a job.

Before Trump, Bannon's political chops were, to put it mildly, marginal. He'd been a Navy officer, a Goldman Sachs guy, and had dabbled in Hollywood. His money came in large measure from owning a piece of the *Seinfeld* franchise.

I never much cared for Bannon; he was an uglier, seamier version of Andrew Breitbart, and nothing about his new nationalist philosophy seemed to line up with any conservative principle. In 2015, Bannon weaponized Breitbart on your author because of my opposition to Trump. My prominence as an anti-Trump conservative led to a series of breathless Breitbart stories, including stories that targeted my children.[3] Bannon emailed a friend that he planned to destroy my career and said, "This is going to be fun."

Bannon's actions made life hell on my family. His minions stalked and harassed my kids and my clients. There was only one solution, and I knew I'd have to find the right moment.

I was going to fuck Steve Bannon so hard his rheumy eyes popped out of his grizzled skull. You come at the king, you best not miss.

In the fall of 2017, though Bannon was gone from the White House, he was still the Hand of House Trump. He'd returned to Breitbart and was rising in media prominence, threatening primaries against every Republican senator except Ted Cruz and a constant source of worry for Mitch McConnell and the National Republican Senatorial Committee. When Bannon bet the farm—every last acre of it—to play the kingmaker and install pedo-curious Roy Moore in the U.S. Senate, I realized that I was about to get a "Fuck me? No, fuck you" moment with Bannon.

While Bannon barnstormed with the wee molester Moore, giving rallies where he grunted out his nationalist populism message to friendly audiences, it looked like Moore had a better than average shot to win. It was, after all, Alabama, the ur-Trump state, the reddest of red, the craziest of cray.

When a SuperPAC contacted us, a key question came up: "Can you help a Democrat win a Senate seat? Ethically, we mean." I'll be honest; I would have done the work just to prevent Moore from serving as a cancer in the GOP and a lunatic in the Senate, but the thought of beating Steve Bannon was deeply compelling. I wanted Bannon's face rubbed in his arrogance and his idiocy not simply because he'd messed with me or because I find his nationalist claptrap to be anathema to conservatism, but because I still treasure running real campaigns using art, heart, and data.

We helped craft a series of ads for a SuperPAC that carefully targeted Republican women in six Alabama counties, pouring in tightly targeted, researched, and tested messages. The strongest was released the night Bannon held his infamous rally in Fairhope, Alabama. You're welcome, Steve.

Our closing ad was simple: a series of pretty, upset girls on screen look straight to camera while a voice-over asks, "What if she was your little girl? Your daughter? Your sister? What if she was sixteen years old? Fifteen? Or even fourteen? Would you let a thirty-two-year-old man date her? Undress her? Touch her? He called it dating. We call it unacceptable. That's why we can't support Roy Moore." Beating Roy Moore was a moral obligation. Beating Steve Bannon was a pleasure. Within days of the loss in Alabama, Bannon went from the GOP's newest kingmaker to political leper. We all piled on, savagely. That's how politics still works, even for people who think they've reset all the rules and defied all the structures.

Steven Law, who runs Mitch McConnell's Senate Leadership Fund, brought out the lead pipe and went at Bannon's kneecaps. "This is a brutal reminder that candidate quality matters regardless of where you are running," he said. "Not only did Steve Bannon cost us a critical Senate seat in one of the most Republican states in the country, but he also dragged the President of the United States into his fiasco."[4] McConnell advisor Josh Holmes chimed in as well: "I'd just like to thank Steve Bannon for showing us how to lose the reddest state in the union."[5] Matt Drudge, no fan of Bannon, hung the loss around Steve's neck with the headline "Bannon Busted!" Your author didn't hold fire either. I tweeted at the time, "Steve Bannon is a cancer. Good people of Alabama were the first dose of chemo."[6]

I was right. Gristle Icarus flew far too close to the sun. His election losses in Virginia and Alabama, his leaking Trump's dirty laundry and stories of White House discord to *Fire and Fury* author Michael Wolff, and his assertion that he might run for president led to a hard break with the White House and the Mercer family. He was fired from his perch at the helm of Breitbart with little ceremony and less mercy. The populist rebellion Bannon personified depended on his having the weaponized Breitbart battle station, a perception he spoke for the president, and buckets of sweet, sweet hedge fund cash from the Mercers. Without it, Bannon crashed so hard there was nothing but a greasy, smoking hole in the desert.

From being the architect of a political movement that he promised would replace a moribund conservative Establishment and a dying Republican Party, Bannon has become a wandering, rootless political gypsy. He was last spotted cheering on the neofascist parties in European elections.[7]

CARTER PAGE

Watching former Trump campaign senior national security advisor Carter Page immolate himself and incriminate a half dozen of his colleagues from the Trump-Putin 2016 campaign was a strange, almost guilty pleasure. Profoundly disconnected, socially awkward, and reeking of late-stage virginity, he gives off the creepy Uncanny Valley vibe of a rogue, possibly murderous android or of a man with a too-extensive knowledge of human taxidermy and a soundproofed van.

Legal scholars watching Page's borderline insane interviews, reviewing his bizarre public statements, and reading the wackadoodle transcripts of his testimony to congressional investigators express various levels of shock. His congressional hearing in October 2017 dismayed his friends in Trump World; it was a long, rambling, performance art piece before the House that opened up entirely new venues for investigation by confirming large parts of the Steele Dossier, which had been assembled to examine connections between the Trump campaign, his business enterprises, and his finances with Russia.

The paper trail of his forays into Russia is an amazing mosaic of comic-opera misunderstandings, grand and petty corruptions, grade-school category errors, and fundamental delusions about Putin's kleptocracy. In short, Page is a perfect example of the ad hoc weirdness of the Trump campaign, Trumpism's deep, misplaced love of Putin's Russia, and the power of magical thinking among the coterie of misfit toys Trump calls his advisors. Page is weird and wrong, and in most campaigns he'd be the weirdest, wrongest dog in the pack. In Trump World, he's in the middle quintile.

A bizarre fascination with Russia as an ally shaped the view of Trump's foreign policy advisors Steve Bannon, Mike Flynn, Stephen Miller, Sebastian Gorka, and the rest of the Foreign Policy Center for Kids Who Can't Read Good and Want to Read Good. Yes, a meaningful fraction of it is informed by an alt-rightish belief that the U.S. and Russia are white Christian allies in the global war on Islam and brown people in general, but some of it is just their natural inclination toward nationalist authoritarianism.

Page didn't just talk the pro-Russia talk; he threw himself into the eager arms of SVR operatives. Like the rest of Trump World, Page brought a kind of Underpants Gnome theory to his bromance with Team Putin. Through some unknown alchemy, he expected to benefit Trump and gain influence and profit from his Russia foray.

It's not that Page is stupid in the same way many Trump voters are mulishly immune to processing empirical facts in the world around them; it's that Page's odd affect and thinking reflect something profoundly off-kilter about him in the same way Trump's entire persona consists of bluster, magical thinking, and willful self-deception.

The delta between Trump's imagination of himself and the brand image that he desperately wants to sell is always wide; he's the "billionaire" lout playing the Manhattan sophisticate who gorges on fast food. He's a man with a lemur wig and a five-pound bolus of chin-wattle who thinks he's irresistible to women. He's the serially bankrupt master of the art of the deal, the TV talk show character who slithered into the Oval Office on a tide of Russian influence and now thinks he won on his merits.

Page was an easy mark for Russian intelligence services because he lives in the same world of willful self-deception as Trump. Carter Page, International Business Man of Mystery, jet-setting wheeler-dealer, and foreign policy savant was an image shared by only Carter Page, world-class dork and sucker. In the FBI investigation of a Russian intelligence cell that sought to suborn Page in 2013, the contempt in which the SVR agents held Page was clear: "This is intelligence method to cheat, how else to work with foreigners? You promise a favor for a favor. You get the documents from him and tell him to go f—ck himself."[8] *Foreign Policy* reported, "Based on the FBI complaint, it appears Page never realized his Russian contact worked on behalf of Moscow's intelligence services."[9] It's not simply that Page was credulous; his credulity was a hot wire inside the already Putinphilic Trump inner circle. Page is just the most obviously gullible of the Trump cadre. Mike Flynn, both venal and bitter, was also easy pickings. Sebastian Gorka would probably shine Putin's shoes in exchange for a gimcrack medal. Steve Bannon, a man better suited to promoting bumfights than grand strategy, thinks of himself as a player on par with Putin, which is an eye-rolling hilarious thought to sane people.

The rest of the jetsam dragged behind Trump's sewage barge of a campaign is little different, and all of them are under the hot lights of Robert Mueller's investigation into Russia's intelligence program to manipulate the 2016 election, and the role Trump and his campaign team may have played in it. Something about the prospect of spending a long time in a federal prison wearing an orange jumpsuit peels away the layers of bluster and pretense. Page's interview with the House was a situation in which he was in little legal jeopardy, but the flop sweat rolling off him came through in almost every strange exchange. Following a Breitbartian anti-Hillary screed at the beginning of his testimony, Page had all the confidence of a whipped dog, lost and desperate.

Like all Trump acolytes and supporters, Page learned a key lesson: once the delusional sales pitch of Trumpism is pulled back, you're on your own. This strange, lost man is one of the most public examples of how ugly the world looks when the con and the crimes are exposed, but he sure as hell won't be the last.

PAUL MANAFORT

Manafort was a Trumpian character in Washington even before Trump. Crooked and corrupting, utterly amoral, he's the tainted wellspring of a dozen Washington and international scandals. Of course he was a perfect fit for Trump. Rumors of bad blood between Manafort and his Russian sugar daddy, Oleg Deripaska, were in the wind by the time he became chairman of Trump's campaign, and his ties to the Kremlin's favored strongmen in the nations surrounding Russia were clear. It tells you a lot that those were his *good* points in Trump's mind.

How cutting must it have been for a man who spent years making millions as a skeezy fixer to have power and influence in Washington in his grasp, only to see it slip away. He was so close to being a respectable éminence grise instead of being a scumbag lobbyist of last resort for assorted kleptocrats, third-world shitbirds, and international criminals.

Manafort is a man who once took briefcases full of cash from Russian billionaires, reduced to wearing two GPS ankle monitors since the Department of Justice and prosecutors view him as an international flight risk. Paul Manafort went from being the campaign chairman of a successful presidential run to a man in the deepest possible legal hole. Rat on Trump and face the wrath of a notoriously spiteful, vengeful president. Flip on Putin's oligarch buddies, he'll spend the rest of his life waiting to be poisoned by polonium. If he flips on neither, he gets to die in jail.

At the end of the editorial process for this book, Manafort's life is grim. He faces decades in prison, and his hanging tough against Robert Mueller depends on faith that Donald Trump will keep his promises and cover Manafort with a swift pardon.

Good luck with that one, buddy.

MICHAEL COHEN

Thug. Loudmouth. Fixer. Michael Cohen is a deeply revolting specimen even by the low standards of the Petri dish of Trump World scuzz.[10] Even the fixer found himself in exile and under investigation by Robert Mueller, a victim of the Trump curse as surely as any other fatality of The Donald's death touch.

Far from becoming a Trump-era superlawyer, Cohen's strip-mall law school degree, mouth-breathing behavior, and really, really terrible legal work in the Stormy Daniels affair left him in exile from Trump, even though Cohen was long reputed to not only know where the bodies were buried in Trump's past but to have been the guy with the shovels and tarps in the back of his car. Cohen, though, should be understood as an almost perfect metaphor for the Trump era, the Trump White House, and everything else orbiting this president like the hot chunks of waste spinning around the central oscillator at a sewage-treatment plant. He truly brings it all: the shoddy, hair-trigger temperament; the indifferent education and understanding of the world outside of dalliance-cleanup duty and real-estate branding deals; the malfeasance, petty corruption, general shitheel behavior, impulsivity, tantrum-as-negotiation style, and overall sketchiness of the Trump administration.

Like Trump, his enablers, and supporters, Cohen thought his position as an inner-circle member would protect him indefinitely. He believed, after so many years of getting away with every kind of shenanigan at Trump's behest, that the facts would never matter, the music would never stop, and the party would never end. Again, he's a perfect metaphor for this administration.

A close friend of Trump's—one you've seen mentioned as a part of his kitchen cabinet and who is a stalwart defender on cable news—once told me that Trump's fixer had a special office in Trump Tower where he handled the legal infrastructure of Trump's bimbo eruptions. A few days after Trump declared his candidacy for president, this friend said to me, "Cohen and that other guy [presumed by me to be attorney Marc Kasowitz] handle the NDAs, the abortions, the payments to all these girls.[11] There's so many of them I don't know how people won't find out about it."

People did find out. Our researchers in 2015 started working the rumor mill in New York, tracing down women who had been in Trump's orbit. All of them were reticent because they feared both the terms of the NDAs they'd signed and Cohen personally.

Cohen thinks of himself as Ray Donovan or Tom Hagen. He sold himself as a super-lobbyist with pay-for-play access to Trump, only to see it all collapse when the Southern District of New York and the FBI kicked down his office, home, and hotel room doors in a massive, simultaneous raid. Cohen suddenly seemed more terrified than terrifying. It was the beginning of a downward spiral for Cohen, who once saw himself as a titan, now reduced to nothing more than a suspect in a constellation of Mueller's investigation, a target of Stormy Daniels's bulldog attorney, Michael Avenatti, and the cause of so many of Trump's emerging legal nightmares.

ROGER STONE

The ubiquitous Roger Stone had been exiled from the mainstream of national politics for a generation, kept on as a curiosity by a few suckers here and there. One of those suckers was Donald Trump. Stone's long descent from Nixon campaign intern and bag-boy to Trump sycophant and beret-clad *Infowars* spinner of lunatic conspiracy theories is a cautionary tale for political consultants and explains much of Trump's style, politics, and rise. Ask his Trump-era fans, and they'll tell you Roger ran the Nixon, Reagan, Bush, and Trump campaigns, made every ad in political history, and is a singular genius in American politics. Not so much.

In October 1999 I was working as a senior advisor to Mayor Rudy Giuliani. I visited my New York politics mentor Ray Harding, the great New York Liberal Party boss, at least once a month. He once said to me, "When they say the Liberal Party is neither liberal nor a party, they're right. It is my personal fucking political machine." He seemed to know everyone and everything in New York politics and skated very close (in the end, too close) to the ethical edge.

Ray's backstory is worthy of a book of its own; it involves escaping the Nazis as a child, being one of the only 1,000 Jews allowed into the U.S. by FDR during World War II, service in the U.S. Army, and a life in politics that was both colorful and corrupt. He was a mighty character.

Our conversations were long, discursive, and educational as hell. One rainy afternoon, the subject of Roy Cohn came up, which led to Roger Stone. Stone is sui generis in American politics. He's become a kind of Zeligesque political figure, appearing when he's least desired and least expected. Like Trump, Roger is constantly burnishing his brand image, writing himself into history, where his role has been, at its very best, tangential.

Ray looked across his desk from behind a cloud of unfiltered Camel smoke and said to me, "Roger parlayed one line of bullshit into a career. The only person who buys his bullshit is that moron Trump."

Ray had known of Roger from some Liberal Party briefcase-full-of-cash shenanigans in which Stone and his mentor Roy Cohn were involved and knew enough of Stone to call his bullshit. I knew of Roger, as everyone in my political generation did. He was always involved in something shady, but in the pre-Google era, it was hard to separate Stone's personal PR from fact.

Stone and Cohn shaped much of Trump's political response behavior, training him never to apologize, always attack, and deploy a torrent of bullshit to cover for the mistakes, disasters, and calamities caused by his *prior* torrents of bullshit.

Stone was exiled even by the Trump campaign, which must have rankled because the ax was dropped by Corey Lewandowski, a man without a scintilla of Stone's political chops, real or imagined.[12] After a few months of intemperate behavior, Lewandowski was himself fired, to be replaced by Stone's old friend, former business partner, and longtime co-conspirator Paul Manafort as the chairman of the Donald Trump for President Campaign.[13]

The installation of Manafort was one of the most consequential of the 2016 campaign. It demonstrates that Roger Stone isn't a far-sighted strategist but a man driven mostly by tactical revenge. Manafort's rise to power inside Trump World would open up ties to Russia, avenues of investigation, and provide a key witness in the Mueller probe to tear into Trump World like an industrial wood chipper.

All so Roger Stone could get a rival fired.

The architect of Trump's victory, if only in his own spin, Stone's infamy had a cost. In October 2017, Stone was banned from Twitter.[14] By late 2016, he had been banned from every mainstream television network save Fox, and even there he appeared only in limited doses.

On the outside of the campaign looking in, Stone raised around $600,000 for a SuperPAC, much of which seems to have gone back into Stone-affiliated firms, but his long-anticipated Powerball-level payday from 40 years of hustling for Trump never appeared. He lives now in a Trumpian demimonde of politics, his game tired, his points spent, and his influence with the White House minimal.

Far from a triumph for Stone, the election of Trump has pushed Roger into a media ghetto from which even his formidable personal public relations skills will never extract him. His connections with the Russian GRU hacker Guccifer and Julian Assange brought him under the eye of Special Counsel Robert Mueller. By the spring of 2018, Stone was running an online fundraising effort to pay his legal bills.

Roger Stone touched Trump's career almost from its beginnings and certainly shaped Trump's political message, ideology (such as it is), and communications techniques. Stone was as close to Trump as anyone.

It wouldn't save him. Stone, a man who has chased the dragon of fame for fifty years in politics, was reduced to hawking conspiracy books, appearances at small local Republican Clubs, and seething about the Deep State with Alex Jones.

STEPHEN MILLER

The ideological zampolit of the Trump administration, Stephen Miller is brilliant, dangerous, and also needs to spend a week getting laid. My God, does it show. All that pent-up fury at Mexicans and Muslims is a bad look on anyone. One-time college besties with pudgy racist thought leader Richard Spencer, Miller is the thinking man's racist on Team Trump.

After Bannon's unceremonious departure from the White House, Stephen Miller and his wing-harpy Julia Hahn (a former Bannon deputy) were two of the last of the white nationalists at 1600 Pennsylvania Avenue, and Miller made the most of it. Like a French courtier, Miller was utterly obsequious toward Trump, utterly vicious with everyone else in sight. He was willing to go on national television—including one spectacularly raw outing in which Jake Tapper threw him off the set—and drill the Trump company line even in the face of reality. He made Kellyanne Conway look like a reasonable and truthful member of the Don Squad, which took some doing.

We reached peak Miller during the shutdown frenzy over immigration in January 2018, as he singlehandedly destroyed a nascent compromise between Trump and Senate members. Miller, seeing a DACA deal in the offing that wasn't sufficiently punitive, engineered the infamous "shithole" meeting, where Trump wrecked an agreement on immigration that led to the first, brief shutdown of 2018. Miller stacked the meeting, prepared the battlefield, and let Trump's ego take it from there.

In some ways Miller has always been more dangerous and more pernicious than Bannon. Bannon's constant autofellation, absurd desire to play the great man of history, and frustration with the boring realities of governance and policy, in the end, helped sink him as a White House power player. Stephen Miller has always been entirely conscious that the immigration fight is racial animus barely disguised as a policy question on who can and cannot come to America. Like Bannon before him, Miller also saw the utility of the immigration scare tactics—MS-13 is gunning for you! A brown wave of cantaloupe-calved drug smugglers is creeping up from Me-he-co!—as the glue holding together the alt-right, the social conservatives, and the blue-collar Rust Belt they-took-our-jobs Trump true believers.

As the classic ideological scavenger inside the walls of government, Miller looks the part: the archetypal sneaky little crapweasel who plays the DC game to the hilt, pursuing his agendas instead of those that would be good for either his principal or the country. Watching Miller, I am haunted by how little humanity is behind those 32-year-old eyes.

I can only imagine what Miller was like when he was at Duke with race-baiter and Nazi fanboy Richard Spencer. Can't you see them in some dorm room bullshit session, smoking weed and working through their plans to depopulate the Rodina of anyone darker than a latte? That, and Spencer trying to find a girl to throw Miller some mercy sex so he could get the dead-eyed creeper out of his dorm room.

KELLYANNE CONWAY

In thirty years in politics, I've known Kellyanne Conway as "the girl pollster." An alumna of Frank Luntz's polling shop, she'd made it a practice area to help Republicans communicate with female voters.

Not an unworthy pursuit, but she was never one of the go-to pollsters in the top tier of the business, which is why no one I knew in politics was surprised when she jumped on the Trump Train after working for Ted Cruz.

Trump, being Trump, fell in love with how thoroughly she worked him and how she stroked his ego assiduously. She doesn't have a job in the White House per se, but she's always game for a TV hit requiring a combination of dishonesty, amorality, and cult-eyed tales of wonder at the healing power of Donald Trump's abiding love.

In the history of White House advisors, not one tops Kellyanne Conway in utter mendacity, though Stephen Miller often gives her a run for her money. A fairly indifferent pollster in her prior career, Conway's complete lack of scruples was a perfect fit for the Trump campaign and his administration.

Aggressively willing to lie, then to deny she lied, then to deny that she denied she lied about lying, Conway is routinely wheeled out to defend the usual panoply of indefensible acts, colossal errors, grand and petit corruptions, and the rest of Team Trump's daily catalogue of disasters. She's magnificent in turning a substantive interview into a Gordian knot of lies, evasions, misstatements, and distractions.

She started early in the administration, uttering the now infamous defense of Trump's inaugural numbers by saying that Sean Spicer had simply presented "alternative facts." It should have been a warning to us all.

Conway hit bottom in the fall of 2017 in her defense of kid-diddling Senate candidate Roy Moore. It took Kellyanne Conway—a woman whose soulless, serial lying has become the entirety of her personality—to grab the controls of the Trump plane and send it crashing to the ground faster than Roy Moore's pants as he lurked under the bleachers at a high school cheerleading practice. In an appearance on *Fox & Friends*, which in the White House is must-see TV for President Trump, Conway argued for Dirty Roy, saying, "I'm telling you, we want the votes in the Senate to get this tax bill through."

Even the Fox News hosts had a moment of stunned silence, perhaps shocked that a senior counselor to the president of the United States was defending Alabama's Uncle Creepy, perhaps hypnotized by the last tiny shred of Conway's integrity being vaporized live on television in service to Steve Bannon's hand-picked candidate.

But there it was. Media outlets who continue to book Conway baffle me. The hosts, producers, and bookers know they're going to stand under a torrential downpour of lies, evasions, prevarications, and eldritch spells seeking to open a dimensional portal and unleash Hell on our plane of reality each and every time she speaks, but they still have her on the air, over and over. It's a peculiar form of masochism, but they keep booking her, and she keeps shredding their credibility for doing so.

She is a woman without a real portfolio beyond a few token issues. Occasionally, when you hear a few words from Donald's maw that don't sound like his usual Trumpian vernacular, you can detect Conway's words, trying desperately to tune Trump's voice into something with dignity and stature. Conway's all-in bet on Trump is the defining moment of her career, but she should know that no matter what she does, no one escapes the Trump curse.

SARAH HUCKABEE SANDERS

Sean Spicer represented one of the Trump administration's few ties to the traditional Washington media relations model. The role of being Trump's press secretary was always going to be fraught with problems. Having a boss with a yawning, ravenous chasm of ego, a lifetime in television roleplaying, poor impulse control, and an itchy Twitter finger make it the Russian roulette of communications jobs. Having one of the world's most notorious liars as a boss was just the icing on the cake.

Sarah Huckabee Sanders's improbable rise was a consequence of Spicer's rapid death from ETTD, the first symptoms of which were evident almost before the first week of the administration ended. Hounded out of the White House for failing to sufficiently immolate himself in increasingly elaborate lies about the wonder, majesty, and accomplishments of Donald Trump, Spicer had burned his bridges with the DC press corps and lost the confidence of the president. He is an early cautionary tale of the professional costs of working for President Trump.

His departure cleared the path for the daughter of noted blowhard and gravy aficionado Mike Huckabee to stand herself behind the podium in the James Brady Press Room in the White House and open the floodgates on a torrent of lies, bullshit, prevarications, and laughably bad excuses for the inexcusable man in the Oval Office. Somewhere, deep in her soul, I imagine she feels a twinge from time to time about the role she's playing, but the powerful magic of the White House apparently gave her a pass on the whole truth thing.

It's not an easy ride.

Sanders went through one humiliation after another. When Anthony Scaramucci's brief tenure as White House communications director kicked off, one of the first things he did was humiliate her from the Press Room podium, saying, "Sarah, if you're watching, I loved the hair and makeup person we had on Friday. . . . So I'd like to continue to use the hair and makeup person."[15]

Scaramucci's desire to glam up Sanders played to Trump's love of the reality-TV aspects of the job, and Sanders was apparently a little too down-market for his tastes. Katie Price, Scaramucci's stylist pick to gussy up Sanders, was his only real White House hire during his all-too-brief tenure. Scaramucci's obsession with Sanders's looks missed the mark. She became one of the least respected White House press secretaries in modern memory because she's a tendentious defender of a terrible president, and Scaramucci's glam squad was never going to fix that problem.

Press secretaries have always engaged in media pushback, ranging from humorous to tiresome, but Sanders took it deep into the fake news jungle in an unwavering defense of Trump that flew in the face of facts, logic, decency, and evidence.

Her greatest hits left the press corps reeling, first with anger, then with derision. When Sanders said, "I don't think it's appropriate to lie from the podium or any other place; my job is to communicate the President's agenda," my Recursive Horseshit Meter pegged at 100%.[16] Aside from the few procedural notes that are demonstrably true, "It is Christmas," and "The president flies to Mar-a-Lago this afternoon," Sanders has been one of the least credible and least persuasive White House mouthpieces in memory.

She doesn't even lie *well*.

When it came to the Russia investigation, Sanders stepped in it time and again. Her claim that Trump's decision to fire FBI director Jim Comey after the White House heard from "countless" members of the FBI that they had lost confidence in Comey led even the normally stoic deputy director Andrew McCabe to respond during a Senate hearing, "We are a large organization, we are 36,500 people across this country, across this globe. We have a diversity of opinions about many things, but I can confidently tell you that the majority, the vast majority, of FBI employees enjoyed a deep and positive connection to Director Comey."[17]

When she claimed that Mexican president Enrique Peña Nieto had called Trump to praise his immigration policies, it was as if she believed no one in Washington had access to a phone or the internet. No such call had taken place, as the Mexican president soon confirmed. Sanders's response was true to her current form: "I wouldn't say it was a lie. That's a bold accusation." No, Sarah. It was a lie.

SEBASTIAN GORKA

Imagine for a moment a ludicrous, Bond-knockoff, straight-to-cable movie villain, status anxiety screaming out of every pore. Imagine a cloud of Drakkar Noir surrounding him dense enough to cause nearby victims to believe they're in the midst of a WMD attack. Imagine attending an Inaugural Ball wearing a black tunic getup that looks like something an old-school *Star Trek* villain might sport. Imagine driving a black Mustang with ART WAR vanity tags.

I know, ladies, try to keep your clothes on, because we're talking the pinnacle of Trump World machismo: Herr Doktor Sebastian Gorka, the Dragon of Budapest, scourge of the savage Mahometan horde, 4-cylinder Mustang driver. If we didn't have a Sebastian Gorka, we'd have to invent him. His outrageous, blustering affect, his Anglo-Eurotrash accccccent, his endless, protests-too-much masculine posturing, and his edge-case policy views are a perfect example of how Trump attracted the misfit toys.

If you're looking for the self-described alpha in the room, look no further than Sebastian Gorka, he of the Eastern European shopping-mall PhD, mom jeans, and terrible taste in firearms. One can imagine Sebastian as a child, busy with his Lil' War Crimes play set, or as a fedora-sporting college incel, solemnly intoning, "Why, no, I don't have a girlfriend. While you were partying, I was preparing for the global race war to come."

A butt of Washington jokes even before becoming a member of the Axis of Assholes with Bannon, Miller, Flynn, et al., Gorka is a "terrorism expert" only insofar as he can insert the word "Muslim" or "jihadi" into every sentence, including questions about the weather. Gorka represents a particular side channel in American national security thinking, and it's one of the reasons he was so attracted to Trump and Trumpism. You see, Gorka's academic and practical counterterrorism credentials are, to put it mildly, nonstandard.

His academic background was roundly mocked even before he took his place in the Trump orbit. Somehow it's hard to imagine previous White House national security staffers whose credentials were "widely disdained" or whose PhD dissertation was considered slightly above something one might get from Trump University.[18] His own dissertation advisor damned Gorka with only the faintest praise.

Stephen Walt of Harvard's Kennedy School called Gorka "the Simon Cowell of Counterterrorism" and said, "Gorka does not have much of a reputation in serious academic or policy-making circles. He has never published any scholarship of significance and his views on Islam and US national security are extreme even by Washington standards. His only real 'qualification' was his prior association with

Breitbart News, which would be a demerit in any other administration."[19] One commentator told CNN, "Gorka was more of a counter-terrorism enthusiast, than an expert."[20]

Ya think?

Gorka represented so much that is just fundamentally wrong about Trump's team in the White House; he combined a lack of knowledge, depth, and qualifications that were matched with a simply astounding degree of hubris, even in a White House not known for its modesty.

Denied a security clearance—an issue that haunted the Trump White House from the beginning—Gorka's duties were undefined, except to appear on television booming out praise for the Maximum Leader. When John Kelly's purges of the Bannonites began, Gorka's days were obviously numbered.

Though Gorka claims he left the White House under his own steam, his security pass was canceled one day while he was away from the building. Gorka's claim that he resigned was contradicted in a White House–wide email that said "Please notify officers of the following staff DNA (do not admit): Sebastian L. Gorka. . . . His pass has been deactivated." In the event someone didn't get the message, a follow-up from the White House rubbed salt in the wounds: "Mr. Gorka is more than likely still in possession of his PIV [Personal Identity Verification] and the WH Pass, as his DNA status was performed without him being on Complex."[21]

You know, just like everyone who leaves the White House on good terms.

Like all serious national security officials, you can now catch Gorka fighting jihad and rocking his thick musk of pure testosterone on Fox News.

– INTERCEPT 6 –

TOP SECRET//SI//ORCON//NOFORN

[BEGIN TRANSCRIPT]

[CALL BEGINS IN PROGRESS]

TRUMP: You're the sweetest.

HANNITY: *You're* the sweetest.

TRUMP: Love you.

HANNITY: Love you more.

TRUMP: Hang up.

HANNITY: You hang up first.

[TRANSCRIPT REPEATS 4 MINUTES]

[TRANSCRIPT ENDS]

15

THE ALT-REICH

IF THERE'S ONE GROUP I'VE DELIGHTED IN SEEING THE ETTD curse hit, it's the alt-right. The rise of an overtly racist, overtly anti-Semitic tendency in modern American politics is revolting and disturbing and needs a pure, cleansing fire to drive it back into the shadows. Fear not, dear readers, this chapter will take the stick to Team Pepe, but first, we have to take a hard look at Donald Trump's role in empowering, elevating, and protecting the alt-right.

This president isn't like any other Republican president in generations. That's not a compliment, as you may have guessed, having read this far. His long, long history of racial and ethnic animus is a grotesque product of a time, an upbringing, and a family that wasn't exactly uncomfortable with racial discrimination and segregation. For Trump's father, it was a central part of their business model in the 1970s and 1980s, leading to Federal investigations and lawsuits over their "no vacancies for blacks" policy.[1] The contrast to Trump's views and actions on race and those of every other modern Republican is striking.

Dwight Eisenhower nationalized the Arkansas Guard to defend the first black students at Little Rock Central High School. Donald Trump retweeted numerous racists ("WhiteGenocideTM," among many, many others) during his campaign and posts videos from the overtly racist Britain First fringe political party.

Richard Nixon stood in Harlem in 1952 and said, "America cannot bear the burden of segregation" and passionately supported the

Civil Rights and Voting Rights Acts. He signed the Voting Rights Act in 1970 and the Equal Employment Opportunity Act of 1972. It took Donald Trump two days to denounce alt-right neo-Nazis, the Klan, and vocal anti-Semites who chanted "Jews will not replace us" and committed terrorist murder in Charlottesville, Virginia.

In 1981 Reagan scorched Klansmen and racists, saying, "You are the ones who are out of step with our society. You are the ones who willfully violate the meaning of the dream that is America. And this country, because of what it stands for, will not stand for your conduct. My administration will vigorously investigate and prosecute those who, by violence or intimidation, would attempt to deny Americans their constitutional rights."

Donald Trump says the protesters and the Klan, the alt-right, and the Nazis they confronted in Charlottesville are morally equivalent. There are, he infamously said, "good people on both sides."

Ronald Reagan's fiery denunciation of the Klan didn't mince words or draw false moral equivalencies. He said it flat out: We don't want your support. There's the door. When Klan leaders tried to draft behind his 1984 campaign, he was blunt: "The politics of racial hatred and religious bigotry practiced by the Klan and others have no place in this country, and are destructive of the values for which America has always stood."

Trump hired Steve Bannon, Stephen Miller, Julia Hahn, Sebastian Gorka, and a host of other alt-right-adjacent racial arsonists and wannabe ethnic cleansers and struggles to clearly, promptly, and with finality put racists and hate groups on blast without days of wheel-spinning, whataboutism, and equivocation.

In 1984 President Reagan spoke at the Republican National Convention and issued a clarion call to tolerance: "In the party of Lincoln, there is no room for intolerance and not even a small corner for anti-Semitism or bigotry of any kind. Many people are welcome in our house, but not the bigots."[2] Donald Trump's commemoration of International Holocaust Remembrance Day in January 2017 left out any mention of either anti-Semitism or Jewish victims of the Nazis.[3]

Donald Trump wants immigrants from Norway, but not from "the shithole countries."[4] I'm sure there's some subtle demographic difference motivating him, but I just can't put my finger on it.

When George H. W. Bush learned David Duke was running for office in Louisiana, he didn't just issue a fiery denunciation. He directed the RNC to deploy money and staff to fight against the Klansman. Donald Trump is, well, Donald Trump. His father, who was once arrested at a Klan rally in Queens, famously redlined New York apartments to prevent African Americans from renting them, and the strange fruit of Trump the Elder's racism didn't fall far from the tree.

Trump claimed Judge Gonzalo Curiel couldn't objectively hear a case involving his scam university because of the judge's Mexican heritage. He called for the death penalty for a group of black and Hispanic young men accused of raping a white woman in Central Park. Even though all the men were later completely exonerated, Trump has never retracted his statement. Trump's aversion to having African Americans visible in his Atlantic City casinos led to a $200,000 fine against him.

"When Donald and Ivana came to the casino, the bosses would order all the black people off the floor," said Kip Brown, a former Trump Castle employee.[5] The obvious and the subtle racism of Trump inspires one of the sharpest cultural and political dividing lines of our era. If the central definition of racism is treating people of different races differently, Trump meets the standard for it, and then some. Oh, occasionally Kellyanne Conway or someone will beat it into him that racism isn't good for the poll numbers, and he'll allow some anodyne "My black friends" press release to slip past Stephen Miller and Michael Anton, but for the most part the White House may as well mount an air-raid-siren-sized racial dog whistle on the roof.

Like an accusation they dare not speak aloud, GOP leaders in Washington and beyond excuse Trump's racism and hide from it, but it's there. They sighed with relief when his staff forced him to walk back his disastrous Charlottesville remarks, only to have Lucy pull the football away from them time and again whenever Stephen Miller gets his ear. His browbeating of NFL athletes who chose to kneel during the National Anthem in protest of police misconduct all just *happened* to be—wait for it—African American was another of his crapulous dog whistles, a display of winking racism disguised as populist patriotism.

Hiring Ben Carson and a few "look at my black friend" callouts in rally halls doesn't change the long thread of personal behavior and actions. It's why the Nazis (neo- and otherwise), Klansmen, alt-righters, and the rest of the residents of our national shame closet hitched their wagons to him. Trump is the disease vector they felt they needed to infect the nation's body politic more thoroughly. The racial hatred was there; they needed Daddy to set the fire.

Let's dispose of one objection right away, because it's an immediate defensive pushback from the clickservative media: "You're just adopting the left's tactics of calling all Republicans racists."

No, not every Trump supporter is a racist, xenophobic, alt-right man-child.

However, every racist, xenophobic alt-right man-child is a Trump supporter. If there's one legacy of his election and presidency we'll spend decades cleaning up, it's the casual ease with which he welcomed them into the daylight. Xenophobic fury at brown people coming here to live a better life doesn't motivate every person who voted for Trump, but every single person motivated by a xenophobic fury at brown people coming here to live a better life was a Trump voter, and he shamelessly, consistently, and viciously plays that card on the campaign trail and in office.

Trumpsplainers have demanded since the election that we listen to the Trump voters and that we understand their economic anxiety and their sense that Washington has betrayed them for decades. These may be true and explicable motivations for their choice of Trump, but those normalizing this president tend to elide and dismiss the centrality of racial animus and anti-immigrant hysteria in Trump's campaign, his government, and his supporters.

The easy explanation is that Trump is the kind of cranky old casual racist 70-something with whom we're all familiar. Far from being an exclusive product of the Deep South, there are people across the country of a certain age who still harbor a kind of background radiation of animus toward black folks. The tragedy of Donald Trump is the pedestrian, tired nature of his racial anxieties, beliefs, and ideas. He isn't a Nazi. He isn't a Klansman. He isn't an alt-righter. It's just that he has no real problem with their beliefs as long as he feels as if they're "on his side" and "nice to him."

I know it's hard to admit, but our president may be the most egregious racist since Woodrow Wilson held the presidency, and that takes some doing. During his defense of the violence and murder in Charlottesville, I was reminded of Wilson's low water mark in post–Civil War race relations. He re-segregated U.S. government offices, dismissed the principles of human equality in American diplomacy, and was basically a shitty human being on the topic of race.

History repeats, first as tragedy, then as Trump. The resonance of this quote from Wilson with Trump's infamous "both sides" narrative is striking: "The white men were roused by a mere instinct of self-preservation until at last there had sprung into existence a great Ku Klux Klan, a veritable empire of the South, to protect the Southern country."[6] If you were a paunchy, polo-shirted torch carrier in Charlottesville, hearing the president of the United States defend the statue of a traitor and revel in Lost Cause rhetoric must have warmed the cockles of your heart and given you an erection you normally couldn't achieve without the proximity of your anime waifu body pillow.

The moral failure of leadership he displayed over Charlottesville alone should have disqualified Donald Trump from managing a Starbucks, to say nothing of leading a great, diverse nation, particularly one where we have struggled so long and so hard to bend that arc of history toward what we can be as a people, rather than where we started. Sadly, the excuse of *those people* is that they now have a powerful avatar in the White House, and he never stops winking, nodding, and dog-whistling to his base.

There's a popular argument among Trump apologists that the

Wall, deportations, and sending the Dreamers back to Mexico weren't linchpins of Trump's campaign rhetoric. This is at best cheap and sloppy historical revisionism.

He opened his campaign with an attack on Mexicans. At Trump rallies, "Build the wall" was the tent pole of his speeches and central to the crowd's Pavlovian call-and-response. His attacks on Marco Rubio, Jeb Bush, and the rest of the 2016 primary field were in large measure about their alleged weaknesses on immigration. Anti-immigrant rhetoric was the political conduit connecting more traditional working-class Republican and Reagan Democrat voters who buy into the modern stab-in-the-back myth that Mexicans took their jobs after the passage of NAFTA.

Trump's anti-immigrant rhetoric was also a talisman among the alt-righters, who believe that allowing immigration (legal and otherwise) "browns" their desired lily-white America. Some fraction of Trump supporters may share his racial hostility in the privacy of the voting booth, but most of them needed at least a little distance between that hostility and overt racism.

Not the alt-right.

Donald Trump didn't create the alt-right, but he coddled it, whispered sweet nothings in its unwashed ear, and helped it burst onto the national stage. Need a little full-blown racism to activate the likes of Richard Spencer, David Duke, and the anime-loving boys of 4chan in service to the campaign? Trump's your man.

Steve Bannon's Breitbart News published loving paeans to the alt-right, stoking its all-male, all-pale audience of cranky trailer park racists, incel weebs, and bronies. Their work in mainstreaming the alt-right and overt anti-immigrant and anti-globalist hostility as a vital and energetic part of the conservative movement is just as repulsive as you might think.

In terms of Breitbart's reputation, the Trump sugar rush came with the cost of Breitbart's brand image; it's permanently stained. It's no longer a transgressive and provocative voice on the right. Under

Bannon, it was *Der Stürmer* with a slightly more modern design sensibility.

"In this way, Breitbart became an incubator of alt-right political energy," writes Joshua Green in *Devil's Bargain*, his profile of Bannon.[7] Bannon even once proclaimed, "We're the platform for the alt-right."[8] Bannon might as well have taken a dump on Andrew Breitbart's grave. Andrew, by Bannon's own admission, may have been a provocateur and a right-leaning troublemaker, but he didn't possess the same kind of ugly racist center found in Bannon's alt-right Petri dish.

While Donald Trump has set back race relations in the country by decades, the ETTD curse struck their movement just as it does everyone else who gets under the white robe with him. The very exposure and influence they expected Trump to provide and the hope that they would have ideological fellow-travelers, if not outright allies, on the inside gave way quickly to the realization that for all America's racial problems, for all our fraught history from the very beginning, the rest of America hates their racial intolerance as much as the alt-right hates people outside their fraternity of pissed-off suburban white-boy virgins.

For many of the leaders of the alt-right, white supremacists and "identitarians," crypto- and neo-Nazis, rebooted Klan dipshits, neo-Confederates, and the rest of their absurd kind, their alliance with and visibility due to Trump turned into a political death sentence.

Some of them wanted to try for a replay of 1930s Munich, hoping to spark violent conflicts with liberal protesters and Antifa. They hoped the provocative, torchlit marches like Charlottesville's and their aggressive Jew-baiting, promises of white homelands, and the "14 words"[9] horseshit would lead to a white uprising. Richard Spencer, in particular, saw himself as the intellectual center of a movement on the verge of tangible political power.

Famously and righteously punched right in his smug mouth on Inauguration Day 2016, Spencer had triggered the alt-right crisis and breakup weeks earlier, when at a Washington, DC, rally of his innocuously named National Policy Institute he burst into a "Hail Trump! Hail our people! Hail Victory!" crypto-Nazi salute.[10]

From there it was only a matter of time. By the summer of 2018 Spencer was lucky to gather a half-dozen local malcontents around a booth in a Waffle House to talk about his glorious new Reich. At every event, counterprotesters outnumbered his followers by an enormous ratio, and for all Spencer has a right to speak, his opponents have the same right, and use it.[11]

After threatening to sue Kent State after they canceled one of his tiresomely overwrought speeches, Spencer quietly dropped his promised litigation.

Richard Spencer saw Trump as a pathway for his more clean-cut, suit-and-tie Nazism to enter the political mainstream, but Spencer was simply a more polished turd than the usual beer-gut-and-man-boobs Klan types. His tweeds couldn't disguise his calls for a white ethnostate. Naturally, he elided the tricky little details of that idea when he told *Vice*, "Our dream is a new society, an ethno-state that would be a gathering point for all Europeans. It would be a new society based on very different ideals than, say, the Declaration of Independence."[12]

Spencer's "Hail Trump" moment marked the end of his dreams of being the godfather of an intellectually compelling and effective white supremacist movement. Discredited and discarded, Spencer is just one more of the bottom feeders Trump attracted, embraced, and abandoned. At that same rally, Spencer said, "No one will honor us for losing gracefully. No one mourns the great crimes committed against us. For us, it is conquer or die."[13] It would be the latter.

Social media platforms finally woke up to the game and started to use their power to marginalize and ghettoize people who advocate deporting, killing, or expelling a majority of their customer base. Social media also exposed their singular weakness, even as they felt they could grow in power under "God Emperor Trump": the vast majority of the movement is forced to remain anonymous. They believe this gives them the power to shitpost, edgelord, and meme a white nation-state into being. What it actually demonstrates is their marginal status, political weakness, and soft jawlines.

Their wailing and lamentations over being "deplatformed" never cease to amuse me. Richard Spencer, alt-right oppo researcher Chuck "Rage Furby" Johnson, Milo, and the rest being tossed off platforms like Twitter, YouTube, PayPal, GoFundMe, and other platforms results in screaming fits about their First Amendment rights being violated, demonstrating they understand neither the Constitution nor private property. Pardon me if private companies don't want to be associated with your scuzzy little Hitler cosplay club, boys.

When fighting back against racism in the real world, the best thing is to put it on camera, and that's what the American media did. Alt-righters saw themselves as shock troops in a movement at least tacitly blessed by Donald Trump. They saw the endless nudge-and-wink of his approval, felt his love whenever he ranted about Walls or immigrants. They expected he knew he was one of their own on some level and believed the white revolution was upon them.

The reality of their pathetic lives and position was a painful wakeup call. They're not Aryan warriors for the most part; they're pudgy white boys from lower-middle-class suburbs who couldn't find a woman's clitoris with a GPS and a magnifying glass. They're not a Kampfbund. They're a chat room on Discord or a bunch of surly drunks shit-talking about the black guy hitting on the white girls in their favorite sports bar.

As they became exposed, largely due to infighting within the alt-right itself, we saw over and over that these were hardly *Mensch und Sonne* models. They were much more likely to own an anime waifu body pillow than a chainsaw. When "Ricky Vaughn," one of the alt-right's vocal Trump fanboys and notorious trolls, was revealed to be one Douglas Mackey, we didn't see a rippling Aryan Adonis but a balding, soft-featured, whippet-human hybrid who had been unemployed for two years.

Tough-talking alt-right leader Andrew Auernheimer, also known as "weev," is a former convict who went full white-supremacist while in prison. Publisher of the *Daily Stormer* neo-Nazi website, Auernheimer once begged of Trump, "Please, Donald Trump, kill the Jews, down to the last woman and child. Leave nothing left of the Jewish menace. It is all on you, my glorious leader."[14] Today the *Daily Stormer* can be found only on the dark web, and Auernheimer's paper-thin legal defense that he's only calling for a new genocide "for the lulz" has made him an international fugitive.

Their reeking, terrible virgin anger is the same kind of thing we've seen in terrorist profiles the world over—angry, lonely, awkward young men told their lack of sex, happiness, and prosperity is from the Evil Other: the Jew, the American, the immigrant, the woman who won't fuck them, the religious apostate. When the torch-bearing Citronella ISIS boys show up in their khakis and white polo shirts, we see a Western version of the black track-suited terrorists toting AK-47s who litter the Middle East and South Asia.

By the middle of 2018, the alt-right had fallen victim to their own exposure and elevation by Donald Trump. In all its themes, variations, and subgroups, the alt-right is like a species of political cockroach; sunlight kills them. Trump gave them the confidence to come out into the light, but the moment the world saw them for what they are, the response was to spray them and stomp them back into the shadows.

PART FOUR

AFTER TRUMP

16

BUT GORSUCH

WHEN MY DAUGHTER WAS SMALL, PART OF THE DEAL WE made if she was to get a pony of her own was that she'd do her part of the barn chores, including mucking out stalls. Ponies are a good lesson in hard work for kids, and one of our favorite jokes was "Keep digging. There's a pony under all that manure."

Trump supporters keep digging through the manure pile of this administration, hoping to find that pony. This quest is a constant, thankless task, in part because Donald Trump keeps producing more chaos and fewer accomplishments than they expected.

The tiresome, Sisyphean defense of Trump by his mob of yahoos is one thing. They're here for the spectacle, the show of a presidential chimpanzee throwing his feces. They're the Idiocracy cosplayers. Trump could eat a live baby on national television, and their only reaction would be "Well, Obummer was such a Kenyan cuck he'd never eat a baby! MAGA!"

Conservative writers, activists, and thinkers most certainly know better but continue to rely on a two-word mantra you've heard over and over: "But Gorsuch."

It's their mantra as they struggle to fit Trump's behavior into a coherent mental framework, stretching and twisting their standards, compromising their principles, eliding every outrage, and ignoring the endemic corruption, grotesque mismanagement, and shit-tier judgment he displays. "But Gorsuch" is a tell, a sign of a mental struggle to justify Trump.

They're digging through a pyramid-size pile of manure trying to find the pony underneath, and it just doesn't work. The list of actual conservative accomplishments in the Trump administration that aren't ephemeral, intangible, or marred with other and undesirable secondary effects is pretty damn short.

At the end of his first year in office, the White House released a list of 81 accomplishments, which is pretty standard fare for most administrations. Very few took the form of "Congress passed, and the president signed the following law." Most of them were policy, executive orders, or unconnected to the administration's actual actions.

This leaves them three primary lines of defense: Gorsuch, the tax bill, and the stock market. It's less to go on than you think.

Neil Gorsuch is a noted jurist, a smart man, and a demonstrated conservative thinker. We should know; he came up through the Federalist Society system where folks on my side of the ideological ledger have done a great job of building up an infrastructure to nominate and install conservatives on the federal bench. It's one of the hidden triumphs of the conservative movement.

Donald Trump had nothing to do with choosing Gorsuch for the empty seat on the U.S. Supreme Court. Gorsuch doesn't reflect Trump's principles, ideas, or philosophy. As Trump has no principles, ideas, or philosophy beyond his narcissism and self-regard, how could he?

Gorsuch was a name on the list given to him by Mitch McConnell, not a choice derived from this president's knowledge, preferences, or ideology. Trump has no judicial philosophy of his own and, in fact, had praised his hyperliberal pro-abortion sister for a role on the federal bench, which was problematic given both the nepotism aspect and that she's to the left of Ruth Bader Ginsburg.

That list was used as a talisman in 2016 to prevent nervous conservatives from wandering off the Trump reservation. The irony is, conservatives could have had a Gorsuch, and other judges of the same desirable conservative stripe, with a lot less drama from a Marco Rubio, Jeb Bush, Scott Walker, or Ted Cruz.

What about the deregulation battle? Isn't Trump engaged in a regulatory war against the hated liberal bureaucracy? Yes and no. The cuts to regulations in some departments may well be desirable. Some are not. Three problems exist on this front. First, those changes are temporary. The next president can, with the stroke of a pen, restore the old regulations, or do worse. Second, the changes so far seem driven by an arbitrary set of demands from corporate sponsors, lobbyists, and industries in good odor with Team Trump. Odd, but I thought Republicans were against picking winners and losers.

Third, they're rule changes, and rule changes are inferior to laws. Passing a law, which takes negotiation, compromise, brains, discipline, and engagement with the actual issues is well beyond Donald Trump's intellectual ken.

Trump's reliance on executive orders is precisely as weak as President "Pen and a Phone" Barack Obama's were. Bragging about something that the next president can wipe away in an instant is a dangerous and pathetic path if you're looking to make a lasting and substantive change in Washington, DC. The inability to focus and work on passing legislation is an ongoing weakness of this administration, and so the cheerleading for these outcomes is inevitably going to be short-lived.

Also, if and when the Democrats take the House and Senate, Republicans should expect a tidal wave of new laws seeking to overturn policies where Trump had attempted to use executive orders. A majority of Democrats in even one chamber will lead to inevitable veto fights, burning more of Trump's already limited political capital, and sink Washington deeper into a sea of political entropy.

Further, many of Trump's executive order–driven "accomplishments" aren't exactly sterling examples of conservative economic policy. Trade tariffs, coal subsidies, and a variety of other big-government economic nostrums pushed by Trump and his cadre of economically illiterate advisors are edging the United States toward a disastrous international economic order where the rest of the world sees us as a target, not a market.

What about the 2017 tax bill? Isn't it a towering Republican win, a brand-new conservative approach to . . . oh, who am I kidding? It's a honking corporate tax cut. It's a bill written by lobbyists for a tier of wealthy corporate and high-net-worth clients, a triumph of the Washington ecosystem of lobbying and paid advocacy.

It's, well, big. That's something, right? Congress raced the bill through the House and Senate in seven short weeks and kept Trump far, far away.

While sold as providing "Trump bonuses" to workers, the vast majority of the tax savings realized by American corporations flowed into buying back stock, improving their cash positions, and executive compensation. I'm no economist, and I'm not even going to argue whether those things have an upside; they do, but at the upper rates and in small numbers of voters.

What I am, however, is a careful watcher from behind the glass of hundreds of focus groups, and what I saw in March 2018 should chill the GOP. In a focus group conducted in a purple, Midwestern state the target audience for the tax cut's PR message sat around a table, and while they liked the bill in a broad, general way, the economic worry had already returned. Sure, they preferred lower taxes to higher in a broad sense but didn't put much faith that this bill would profoundly change their lives. The continued belief that Washington was working for lobbyists and special interests blunted the bill's political uplift.

Public polling showed high-income earners were delighted with the tax cut, and middle-class voters, well, not as much. Only 25% said they'd seen a boost in their paycheck as a result of the tax law. Of that 25%, 58% said it made them more likely to support the GOP. That's 14.5%, and while necessary, it isn't necessarily sufficient.

The idea that the bill would provide such a tangible sense of benefit and a concomitant political push for the GOP wasn't wrong, but it also wasn't enough to offset the negatives Donald Trump had imposed on the GOP. Even "Trump bonuses" appearing in paychecks—and they were more than the Democrats spun and less than the Republicans promised—didn't change the broader political calculus.

The other mistake the GOP made was believing that the tax bill guarantees the stock market's eternal, upward trajectory. The market had largely already priced in the tax cut to its performance for the year before the bill passed in Congress. It was baked in the proverbial cake.

Republicans took the tax bill's political upsides for granted, despite the fact that it blows a trillion-dollar hole in the deficit and presumes ludicrously high growth rates, and while the corporate rate reductions are permanent, the individual tax rate reductions are temporary. It's chock-full of cherry-picked goodies for specific industries, like the carried-interest loophole, and ends local and state tax deductions.

There's a cost to bad policy. There's a cost to government where the executive either ignores, bypasses, or intimidates the legislative branch into doing his bidding. Part of the short-shortsightedness and magical thinking of the Trump era is this idea that there will never be another Democratic president or a Democratic majority in the House or Senate.

Someday a Democrat in the Oval Office who combines an ambition to expand government power will run wild with executive power, and Republicans will be caught slack-jawed and stunned. We looked away and giggled with glee as Trump ran roughshod over the balance of powers and the limits of executive authority, and we'll pay for it down the line.

That we haven't achieved conservative perfection in government with any president before Trump is a feature, not a bug in the dysfunction of today's GOP and conservative base. No, we didn't deliver the perfect wish list of the further edges of our coalition in any spot. The foreign policy hawks didn't get trillion-dollar defense budgets. The social conservatives didn't get a ban on abortion, gay marriage, or *Fifty Shades of Grey*. The small-government guys didn't get reductions in government to the point they could drown it in a bathtub. Trump isn't going to deliver those things either, and what his supporters never understand is that he doesn't want to.

Trump turned on its head the old paradigm of liberals wanting to grow government and conservatives wanting to constrain it. The "But Gorsuch" premise comes down to one dangerous thought: that Trump is worth all of the excesses, deviations, and risks to the movement, the party, and the country. As Trump's departures from conservative ideology leave consistent conservatives reeling, his evident personal instability becomes more marked. He's not growing into the job, and scandals of his own creation have paralyzed his agenda. It's difficult to see how the trade-off is worth it.

Do Gorsuch and a handful of court nominations make up for the seemingly enormous, looming political costs? Do a few regulatory rollbacks compensate for setting a new precedent for the broad use of executive power? Does having an ongoing war with the media off-set losing female, and suburban voters in record numbers? Does "he fights" make up for the fact that when he enters the discussion the result is more likely "we lose"?

Does Trump's campaign to weaponize and expand federal power against immigrants offset the fact that we are permanently scarring the reputation of this country and our party with Hispanics of every description?

Does a tax bill offset the damage done to race relations and the permanent alienation of African Americans from the GOP? There may be good people on both sides in Trump's mind, but in the minds of minority voters, the game is over.

Do Trump's shallow, dick-measuring juvenile feuds with everyone who has ever looked at him cross-eyed make America look more or less like a nation led by a serious person? Does Trump's obedience to and bizarre love affair with Vladimir Putin make our country look stronger, or weaker? Does the glaringly overt culture of corruption designed to enrich Trump and his family make foreign powers think that we're incorruptible or that there's a gigantic For Sale sign on the forehead of the leader of the free world?

Life is full of trade-offs. Life is full of compromises. The best shouldn't be the enemy of the good. The differences in perception between Trump voters and people who live on this plane of reality are stark. Trump fans view every statement, tweet, speech fragment, and half-formed word-fart out of Trump's mouth as a final, permanent, brilliantly conceived and executed policy. His critics on the right wonder about how the expansion of state power and his role as our first modern president with genuinely authoritarian inclinations plays out in the long haul. His fans believe Trump already built the Wall, the economy will never be better, and the only thing we have to fear is Robot Hillary 2020 and the fake news media.

The Democrats, never strong on irony, are finally feeling the sting of worry about expanded government under Trump after decades dreaming of an all-powerful do-gooder technocracy, where Nanny Sam subsumes the rights of the states and individuals. In the strangest, most backhand way, they might learn a lesson about being careful what you wish for in this world.

A conservative Supreme Court is an important and significant victory, but if it's the last major victory before sweeping Democratic gains, the costs to the party and to the conservative movement may be steeper than we've yet imagined. I think about who will weigh those costs in the future, and I find it hard to imagine anyone saying, "But Trump."

17

TRUMP IS ELECTORAL POISON

DONALD TRUMP IS ELECTORAL POISON. I KNOW I'M TAK-
ing a bit of a gamble saying that, as this book will go to print before
the 2018 elections, and externalities, Democratic Party incompetence,
zombie apocalypses, and other factors may conspire to bite me on
my predictive ass. Still, the signs and portents of a Democratic-wave
election are building, and have been by the day. Donald Trump's approval ratings are somewhere above genital warts and below every
other president in modern history, so that's nice.

"Win the Trump primary" has become a common term of art,
with the wholehearted belief that Donald Trump's hold over the base
is not simply *a* factor in elections from U.S. Senate to the local Mos-
quito Control Board, but *the* factor. Campaigns pandering for the love
of the Trump base (and in some cases, Trump himself) may feel narrow and tone-deaf, but look at any primary election on the GOP side
of the ledger in 2017 and early 2018 and you'll find candidates working
diligently to out-Trump Trump.

While imitation of Trump is the stupidest form of political flattery, the plague of Trump-like candidates racing toward their own
doom keeps growing. Republican primaries have become contests for
the Darwin Awards, a political version of hold-my-beer-watch-this
bubba-ism.

In their brave, stupid new world, it's not enough to build the Wall; they want a 3,000-mile lava moat with robot alligators programmed to eat Mexicans, then a minefield to stop the stragglers, and finally laser turrets to fry the ones that escape the alligators and mines. They've adopted the swaggering fabulism, grunting populism, short-temper, short-attention-span style and overall affect of Donald Trump in every way but the blond wig. Their cries of "Fake News!" rend the air.

What could go wrong? Um, everything. And it's all the fault of my colleagues in the Republican consulting class.

My friends, competitors, teammates, and acquaintances in the GOP consulting community have a terrible, horrible, incurable case of ETTD, and these Typhoid Atwaters are spreading death to the Republican candidate pool.

You should understand something about Washington's consulting community before we dive in. Individually there are brilliant strategists, ad makers, pollsters, speechwriters, communications wizards, and lawyers in the Republican consultocracy. There are also a few talentless, venal, backstabbing shitheels, of course. Collectively, they live in a city that encourages pack behavior, conformity, and caution. The campaign community is particularly sensitive, their gazelle noses sniffing the wind for the slightest changes in the town's mood. Is that a lion in the tall grass? Are there crocodiles in that grassy verge near the watering hole? Are we Tea Party this week, or back to Bush Republicanism? It's become a corporate sector, and iconoclasts aren't particularly welcome.

Being inside the system is ludicrously profitable. It's all Other People's Money, and there are rarely penalties for failure. In the Super-PAC age, the business got so much easier. There are few incentives to play outside the lines, and the campaign committees—the NRCC, the NRSC, and the RNC itself—are a cozy blanket for even the mediocrities in the business.

During 2015 you would have been hard-pressed to find a pro-Trump consultant in the entire GOP infrastructure. Driven by ideology, experience, and practicality, their contempt for and disgust with Trump were vivid and justified. I wasn't some lone genius who uniquely understood the damage Trump would do to the party, the conservative movement, and the nation. They saw how much was at risk and for the most part were vocal in their positions.

Even the consultants who worked for Trump treated him, at best, like a paycheck and a source of future steak-dinner war stories that would take the form of "You will not fuckin' believe what that fuckin' moron did." Once Trump secured the nomination, however, the official apparatus of Washington was, according to the rules of the game, his. Every consultant with an RNC contract was suddenly Born Again Trump, their criticisms of the nominee forgotten. Red hats suddenly blossomed, some from pure party tribalism, more from financial considerations. Honestly, I understood it but warned them against the downstream blots on their political copybooks.

Because packs move as packs will, after the election there was a panicked rush to Trump, a Kabuki dance of elaborate apologies and explanations to anyone they could find in Trump's orbit. Again, it was almost understandable. They had bills to pay, and if their clients were Republican Party committees or SuperPACs, no ideological deviations from Trump juche were allowed. Many settled into new roles as Trump cheerleaders and defenders. Alex Castellanos, a former Bush and Romney strategist, was a member of the Old Guard of GOP media consultants. Once a vehement critic—mirabile dictu!—he swiftly became a defender of the Trump True Faith in June 2016. I'm sure being hired by a pro-Trump SuperPAC had nothing to do with it.[1]

Castellanos wasn't alone. The social pressure of the New Washington, lubricated in equal parts by money and fear of being ostracized, brought many former Never Trump rebels to heel.

Then the curse hit.

In 2017 it became evident that these smart, crafty, and experienced consultants were advising their clients to "go Trump" and embrace the folly and absurdity of Trump's style and to cling tightly to the man beloved by the base. These folks knew Trump doesn't translate outside the base. We're all reading the same polling results over and over again; the hard core of the GOP loves Trump and hates everyone and everything that doesn't. Everyone else will crawl through broken glass to vote against anyone even Trump-adjacent.

These consultants understood that Trump was poison with voters outside the base and that you can't go with a "just the tip" approach to Trumpism. To put it in terms Mike Pence might like, you either abstain or marry it.

The DC consulting community got hitched to Trumpism and obsessed with winning over Trump voters. That's why you saw ineffective, centrist-repellent ads about MS-13 and illegal alien criminals in states like Virginia, where the blowback cost Republicans the election. The desire to draw The Donald's favorable tweets and perhaps win the coveted Rally with the President overcame judgment and experience.

For these folks, winning the Trump primary, while necessary, is not necessarily sufficient. As the losses started to stack up in 2017 and 2018, and a bleak 2020 election cycle loomed on the horizon, the DC campaign advisors who have bound themselves to Trump are looking at long odds, sweeping electoral losses, and a trip into the political wilderness, but because they've sold themselves on the fantasy that Trumpism—with or without Trump—is the future, they won't change a thing about it.

It's political malpractice of the highest order.

Trump's unlikely win, driven by his shambolic, half-assed campaign, has convinced a generation of Republicans that the careful use of data, polling, analytics, and media placement can be replaced by grunting, atavistic "Build duh wall, deport 'em all" populism, Twitter, and rallies. They've convinced themselves that everyone who votes is a Fox News viewer.

In the Reagan era, the tools of campaigning were still recognizable from 50 or even 100 years before, except for a deeper reliance on television advertising. In the Bush era, we started to understand the primacy of data and targeting. With the two Obama elections, we recognized that the Democrats had a data and analytics advantage over us. As a party we—and by "we" I mean both the GOP inside data team from the Data Trust and the Koch-funded i360 data archive—started to insist campaigns and candidates focus their message, target their resources, and hit the right targets at the right time with the right message. You think campaigns are hideously expensive? Imagine them without targeting and data.

That's fine with Trump's acolytes. They don't need all that modern-day witchcraft and science. They'll just outsource that to Moscow.

Now we're about to see a generation of candidates driven by rage, with Fox-level intellectual constructs (mostly simple, brightly colored pictograms) that have all the subtlety and introspection of the Breitbart comments section. A pollster friend of mine lamented that his otherwise bright candidate is convinced that if he can just be on Fox enough, the rest of the campaign doesn't matter. They've sold themselves that the rest of America sees Trump's chaotic, sloppy behavior and his clown-show government the way they do; as a charmingly eccentric slap in the face of the politically correct and moribund Establishment, not as a calamitous shitshow.

They've also come to believe that the base, and only the base, matters. They're looking away from a universe of survey data that show Donald Trump is narrowing the base into a demographic box canyon. There are only so many white dudes over the age of 50 with a high school education or below, and they're a shrinking pool.

Well, I'm just a simple country campaign consultant who's run ads in 38 states and been to the electoral rodeo a time or two, and I can tell you, the idea of running as a Trump Republican if you're not Donald Trump is a catastrophically long reach anywhere outside of seats the best redistricting money can buy. If you're in a safe seat in a district with a 15% GOP voter registration advantage in Asscrack, Arkansas, that might work. Almost everywhere else, the lesson from January 2017 until today has been that Trump is a mighty headwind for GOP candidates.

In 2017 Republicans had two chances to either hold or take governor's mansions. New Jersey and Virginia were outstanding object lessons in the ETTD effect, and Republicans stubbornly refused to either learn from them or even acknowledge that Donald Trump's divisive leadership and character led to their defeat.

In New Jersey, Chris Christie's designated political heir was Kim Guadagno, his lieutenant governor. New Jersey hasn't been a Republican stronghold for a long while, and it was never going to be an easy race for Guadagno, but as a moderate voice in the GOP, she would have at least had a fighting chance. After running a campaign about menacing illegal aliens (where have we heard that before?), she got her ass handed to her in a sound defeat. It wasn't a shock, but the signs were building.

It was in Virginia where we learned how bad it was about to get.

OH, VIRGINIA

In a painful case of ETTD, Virginia's Ed Gillespie learned the hard way that keeping the Trump base happy is a short path to a humiliating loss. The Democrats held on to the Virginia governor's mansion in a race that was a teachable moment on the utter political poison of Trumpism, and yet another example of a decent, modern, smart Republican trapped in a vise between disqualifying himself with the Trump base or disqualifying himself with the other 64% of the electorate.

As a candidate for governor, Gillespie was surrounded by a team of smart, practical, experienced campaign hands. Two of his most senior consultants are among my closest friends. And yet the virus of Trumpism caused the campaign to fixate on themes that kept the Trump base happy while ignoring the simmering mass of voters who would move heaven and earth to vote against anyone running in the ideological or stylistic footsteps of Donald Trump.

Gillespie ads against the overhyped threat of the MS-13 Central American drug gang were fodder for the Trump base and poison for the enormous northern Virginia population of independents and moderates. (As an aside, independents and moderates are not the same things, though they are commonly conflated in the mind of many analysts. This simple category error leads to much campaign heartache.)

The grumbling from the Trump base before and after the election was that Gillespie wasn't sufficiently fulsome in his praise of Trump, even though poll after poll showed that Trump's numbers in Virginia were execrable: 57% disapproved of Trump, and of that 57%, 87% voted for Democrat Ralph Northam. The Trump headwinds were powerful; running a campaign that recapitulated Trump's shittiest themes made it impossible to win.[2]

Afterward, in a moment that must surely have stung the decent, dedicated Gillespie, Trump tweeted, "Ed Gillespie worked hard but did not embrace me or what I stand for. Don't forget, Republicans won 4 out of 4 House seats, and with the economy doing record numbers, we will continue to win, even bigger than before!"[3]

Virginia was an important lesson; in purple states, Trump activates low-propensity Democrats, and the themes and style of Trumpism activate them more, even from candidates who aren't explicitly running as Trump Republicans. Oh, and while Democrats were at it, they took 15 seats in the Virginia House of Delegates, moving from the GOP 66–33 majority to a 51–49 split.

SENATOR PEDOBEAR

In my 30 years in politics, I've worked against two Republican general election candidates. The first, as I think you may have picked up on by now, was Donald Trump.

The other was pedo-curious mall stalker and overall creep Roy Moore. The Alabama race tested a number of Republican electoral verities, and one of the most important was that even in the deepest of deep red states, there's a limit.

Roy Moore was a stain on the American political system not simply because he stalked and molested underage girls but also because he was defiant toward the rule of law, ignorant of the Constitution, and—I know you'll find this surprising given he was from Alabama—not a fan of African Americans, Muslims, immigrants, or gays.[4] If it hadn't been for the girls, though, Roy Moore would be in DC today being hailed as part of the nationalist populist revolutionary front in the pages of Breitbart, the *Der Stürmer* of our time. It was a delight to be brought in to do SuperPAC ads against him.

The election was full of warning signs for the GOP. Even in the most heated of races, Republican and conservative turnout was flat. African American turnout, never a sure thing in off years (or even in on years—as Hillary Clinton learned), was stratospheric. Younger voters showed up for once and voted strongly against the Republican candidate. Even in the reddest state in the nation, Trump couldn't juice the numbers.

The other factor that stood out was also seen in Virginia: college-educated voters have broken hard for the Democrats, even in red areas. In 2012, Mitt Romney took 64% of Alabama's college-educated vote. In 2017, Roy Moore won just 43%.[5] Though Steve Bannon, who was then still very much in the Trump orbit, campaigned passionately for Moore, the corollary to ETTD applies to Steve: everything he touches gets infected with something that oozes and smells of rotting meat.

A SMALL RACE. A BIG LESSON

The statewide elections are interesting, but sometimes the devil pops up more clearly in the details of small races in places you know best. It's why I paid particular attention to a mayoral race in my old neighborhood. It's the story of Rick Baker, Rick Kriseman, and the job of mayor of St. Petersburg, Florida. I know the area well. I was born and raised just across the bay in Tampa, and I was a field director for both Senate candidate Connie Mack and George H. W. Bush.

Pinellas County was one of my early political stomping grounds. Once reliably red, it had drifted into the center lane, giving Obama wins in 2008 and 2012. It went for Trump by just 6,000 votes. The city of St. Petersburg, however, is different from much of the rest of the county. It has African Americans.

Republican Rick Baker held the mayor's office for two terms and was wildly popular. He was called America's best mayor for a good reason; he was the kind of local leader Republicans saw as the future. Baker was a diligent, honest force in working with the African American community, something Republicans locally had not, to put it kindly, been terribly motivated about in the past. He really engaged, built relationships, and reached across party lines to treat African Americans with respect and to address the needs of their neighborhoods and families.

Baker won wide support in the African American community at the ballot box because he put in the work by doing more than just talking the talk. He won 90% of the African American vote in one election. He was the crossover-vote dream, where our rhetoric was consonant with political reality. Rick Baker was, and is, a man who did well while doing good.

On housing, education, crime, and race, Rick Baker was the kind of Republican Republicans claimed they wanted and needed to be to win over African Americans. His book *The Seamless City* was a cult favorite among Republican leaders from Jeb Bush to Mitt Romney.[6]

Then came Donald Trump.

Baker and his Democratic opponent, Rick Kriseman, who was then mayor of the city, fought to a draw in the ugly primary election in an ostensibly nonpartisan race. Kriseman beat Baker by 69 votes out of 56,500 cast. The razor-thin 48.36 to 48.23% meant a runoff election, and unfortunately for Baker, his running mate was Donald J. Trump.

This was Baker's race to lose. Kriseman had been a frankly terrible mayor, beset with a record of city projects that flopped or hung in limbo and a record of delay, incompetence, and mismanagement that would make a 1950s Soviet bureaucrat proud. In the end, though, the petty scandals and failures didn't matter. Kriseman could have stayed in bed eating bonbons and still won because Donald Trump couldn't help but defend his base in Charlottesville.

The moment Trump drew a moral equivalence by using the phrase "both sides" the die was cast. African Americans in St. Petersburg and across the nation heard loud and clear that the president thought there were some "fine people" among the Klan, the neo-Nazis, and the white separatist scum in Charlottesville, and that they were morally equivalent to the people protesting them.

All Rick Baker's work was washed away. All his relationships with the African American community were broken. Rick Baker hadn't changed. He was still the good-hearted and proven leader he was before. There isn't and wasn't a single iota of racial animus in Baker. Rick Kriseman certainty didn't suddenly become less of a moron and terrible leader.

Baker faced the same terrible problem every other Republican outside the most lily-white district faces: the Scylla of large majorities repulsed by Trump's overtly racist dog-whistling and the Charybdis of a Trump base that will turn on anyone who utters the slightest condemnation of him.

Baker had two and a half months to denounce Trump's position with passion and clarity. That's a lifetime in politics, but his advisors lived in terror of losing the Trump vote, blind to the costs of holding it in the first place. Baker simply couldn't do it. Ignoring the 800-pound Klansman in the room doesn't work; African Americans and independent voters were listening and never heard Baker say the words they needed to hear.

The *Tampa Bay Times* political editor Adam Smith captured it perfectly:

> In fact, it would have been political malpractice for Kriseman not to wrap Trump around Baker and nationalize the race as he did. Baker made a terrible, and perhaps cowardly, decision to do little to distance himself from the president. The race effectively ended in August, when President Trump spoke of the "fine people" who participated in a neo-Nazi march

in Charlottesville, where clashes led to a woman's death. . . . Baker is a Jeb Bush Republican and anybody who knows him understands that he shares few of Trump's values. Baker was so scared of antagonizing Republican voters, however, that he wouldn't criticize the president's Charlottesville comments, not even as mildly as House Speaker Paul Ryan and Senate Majority Leader Mitch McConnell did.[7]

Baker's political tragedy is the story of a good man trapped by a bad president and his own fear. With all his good works in the African American community blown away by a tide of hatred and racial animus that Donald Trump slammed back into the American political dialogue, I'm sure Baker today ponders the counterfactuals of a robust, sharp attack on Trump and riding out the anger of the Trump base.

It's a lesson for other Republicans, one that I am certain they'll ignore.

THE PANIC OF PA-18

The signs of trouble in the GOP were all over the board in 2017 and 2018. They clung to a handful of easy-lift Congressional races in heavily red seats, but the cracks were showing; Democratic turnout was up, GOP morale was down.

It was a special election in the spring of 2018 that chilled House Republicans to their core. If a generic, conservative Republican couldn't win in a generic, conservative Republican district, what did the future hold? Pennsylvania's 18th district wasn't the loudest or the most expensive race in the Trump era, but it was one of the most telling.

The various Coal Country Kristofs told us this part of America had been politically transformed by Trump, who cast its residents as the ignored, salt-of-the-earth working Americans who had been abandoned by Washington, the powerful and economic elites. These voters were described as a people singularly activated and motivated by Donald Trump. Working-class Republicans and Democrats were ready to MAGA. Nothing could sway them from his populist message, because only Trump had . . . oh, who am I kidding?

It turned out to be a political exercise that scared the GOP, but not nearly enough.

The 18th, comprising Pittsburgh's southern suburbs and parts of Allegheny, Westmoreland, Washington, and Green counties, was a deep red district from the start, with a Cook Partisan Voting Index of 11. The Democrats hadn't even bothered to field a candidate in the previous two election cycles. In 2016 it had voted for Trump in a 60 to 40% blowout. This was Trump country, writ red.

Rick Saccone is a Republican cut from central casting for the district—ex-military, solidly middle class, solidly to the right across the entire spectrum of conservative issues. He is almost ridiculously generic. No major scandal marred his record, and his tenure in the Pennsylvania legislature was unremarkable in every way.

For once in their lives, the Democrats told their own progressive purity posse to shut up, sit in the corner, and let the grown-ups work. Conor Lamb was by no means a Nancy Pelosi Democrat, and that's what made him a competitive force in the race. He split the difference on abortion, and as facile as "personally pro-life, politically pro-abortion" sounds, it's also where a majority of Americans fall on the issue. He stood by the Second Amendment, even though the horrific Parkland shooting took place three weeks before the end of the race. He is a military veteran, and right for the district.

He didn't even make it about Trump, showing a degree of political sophistication that belied his years. Lamb was engaged in the strategic play of permission politics; knowing he wasn't a perfect fit with the politics of the district, he gave voters permission to consider him by not disqualifying himself to conservatives. It was, in the words of *Vanity Fair*, "Trump Kryptonite."[8] The other elements of his campaign persona were good enough for a look; by not responding to Saccone or Trump on their turf, he gave independents and Republicans a chance to say, "Okay, I can live with this guy." It was the same trick we pulled in New York, giving liberals permission to come to Rudy. In contrast, Saccone's messages was "All Trump All the Time."

If you want to know why the GOP is in a panic in the spring of 2018, it's this: they finally realized Trump's negatives outweigh everything they try when it comes to paid advertising. The NRCC's and allied groups' usual portfolio of attacks was a complete failure in Pennsylvania. They spent $7.4 million on paid media; Lamb and supporting groups spent only $4.4 million. A nearly 2:1 paid media (broadcast television, cable, and digital ads) spending advantage was one of those old rules of thumb that died in the Trump era. So too did some of the thematic plays that had long worked wonders.

The NRCC and the Congressional Leadership Fund, Paul Ryan's personal PAC, launched their advertising assault with something they thought was a guaranteed winner: the massive Republican-passed tax bill of 2017. It was, we were assured, the thing that would fix what ailed the GOP. The themes were, to boil it down, "Evil witch Nancy Pelosi wants to take your few remaining pennies, and Conor Lamb will help her. Aren't you loving your Trump Bonus?" People weren't. The tax cut ads supporting Saccone flopped in focus groups and were pulled from heavy rotation and, finally, after burning through a $2.5 million stack of cash, taken down altogether.[9]

I know what you're thinking. How could a tax bill that was written by Wall Street lobbyists and designed to protect hedge funds, major investment banks, and real estate developers not persuade Rust Belt voters? How could they not drop to their knees in praise of and thanks to Paul Ryan when they're looking at as much as $15 per week more in their paychecks? Didn't they get the news that major corporations were engaged in a wave of stock buybacks and executive bonuses that would—wait for it—trickle down?[10]

The failure of the ads praising the GOP tax cut was inevitable; you can't sell bad dog food with good PR because the dogs don't care about the PR, only the taste. This wasn't even good PR. Generic, gauzy, "Thanks for muh tax cut" montages of workers, scare shots of Pelosi, and over-the-top voice-over work wasn't going to cut it, and didn't.

It was an article of faith among DC consultants that passing *any-thing* in 2017 was better than passing *nothing*. "We have to give Trump a big win, and this helps us, too," was an argument made with a straight face by ostensibly intelligent adults. This was always arguable, but most Americans weren't screaming for the protection of the carried interest loophole and for private equity guys to pay the same tax rate as a greeter at the Olive Garden. Then the argument morphed into "Wait until they see the benefits in their paychecks." That fell flat when the numbers weren't as sky high as they expected and when voters started learning that they could no longer deduct state and local taxes.

When those ads failed, the GOP's argument seemed to be "Well, we've screwed that pooch. How can we do something that everyone outside of Trump's base hates?" You guessed it; immigration reared its ugly head again, despite the painful lessons of Virginia, New Jersey, and other races in 2017. Of course, when you're going to fuck it up, do so with gusto, right? The next wave of ads did everything but Photo-shop MS-13 face tattoos on Lamb.

It was pure Trump immigrant scaremongering and included bonus footage of Nancy Pelosi in almost every frame. Both of those tactics once scared Republican voters into line. I'll freely admit to put-ting Nancy in dozens of candidate and SuperPAC ads over the years because GOP voters hate her with a fiery passion. Ryan, the NRCC, and Saccone failed to answer the most important question of any ad: Does it work?

Those ads, as noted elsewhere in this chapter, work on one group and one group only: Trump core voters. They're less compelling for softer Republicans, and both independent and Democratic voters find them repellent. They close the door to even considering the other can-didate. The ads were politically tone deaf, generically clunky, and, by the end, clearly not working. While Conor Lamb's ads were talking about how he'd defy both sides in Washington to do the right thing for his district, Rick Saccone and his allies were screaming about the imagined scourge of deadly Mexican immigrants.

At the close of the campaign, Saccone got two things only the president could deliver: Trump declared the opening of a global trade war by the unilateral imposition of a 25% tariff on imported steel and a 15% tariff on imported aluminum. The conventional wisdom was that trade policy was a giant vote-getter for Trump in the Rust Belt and that the PA-18 audience would be similarly entranced, but it didn't move the numbers; only 3% said it made them more likely to support Saccone.[11] While it was a net positive in the district, voters had other things on their mind.

Then Saccone got the Trump Rally for which he'd been waiting. You know . . . a *rally*. How could poor Saccone not have seen how this would end? Instead of making a political case for his candidate, Trump stood on stage for 70 long minutes doing his usual Borscht Belt Mussolini shtick, bellowing, strutting, and doing everything but grabbing his sack on stage. It was a disaster, and Trump only mentioned Saccone in passing in the last moments of the event. The spectacle was for Trump's needy ego, not to elect another Republican.

When the president arrived in western Pennsylvania the Saccone campaign was on its last legs, unable to understand why his numbers against Lamb were cratering, unable to understand why the ads darkening the sky like a thousand B-2 bombers weren't working.

By the last night of the campaign, Saccone had cracked. With Donald Trump Jr. by his side, the beleaguered Republican said, "I've talked to so many of these on the left. And they have a hatred for our President. And I tell you, many of them have a hatred for our country. . . . They have a hatred for God. It's amazing. You see it when I'm talking to them. It's disturbing to me."[12]

Saccone missed the point by a mile. It wasn't hatred of God. It was hatred of Trump. Trump's actions gave Lamb the latitude to run as a centrist Democrat without pressure from the left. Lamb may have won by only 0.28%, a mere 600 votes, but the size of the swing toward the Democrats sent a ripple of terror down the spine of the National Republican Congressional Committee and House leadership. One GOP congressman told me, "I'm only in a swing seat. Is Paul going to spend $10 million on me?"

The post hoc rationalization gymnastics on the part of Paul Ryan and the Republican caucus were spectacular, and telling. Some argued Lamb ran as a centrist, or even as a conservative Republican—you know, the usual pro–universal health care, pro-union, anti–entitlement reform, pro-marijuana conservative. Some noted Saccone's wispy porn-stache and terrible fundraising, or was it his wispy fundraising and terrible porn-stache? Some used the classic DC blamestorming technique: "It was a bad candidate, not a bad message." Representative Steve Stivers, head of the NRCC, was more honest. "This is a wake-up call," he said. "Prepare to bear down."[13]

The White House whispered, "If only Saccone had really embraced the president." Trump advisor Jason Miller told CNN, "Saccone came across as Establishment and not close enough to Trump." Saccone had been "Trump before Trump was Trump" from the start, and the president's children, surrogates, and allies had vigorously campaigned for him.[14] The advertising, previously described, was unadulterated Trumpism.

In the end, Trump's death-finger touched Rick Saccone from the moment the Republican candidate entered the race. He had demographic, political, behavioral, and financial advantages from the very beginning. It was Saccone's race to lose, and Trump helped him do just that.

MORE WARNING SIGNS

It isn't just the direct win-loss scoreboard that counts; you should also look at the partisan swing; in all seven 2017 special elections, Democrats improved their vote by an average of 18%. Even where the GOP won, the Democrats closed the gap due to their level of motivation. Democrats are eager, activated, and determined to vote against Trump and Trump-allied candidates. They've posted record-breaking performances in districts that voted strongly for Trump, defying much of the political modeling for generic voting behavior.

This special election swing has traditionally had a solid predictive effect; in 1994, 2010, and 2014 special election swings presaged solid pickup years for the GOP. In 1998 and 2006, the Democrats saw the same effect.[15]

Another factor pointing to the Democrat wave elections is simple: Republicans are bailing out of Congress like a fighter pilot ejecting from a flaming jet. In the Senate, Jeff Flake, Bob Corker, Orrin Hatch, and Thad Cochran announced their departures.

For Corker and Flake, the sheer irritation of working in Trump's Washington and watching the institution they served become one more part of the Trump cheering section was too much to bear. Both men were outspoken critics of the president, with Flake and Corker making remarkable and impassioned speeches against Trump on the Senate floor.[16]

Trump returned the favor, unleashing his band of merry lunatics to attack them. If you're ever looking for proof that Trump hates his fellow Republicans more than he hates any Democrat or foreign dictator, his attacks on Corker and Flake should do it.

For Hatch and Cochran, age and health factors played a role, though both men came from a more genteel wing of the party that has disappeared in a constant screech of Trumpian vulgarity and fury.

In the House it was like a stampede toward a dessert bar at fat kid camp; while 16 Democrats were leaving, 45 Republicans declined to seek reelection.[17] In state legislatures, Republican retirements and open seats were running roughly 2:1 ahead of Democratic retirements and open seats.

I always say that off-year elections and long-lead polls should be seen as portents, not inevitable facts. The Democrats, long experts at snatching defeat from the jaws of certain victory, can still blow it in a hundred ways we can't even anticipate yet. After the election results of 2017 and 2018, though, the patterns in the polling, fundraising, and candidate recruitment are bright-red flags, klaxons so loud they're screaming to even the most politically tone deaf. Republicans hoped to campaign on a popular tax cut bill, but by early 2018, though it was popular, it was also far in the rearview mirror, politically speaking.

A one-issue legislative portfolio isn't much to run on in 2018. In the minds of the voters, the tax bill's effects are a marginal net positive, but that's contingent on the stock market's robust condition. Even after the passage of the tax bill, national polling gave Democrats a 46 to 42% advantage on handling the economy, 43 to 39% on handling the budget, and 46 to 41% on handling taxes.[18] Ooopsie.

On every other issue, Trump hangs over Republicans' campaigns like a dark cloud. Republican candidates no longer have the power to define themselves individually or to tell their own story. On the issues Trump loves and that make his base squirm with pleasure—immigration, deportation, and the Wall—the voters are substantially to the left of the president. While 16% of Republicans say immigration is their top issue, only 4% of Democrats and leaning voters agree.[19] It's another "Please the base, lose the rest" game.

What else do Republicans have to show for their work in 2017 and 2018? A full-throated defense of Donald Trump over the Russia issue and little else. Devin Nunes and the DC Vladimir Putin Tiger Beat Fan Club have spent every waking hour trying to generate phony counternarratives to the doom that Mueller brings.

The polling shows it: 55% disapprove of Trump's handling of Russian interference in the 2016 election, while just 30% approve; 61% believe the Russia probe is a serious matter, compared to 34% who think it's just politics to discredit Trump; 55% believe he's interfered with the investigation, and 58% say he's not taking it seriously.[20] If you're a Republican candidate running on how mean Bob Mueller is to Donald Trump and how the fake news is keeping us from debating the real issues, like Seth Rich and the Awan Brothers, strap in, because it's gonna get bumpy.

Republican candidates' entire political destiny is now in the wee hands of Donald Trump. Their fate is contingent on his actions, statements, beliefs, and—God save them—tweets. Every day of their campaigns will be a waiting game, praying that some lunatic tweet won't blow up the last several weeks of their messaging or advertising strategy. Every day will be a day they hope indictments don't drop or that

Trump doesn't decide to wander naked in the Rose Garden or nuke Bermuda.

The conceit that Trump's rabid base will be motivated to support Republican knockoffs of Trump is one of the dumbest things I've ever heard in my life because the Republican base hates one thing more than Democrats and liberals, and that's other Republicans.

We see doors closing to Republicans in swing states and purple states because they're caught in a reflexive defense of the indefensible Trump and terror of what happens if they defy him. The Senate map of 2018 is largely favorable to the GOP simply for structural reasons; they're playing defense in only 8 states, while the Democrats have 24 seats in play. In the House, the sense of doom in swing seats in affluent suburbs is palpable.

At this writing in the spring of 2018, it's still not too late for Republicans to hearken to some better angels, but in the era of Trump, it looks unlikely. If they don't choose another path, the warning signs of today may lead to political catastrophe tomorrow.

18

MY PARTY AFTER TRUMP

If the Republican Party is to survive, remain relevant, and be true to its founding principles, our leaders and our members will need to recall that before the spectacle of Trump we believed all men and women are created equal and endowed with the same inalienable rights to life, liberty, and the pursuit of happiness. We believed that government has no lawful power over us except by our consent. We believed that vigilance in the protection of the rights and freedoms of every American was not only our right but our obligation.

Let me be very clear about one thing: I'm not the arbiter of what constitutes pure conservatism, but I know what we've got in Washington today is a long way from it. For modern conservatism and the Republican Party to recover in the aftermath of the Trump era, I'd like to offer a few straightforward policy recommendations that combine a return to conservative principles and some practical political fixes. These fixes are for the heart, and the head.

In this time of nationalist populism, many of Trump's supporters believe Americans are a race, not a nation. This should offend conservatives who believe in the propositional nature of American citizenship, but the Volk and Rodina crowd is in the ascendance, as are state capitalism types. Let's see if we can fix that, shall we?

A PARTY OF HOPE, NOT HATE

The fundamental nature of conservatism is, in William F. Buckley's famous formulation, to stand athwart history and yell "Stop!" But what radically accelerating technological, social, and demographic change has left is increasingly leaving the possibility of stopping progress far in the rearview mirror of our national Tesla.

Republicans need to become a party of militant optimism about the future. Right now we are a party of doom and gloom, screeching about the imminent collapse of the West under the sensible heels of Hillary Clinton, the machinations of George Soros, Islamic terror, and the usual pantheon of Trump's scaremongering closet of horrors.

We've always been a nation with our eyes cast to the far future. We've always believed that the U.S. system and values and the propositional nature of what it means to be an American have a kind of alchemical felicity that leads to an arc rising toward better lives, more freedom applied more broadly, greater economic prosperity, and institutions, based on laws and norms the world can envy. In 2010 we stopped talking about the shining city on a hill and started screaming about sharia law coming to your local day-care center.

A GOP looking backward, desperate to restore the economy, racial composition, and social structures of the 1950s, is bad for the brand, and the kind of nostalgia that is both pointless and cruel. Democrats learned this lesson in Bill Clinton's election of 1992, and again with Barack Obama in 2008. Both men were more optimistic than their Republican counterparts, painting a vision of an America that works and moves forward without fear.

We need to start telling Americans we believe in them again. Look up. Look ahead. Tell people you have faith in them. Teach them we believe we can lift people up and that no one is a prisoner of their past. Tell them that the city on a hill is still there, radiant and beckoning.

REFORM FROM WITHIN

As a party, the GOP became very comfortable in Washington within months of our sweeping victory in 1994. The army of K Street and Capitol Hill lobbyists who had previously been besties with every Democrat under the sun suddenly started stroking checks so fast their manicured fingers cramped. With majorities in both houses, the tidal wave of money flowing to the GOP has had precisely the corrupting and corrosive effects one might expect.

Campaigns became less about a set of principles reflecting the values and needs of the districts and states in which candidates were campaigning and more about tailoring messages, policies, and outcomes to specific corporate benefactors. Lobbying is a business, and under the GOP, business has been good.

Americans are convinced down to their very souls that Washington's corruption is so endemic, so bred in the bone, and so intractable that payoffs, special favors, and logrolling define the capital city more than anything else. Public corruption is the single most dangerous perception for a majority party—to wit, 1974, 1994, 2006, 2010—and the GOP is running headlong into deep ethical waters.

We need a return to strict ethics rules for elected Republicans, whereby both personal and fiscal violations lead to actual punishment and, if merited, expulsion from the body. We need to forbid members of Congress from lobbying after they leave. We need to tighten up financial disclosure rules so members voting on legislation that benefits their own bottom line face sanctions.

These aren't hard to do, but they won't be popular. After all, the man at 1600 Pennsylvania Avenue is a walking conflict of interest, and some Republicans seem hell-bent on emulating him. We'd better clean up our own house, or the voters will do it for us.

THE CONSTITUTIONAL
OPERATING SYSTEM

We continue to stubbornly cling to the illusion that the Republican Party is the party of adherence to the Constitution. In the era of Trump, that's become a risible lie. We need to start walking the walk on reverence and adherence to the Constitution. It's central to our philosophical priorities as a party.

It's the national operating system, and its past time we stopped simply paying lip service to it in the conduct of the business of the American people. Republicans tempted to use government to achieve their policy ends will have a higher hill to climb, but the bills they pass will be less subject to the whimsy of the courts.

Republicans need to restore the divisions between the three branches of government. Under Trump, Congress has abandoned its role as a coequal branch and acted like a Trump houseboy. Congress must exercise its prerogatives and responsibility; the Executive must respect its boundaries under the Constitution; and the courts must play in their lanes. The dynamic tensions between the branches are a feature of a functioning Republic, not a bug.

This also entails respect for all the amendments, not just the 2nd and 10th.

TALK MAIN STREET—AND MEAN IT

The vast and increasing disparity in wealth in this nation has been shrugged off by Republicans for a generation. It's time to be honest about it with the people who haven't enjoyed corporate tax breaks, preferential regulatory treatment, and Wall Street bailouts. We talk a good game about putting Main Street before Wall Street, but talk is all it's been.

We've been parties to bleeding dry the middle class in this country, confusing "good for business" with "good for people." The market we've been a part of creating isn't free. It's shaped in Washington's regulatory structures, and we've been paid lavishly to build it for the sectors with the best lobbying money can buy. We'll fight over supply-side economics another day, but the economic realities of today leave Americans feeling pressured, stressed, and powerless. Sit in on any focus group of likely voters in an affluent suburb, and when the pretense of "we're good" falls, the intensity of the pressure they feel and the burdens they face come screaming at you.

The economic populism of the Trumpist variety and liberal technocratic fantasies are both dead ends in a modern global economy, but the crony capitalism and rentier economy being created with our compliance are economically artificial, frankly cruel, and eventually politically poisonous.

Free markets, economic prosperity, the uplift of a real economy that is structured for growth, modern job creation, is resilient in times of crisis and responsible to the people of our nation would be a lasting legacy for a revitalized Republican Party.

THE RULE OF LAW

Stretching back to the most fundamental Burkean conservatism is one value all but shredded in the age of Donald Trump; respect for the rule of law.

His constant attempts to obstruct justice in the Mueller investigation with only the slightest pushback from Republicans set a precedent so dangerous that we haven't even seen the possible scope of the damage yet. Recommitting as a party to the rule of law seems like pretty basic conservatism, but in the era of Trump it's a radical commitment.

Trump's desire to fire, suborn, or destroy anyone investigating him or his administration is an outrage that will echo longer than Watergate. As a fundamental reform, we need to make a more explicit commitment to not only obeying but honoring and upholding the law, no matter where it takes us. There is no excuse for the direction we've chosen; a commitment to restoring respect for the law is fundamental.

SMALLER, SMARTER, AND
BETTER GOVERNMENT

Republicans talk a great game about limited government, reducing the scope and power of the state, and keeping the hated Washington bureaucracy out of the businesses and lives of Americans. In practice, however, we expanded the federal government radically, both in power and in size, even before Trump.

The vast halo of consultants surrounding Washington, DC, and its environs may not have increased the official head count at the agencies, but the government has grown like kudzu in the past 30 years. It grew during Clinton. It grew during George W. Bush, in dramatic ways that seemed sensible then but are disquieting now. It expanded during the Obama era, and it's growing during the Trump era.

Merely bleating about cutting the size of government isn't enough. Republicans need a new commitment to reforming government, altering its contours and missions to modernize and streamline it. We need to build a customer bill of rights into every government agency that interfaces with the taxpayers directly, ensuring Americans are treated with respect and courtesy. We need to take a meat ax to the legions of consultants conducting the business of government without any real accountability to Congress.

This isn't about across-the-board wholesale cuts, but a serious, mission-driven reform. The bureaucratic immune system is powerful and still wildly dysfunctional. Republicans can lead this charge, reduce the costs and power of the state, and deliver more of the services government should provide to the taxpayers.

BUILD A DIVERSE PARTY

No, I'm not off on some PC SJW rant.

The founding model of our Republic never envisioned members of the House and the United States Senate as members of an ideological monoculture, each responsible not to their state or district but to a single national menu of policy choices. Starting with the post-2010 Tea Party triumph, a growing number of Republicans began to fall into a single ideological frame. The Founders expected the people's representatives in Washington to reflect the values, views, and interests of their state, not simply the positions du jour of Fox News or Mark Levin.

Ideological monocultures right and left kill political creativity, experimentation, and innovation. They close off prospects for victory. The Democrats suffer from this constantly, insisting every candidate hew to the pro-abortion, antigun politics that would get a nod of approval in California but howls of derision in about 40 other states.

A Republican running in Vermont shouldn't have to meet the same purity tests a Republican from Alabama might. A candidate in Florida shouldn't have to conform to the same positions as a candidate in Wyoming.

By increasing our ideological diversity we'll expand the places we can compete, offer Americans more choices in more communities, and enrich the scope of candidates who enter politics.

With that in mind, it's time to make real efforts to recruit African American, Hispanic, and female candidates, not as stunt casting or on a quota basis but as a sign we're serious about voices with new perspectives and ideas. Tim Scott, Mia Love, and Nikki Haley are rock stars, but still all too rare.

But we can't even start to do that until we do what I outline next.

PURGE RACISTS, CONSPIRACY NUTS, AND LUNATICS FROM OUR RANKS

The Republican Party has a race problem, and pretending it doesn't exist has become impossible. We've lost African American voters for decades, and now Trump, Trumpism, and his alt-right allies have turned them into the most powerfully motivated demographic in American political life. In Virginia, Alabama, and other contests in 2017, African Americans—particularly African American women—

have turned out in droves to vote against Republican candidates in levels that exceed their performance for even Barack Obama.

I wrote in an earlier chapter about the history of Republicans standing firm against racial animus and hatred. Donald Trump took every single cliché used by Democrats against the GOP on race and made them a central part of the Republican brand. It's the nadir of an already low point in America's recent history of race relations.

We're not going to have even the slightest chance to win over African Americans until we aggressively, consistently, loudly purge the racists in our midst. Zero tolerance, pack your shit, and hit the road, buh-bye.

I'm rarely at a loss for words, but the fury I felt after defending my party for decades from attacks that it was inherently racist, only to have it elect a man racist in deed and word, tolerant of even more vile racists, and a hero to racists, white supremacists, and anti-Semites leaves me almost speechless with rage.

The purge of racists in our party can't be subtle, it can't be delicate, and it can't be delayed. Ties to the alt-right? You're gone. Ties to the Klan? Gone. The national and state parties need to adopt bylaws that disqualify folks who hold these beliefs from running under our banner. Want to run under the flag of the Racist Dumbfuck Party? Be my guest, but get used to pulling .02% on election day.

The single greatest risk to conservatism, the Republican Party, and the nation is if the alt-right virus spreads deeper into the political system. Racial division and hatred and political movements built around them would be an insult to the long journey our nation has traveled from the original sin of slavery until today. I've outlined the vital necessity of conservatives resisting the alt-right temptation. If we fail, the future won't be simply awful; it will be filled with pathways that lead to some of the darkest forms of violence and hatred.

The next purge required is to end our reliance on and tolerance for conspiracy lunacy. The hatred of the media so common on the right has led millions into a box canyon of inflammatory kookspiracy so far into the extremes that it makes agitprop look like the *New York Review of Books*. Congressional press releases read like *X-Files* spec scripts. Millions of conservatives believe in conspiracies so baroque and Lovecraftian that even trying to explain them makes me feel like I'm taking crazy pills.

Conservative authors, news outlets, and broadcasters need to outgrow the fever swamp of conspiracy and madness. Republican elected officials need to stop playing ball with these sites and writers. In a sane world, Congress and the White House would never credential outlets like *Infowars*, lisping, human flounder hybrid and edge-case lunatic Mike Cernovich, or dim-bulb kookspiracy theorist Jim Hoft. It's time to get back to some professional rigor when it comes to who and what we cover and believe. Stop feeding the conspiracy monster, and it starves.

DECENCY, HUMANITY, AND TOLERANCE

These aren't liberal excuses; they're foundational conservative values. The fashionable cruelty of the Trump era—degrading opponents, deporting people of the wrong ethnicity, the endless stream of dick-joke-level insults and offenses—aren't the character of a president or of a party deserving of respect and support. Respect, courtesy, noblesse oblige, reciprocity, and honor may not seem *à la mode* in the Trump era, but they're powerful social forces a smart party would wire back into its DNA. President Shithole may not get it, but we can, and should.

The increasingly hideous tone of the GOP is a long-term brand killer; we need to stop reveling in the fuck-you culture of constant, always-on outrage and offense. It's juvenile, repellent, and self-limiting. Outrage has a reason, and a place. When it's over everything, it's about nothing.

RESPECT AND HONOR
AMERICAN INSTITUTIONS

In this post-everything world, Donald Trump is wrecking our institutions in ways more corrosive, insidious, and permanent than the wildest visions of our worst enemies.

One of the points of deep anxiety in American political life is the constellation of institutions on which we once relied have fallen into disrepute, one by one. Business, finance, the church, the education system, Congress, and many others have transformed from being the sinews that connect a society to corrupt echoes of what they once were. Trump has corrupted and broken the entire idea of the American presidency, an institution so vital and so central to American governance at home and abroad.

This is one of the biggest of big lifts in the path out of this crisis. How about a party that advocates for a world where serious people take on serious tasks in a serious way and are accountable for results? Restoring faith in institutions rests on accountability, but as a nation we've become great at ducking it. It's become a structural feature in every domain of American life, and it's wrecking the country.

The failed teacher gets promoted to a bureaucratic job with higher pay. Wall Street CEOs who make bad bets on absurd derivatives incinerate billions in the pensions and 401k accounts of Middle Americans get government bailouts and a golden parachute, not stainless steel handcuffs and a stretch in federal prison. The congressman who gets caught taking a sack full of cash to pay for his intern's abortion may lose his office, but he's back lobbying for seven figures the next year.

We blame society, genetics, the media, bad parenting, and the Colonel's addictive fried chicken, but at root, we've become comfortable blaming others for our failings. At every point on the spectrum, we want to move from failure to exoneration to reward, with never a hard look at why and with no one being held to account.

Many Trump voters have told focus groups they backed him because everything else was broken, so why not let a madman disrupt the system and drain the proverbial swamp. Their feelings came from the broken institutions around them.

A better, smarter, restored GOP can't fix every institution, but we can start by fixing ourselves. We can start by adopting and holding to a set of ethical, managerial, and behavioral standards as a model. We can become a party and a movement that stops letting our own "fail up" into positions of greater reward and consequence.

GOVERN LIKE GROWN-UPS

Trump's raging, vulgarian insult-comic shtick wore thin for most Americans during the campaign. Many more reached their limit in his first year. For too many Republicans, the desire to emulate Trump as a play to the base was all too tempting.

The House Clown Caucus of Devin Nunes, Matt Gaetz, Steve King, and others turned the formerly staid GOP into a party of derision. From the Oval Office on down, future Republicans need to consciously, mindfully conduct themselves with dignity, probity, and care. The old, abandoned face of politics that emphasized smarts, seriousness, and stature needs a comeback over the Trumpian politics-as-professional-wrestling model.

Decorum is boring, and manners are passé in the Brave New Trump World, but behaving in a way that isn't deliberately asinine and vulgar might—even for a moment—let Americans look at Republican politicians as leaders and not conspiracy-addled clowns intent on showing their asses at every turn.

Congress has become so paralyzed with its ideological rigor mortis that Americans are right to believe Washington is a place where good ideas go to die. We might start by getting back to regular order in the House and Senate, passing a budget every year, and governing like adults. Voters look at Congress as immature, messy, ineffective, and pointless, and the current crop under Trump is doing little to change that.

Both the House and Senate leadership must also discipline their members in areas ranging from ethics to affect. The majority leader and speaker have tremendous power. It's important they start to use it to impose a necessary dose of maturity and gravitas in both bodies.

KILL CRONY CAPITALISM

As a party, we've talked a great game for a long time about ending crony capitalism, the reviled system by which battalions of lobbyists advocate for tweaks to federal law and regulations for the specific benefit of their corporate clients. From the virtuous to the skeezy, from Big Corn to Big Tech to Big Sugar to Big Banks, American corporations have learned that market dominance and guaranteed profits can be ensured with Big Lobbying.

Americans know and feel that the deck is stacked against them when it comes to Washington offering the biggest, wealthiest, and most irresponsible players the power to define markets, protect themselves from risk, and leave taxpayers with the bill.

It's time to stop it. Picking winners and losers in the American economy was derided under Obama and Clinton but has become an article of faith in Trumpian economic nationalism. If we believe in free markets, it's long past time to hit the brakes on corporations using Congress to ensure their bottom lines, executive pensions, market positions, and supply chains.

STOP FIGHTING THE LAST WARS

Americans have made up their minds on gay marriage. They're fine with it, and that's not going to change in any foreseeable future. As a conservative, I don't want the state to decide who can and can't get married, but ironically there are still Republican leaders who believe that gay marriage and gay adoption are moral horrors so extreme that government must stop them. They're a shrinking number, but it's time to tell the evangelical cohort in the GOP that since they've shown their true colors by giving Donald Trump a series of mulligans on his porn-star-screwing, pussy-grabbing, serially adulterous life, they've lost their moral authority to scream at the rest of us.

Americans have also decided that they're fine with marijuana. The states have made up their minds and gotten to work taxing, regulating, and prospering from medical and recreational marijuana. The GOP needs to end the War on Drugs absurdity that costs billions, incarcerates far too many, and profits no one except the booming private prison industry.

POST-TRUMP AMERICA

THERE ARE TWO PATHS FORWARD IN OUR POLITICS: A BIG
Reset or a *Mad Max* political hellscape. I don't know yet which one is
going to happen.

THE *MAD MAX* OUTCOME

Let's get the bad news out of the way first. As poorly as Trumpism
scales, and as strongly as it repels most people who have a conscience,
there is something attractive about casting off the boring strictures
and structures for those who think this is their one shot at permanent,
transformative power. This is how authoritarian regimes boot up: the
self-fulfilling idea "This is our one shot, and damn the rules." The slope
is slippery, the descent is fast, and the regimes that slip away from
democracy and freedom do it a little at a time, and then all at once.
You'll pardon me for being skeptical after the past two years that any
meaningful firewall exists in the corridors of Washington power to
stop the transition from America to something . . . darker.

Always plan for the worst, prepare for the crash, expect the disaster, and be ready for Murphy's law to obtain in any political crisis. A
plan beats no plan, every time, and even if it's a plan for the end of the
GOP and conservatism as we know it, it's a useful exercise to wargame
out the worst case.

Join me for a quick tour of American politics in October 2024.

Trump himself died of a massive stroke in December the year before. Sarah Huckabee Sanders insisted to the press for months that the
president had not died after eating two buckets of KFC and slugging
down a magnum of gravy, but leaked photos from Barron Trump's
iPhone XII disproved this.

Donald Trump Jr., the current Republican nominee, had replaced
Mike Pence as vice president shortly after the 2020 election and had
been named president after his father's death. As an aside, Pence was
happy to finally leave the White House and spend more time with
Mother and the Pence Center for People Who Are Totally Straight
and Don't Need Anyone Assuming Their Anxiety About Gay People
Means They're Curious about the Touch of the Same Sex.

Don Jr.'s campaign eschewed the trappings of the traditional race.
Relying on rallies closed to the media but broadcast on the Trump
TV network, Fox, and Facebook Live, the younger Trump's campaign
enraged the press. He had become an even more inflammatory social media presence than his father. Media outlets opposing Trump
had increasingly come under pressure from all sides, including a slow
increase of political violence against reporters from publications considered hostile to the White House.

The worship of Donald Trump the Elder by his small but intense
core had taken on a religious fervor. Trump supporters recounted
miracles of how Don Jr.'s father's touch healed scrofula, restored sight
in the blind, raised the dead, and generated miraculous meals of over-
done steaks and Filet-O-Fish.

From 2016 until 2024 the Republican Party and the conservative
movement had slowly become entirely defined by Trump and Trump
juche. Wrote one conservative opinion leader on the pages of the recently merged Breitbart-Federalist–Gateway Pundit site, "Those laws
and principles that made the GOP so impotent and weak are for a
nation that is impotent and weak. Loyalty to the Leader, the Party, and
the State are now the principles that define conservatism."

Another wrote, "We were too cautious about embracing strong
state power and a dominant executive. We know Trump's leadership

has saved America and Trumpism is the future. It needs a powerful government to match a powerful man's legacy. Even our 'allies' in Congress hid their cuckish cowardice behind a phony love of their 'coequal' branch. If they want to be coequal, they should run for president."

Articles like "Is It Time to Kill the Cucks? (Politically)" and "Trump Poll Shows Trump Voters View Trump as Greatest President in History of World Because MAGA Hillary for Prison" proliferated. Sarah Huckabee Sander's Pepe the Frog lapel pin caused quite a stir.

Conservative media outlets had fallen, one by one, as they had been bought out, sued to death by the Peter Thiels of the world, or seen their audiences slip into the warm embrace of stupid. Republicans cheered the end of legal accountability for the president and viewed the ruthless will to power and a boundless sense of outrage as the only metrics of leadership.

Trump found, and Americans learned, that there was nothing he could do that struck the conscience of congressional Republicans. There was nothing he couldn't escape by stoking resentments against either the news media or the hated Establishment. While scandal after scandal built around Trump, it seemed only to harden the resolve of his legions of fans and his diminished cadre of congressional allies.

As Mueller's probe put Trump associates and family members in jail for both obstruction of justice and conspiracy, they screamed louder about Hillary's emails and Uranium One. Though Manafort, Stone, Cohen, and others were left to die in jail, Jared had been pardoned after 11 months of his sentence, after his father-in-law had sufficient time to "comfort" Ivanka.

Evangelicals confronted with Stormy Daniels, various baby mama dramas, and then a string of other Trump affairs with porn stars, escorts, models, and other women shrugged and offered mulligan after mulligan. Melania's departure from the White House, and the return of Hope Hicks, this time as First Lady, in the weeks before his death left them gushing about how Donald Trump *truly* loves the institution of marriage.

The slow-motion divorce from the mainstream of American politics with the adoption of Trumpism was an electoral death wish for the GOP. Democrats dominated the U.S. House, and Speaker Pelosi at age 84 still clung to office, frankly intimidating in her robot exoskeleton. Democrats had gained back vast power in the states as GOP legislative offices fell.

African Americans, traditionally a lost cause for the GOP, became even more so, their GOP support numbers in the 2% range. Trump Jr. continued his father's flirtations with the alt-right, and few forgave his remark that Richard Spencer "had a lot of good in him" after the white nationalist had been found dead of autoerotic asphyxiation while wearing an SS uniform and a tutu.

Hispanics built a Wall, all right, an electoral wall in a dozen states that switched from Republican to Democratic control. California, Oregon, and Washington had seceded from the nation in all but name, largely ignoring Federal law on marijuana, immigration, and the environment. The 2018–2021 Trade War, $6-a-gallon gas, and sky-high health insurance premiums left the economy reeling.

A rising tide of slightly less liberal centrist Democrats took seats in the Midwest and the suburbs of major cities throughout the Deep South. They were propelled there by a wave of educated women fleeing the GOP for good. Educated men were following quickly, leaving the Party of Lincoln as the Party of the GED. Millennials, long a target of every political interest, were displaying solidly Democratic voting behavior.

The people who clung to Trump ran the Republican Party, though. Their desire to defeat Democrats after three consecutive legislative beat-downs was nowhere near as passionate as their hatred for anyone even slightly Trump-skeptical. The Trump cadre's atavistic lust for the purge, the long knives, the broken glass, the savage blog post, and the whiff of grapeshot led to many moderate GOP elected officials caucusing as independents. Others fled for third parties, a small but fast-growing contingent on the American political landscape.

Primary elections became heated contests as to which candidate had been with Trump sooner and more passionately. Trump stamps and MAGA tattoos were a frequent sight, and the number of candidates who had named their children Donald, Ivanka, Eric, and Melania was remarkable. Candidates stopped pledging allegiance to tired things like the flag and the Constitution, and instead pledged to always serve the Trump agenda and their undying loyalty to Trump and his family. Violent altercations were increasingly common.

Bob Mueller's death in mysterious circumstances just after he indicted Erik Prince and Steve Bannon remains unexplained. Jim Comey's disappearance, a wave of assassinations of media personalities, and the plane crash that killed Rick Wilson and Bill Kristol raised eyebrows, but were mostly greeted by Fox headlines celebrating the end of a last few noisy voices critical of The Trump Dynasty.

THE BIG RESET

I do know that for all the trauma, stress, pain, humiliation, embarrassment, and bad hair role-modeling Trump has given this nation, there are many reasons to remain militantly optimistic about our future. America's political immune system is resilient, but we often have to hit the highest fever, the worst pain, and the deepest shock before the T-cells of our values, history, and national character kick in.

I continue to believe that in the future Trump will be viewed as an aberration, a deviation from an arc of history that has produced leaders who, however flawed, were eventually constrained by a basic, deeply wired respect for the nation, the Constitution, and the rule of law. After all, even Nixon chose not to destroy the nation.

I believe that we've entered an era in which the policies of both parties, particularly in economics, are overcome by events, swept aside by technology, and joyously and painfully disrupted. No, Republicans aren't getting a million coal miners going down-pit again. No, Democrats, you're not going to get a massive technocracy telling me what kind of toilet paper and lightbulbs I should use.

I believe that the cranky, geriatric conservatism of the post-2010 era—oppositional, increasingly comfortable with racial hostility, closed to the world, revanchist, and addled by conspiracy—is a deviation from, not an alteration of conservative principles. Some of the conservative movement's "leaders"—a term now fraught with images of weakness, compromise, and hypocrisy—will need to be exiled or at the least parked for a time in some kind of political lazaretto until they see the error of their ways.

I believe there's so much to be done, so many challenges, and so much more to achieve as a nation in a complex world because the demise of Trumpism is as inevitable as it is desirable. It's a 19th-century political movement in the era of technological and social uplift that was unimaginable a few decades ago.

Being such an acid-tongued bastard, it sometimes gets lost that it's not simply that I hate Donald Trump. It's not simply that I loathe his status as a shit-tier human in every measurable axis and think he's a stain on the presidency. It's that I love this big, messy, chaotic experiment we call America. It's because deep in my heart, I know that the country I love is tougher and vastly better than he is and, when called to its higher purpose, always answers.

We've almost blown it a dozen times in history, but some providential hand steers us away from the cliff. We've been hit hard by foreign powers—Pearl Harbor, 9/11, the Russian information war of 2016, and Milli Vanilli in the 1980s—but we always rally. We always recover. We always rise from the wreckage. Churchill was right: Americans will always do the right thing after exhausting every other option.

Trump is a problem we'll be a long time in solving. The damage to our institutions, our hopes, and our reputation in the world won't be undone overnight or with a few sweet words. It will take work and commitment from people on the conservative side of the equation to admit and rectify the dangerous flirtation with authoritarian statism Trump represents.

It's not impossible. Far from it; it's vital.

On the eve of the Civil War, Ulysses S. Grant wrote his father, then living in the South, a brief letter. At that moment, South Carolina had seceded from the Union and Fort Sumter had been fired upon. The cataclysm of the War between the States was upon us.

At a dark moment of my own just after election day in 2016, a mentor reminded me of Grant's letter. One paragraph struck and comforted me then, as it does now:

> Whatever may have been my political opinions before, I have but one sentiment now. That is, we have a Government, and laws and a flag, and they must all be sustained. There are but two parties now, traitors and patriots, and I want hereafter to be ranked with the latter, and I trust, the stronger party. I do not know but you may be placed in an awkward position, and a dangerous one pecuniarily, but costs cannot now be counted. My advice would be to leave where you are if you are not safe with the views you entertain. I would never stultify my opinion for the sake of a little security.[1]

Resistance on the right to Trump isn't just out of stubbornness. It would be easy to say conservatism will survive under the moral and political disaster that is Donald Trump, but it wouldn't be honest to do so. Team MAGA and the Trump GOP would love for us to shut up and let the world burn.

The Never Trump movement was catalyzed in the 2016 election, but it exists today for a bigger purpose; we've committed to conservative, constitutional leadership for the future. We reject an all-powerful state, whether it's in the hands of a leftist technocrat or a bright-orange alt-right-curious neofascist. That's the core of Never Trump that Trump's fans don't understand. It isn't just that we loathe him personally (though that's easy to do with his horror-show affect); it's that we reject his core political tendency of authoritarian statism.

Every day that passes gives us additional evidence of how much Trump believes he can govern not under the Constitution and laws of this nation but by fits of pique, fiat, diktat, and by force of will. He either doesn't understand or doesn't respect the separation of powers and the structure of government the Founders built.

Never Trump was intended as a kind of Dunkirk for principled Republicans and conservatives. In the short term, the evacuation of Dunkirk was a victory for the Germans; they rolled into Paris unopposed on June 14, 1940. They controlled Europe until 1944. The French government capitulated, and the Vichy regime, led by Marshal Pétain, collaborated with the Nazis at every level, including playing their role in the arrest, deportation, and murder of Jews.

I know, I know. The clickservatives reading this are huffing and ready to scream that I'm violating Godwin's law and that the analogy between the GOP and Vichy is too much. Tough shit. Your willing blindness to the slippery slope of history when it comes to authoritarianism and the prospect of it in this nation disqualifies you from the discussion.

Collaboration with evil comes in many forms: grudging, tacit, overt, and enthusiastic. France experienced all those variations of cooperation with the evil of the Nazi regime. Charles de Gaulle, the Free French, and the Resistance never faltered, never accepted the Pétain regime, and never stopped fighting to recover their nation. Their privations were long, and sacrifices many.

Our effort to hold the conservative movement together by rejecting Trump as the nominee was the opening act. Those of us still standing, still able to wake up and not wonder where our souls have gone, oppose him as president not because we don't like who he is, but for what he does and fails to do.

It is to this moment a resistance of people who genuinely believe in conservative ideas and oppose politics redolent with authoritarianism, anticonstitutionalism, and personality-cult fervor that has no place in our Republic. It isn't just an aesthetic or a stylistic choice. It's about the future of the nation and about the future of conservatism.

We couldn't defeat Trump in 2016, but we refuse, no matter how much you throw at us, no matter how much venom and ire you pour down on us, to make those last compromises, to put this man and this mob ahead of this country.

We don't love this mission, but we're on it. Our Dunkirk may not be seen as a victory today in the era of raw, swaggering triumphalism and a hermetic personality cult, but it's essential to the survival of conservatism and a principled Republican Party with a brain, a heart, and a spine.

We'll fight because the risks Trump poses are too great, even if our own party brethren have sunk so deep in the comforting, expedient politics of the moment. We'll remind them that freedom isn't some easy birthright, some soft insurance policy that a Republican president could never compromise. They won't like it. They won't appreciate it. But we won't stop. Unlike Trump's collaborators, explainers, and excusers, we'll keep Reagan's words in mind:

> Freedom is never more than one generation away from extinction. We didn't pass it on to our children in the bloodstream. The only way they can inherit the freedom we have known is if we fight for it, protect it, defend it and then hand it to them with the well thought lessons of how they in their lifetime must do the same. And if you and I don't do this, then you and I may well spend our sunset years telling our children and our children's children what it once was like in America when men were free.[2]

Like the Guilty Men of Great Britain who sought peace at any price with Herr Hitler, the new establishment conservatives who seek Trump at any price to the country, the movement, and the party will have to contend with the stubborn, angry, determined minority of us who still stand for something more than Nielsen ratings and the Twitter fury of a game show host masquerading as a president. Perhaps none of us who remain on the right and still standing is a Churchill, but all of us believe this fight isn't over, isn't optional, and isn't going to end without blood, sweat, toil, and tears.

Everything about Donald Trump's presidency and character is a disaster for America. The victories Republicans think they have achieved are transitory and ephemeral and come at the cost of their principles and, probably, their immortal souls. He is a stain on the party, on conservatism, and on this country that won't easily wash out.

Our goal is not simply to stop Trump's excesses, corruptions, and degradations of what America is and should be. It is to stop the rise of another Trump from those who would follow in his footsteps, to kill in the political cradle those with better social skills but the same agenda of discord, division, and radical, anticonstitutional statism. Our goal should be to end the era of entertainment conservatism and to select candidates for their quality, not their celebrity.

If I hadn't taken up this fight, I would be richer, still loved on the right, and able to stay in the same lane I'd been in for years as a partisan warrior who took up the fights of my tribe without a second thought. I could have kept my stable of clients, kept moving forward in a world where the compensation for discarding my principles had a lot of zeroes behind it.

The attacks on me, my family, and my clients were a cost I've paid in full for opposing Donald Trump from the right. There were days where I feared I'd lose everything in this battle, and yet some stubborn love of my country and my party kept me pushing forward. The oddest part of this battle is the feeling of liberation and serenity I have felt from the very start. When challenged once with the question "How's that Never Trump thing going, Rick?" I replied, "Fabulously. I never have to defend a verbally incontinent, psychologically unbalanced, grotesquely ignorant failure who is reviled by his country, mocked by the rest of the world, and who embarrasses himself and the nation with every crude, impulsive act."[3]

I have never been alone in this fight, and the support of friends on the right who are both openly and secretly opposed to Trump has consistently been a source of strength. The network of people who understand the risks and the dangers we face and are working tirelessly to oppose him is broader than Trump's supporters know. (P.S. Don, some of them work in the White House.)

I sleep well at night and wake up ready to be in the fight every day, and with the certain knowledge that men and women of good faith on the right are in that fight with me.

Though there are days I miss the camaraderie of people I fought long and hard with in elections and policy battles for 30 years, the comfort of that tribal campfire has faded. The Republican Party I knew and loved now feels like an armed camp in a third-world nation, full of informers and enforcers all seeking to curry favor with the Maximum Leader. The cultlike edge is not a flavor of conservatism with which I will ever be comfortable.

I'll leave you with another Churchill quote, as true today as it was then: "I have, myself, full confidence that if all do their duty, if nothing is neglected, and if the best arrangements are made, as they are being made, we shall prove ourselves once more able to defend our island home, to ride out the storm of war, and to outlive the menace of tyranny, if necessary for years, if necessary alone."[4]

Also, Trump has tiny, tiny hands.

A NOTE ON THE PAPERBACK EDITION

THE ORIGINAL HARDCOVER VERSION OF THIS BOOK WAS submitted, with me kicking and screaming, on April 15, 2018. My editor and agent had to pry me away from the keyboard because the endless, gushing sewer of Donald Trump's presidency provided a constant stream of new excesses and outrages to chronicle, new stumbles by this incompetent and corrupt president to ridicule, and daily proofs of my ETTD theory.

Reaction to the book has been beyond my wildest expectations. My travels around the country promoting it have given me a window into the deep pain, searing anger, and profound resilience of this nation in the era of Trump. I'm profoundly grateful for the thousands of emails, letters, and encounters with folks touched by the book. I've also continued to get more death threats than the average Afghan government official and have dealt with my share of angry Trump cultists (but that's redundant), including one charming fellow who almost lost his last few teeth when he decided to spit on me in an airport. My stalker emails continue to be spectacular, if mostly incoherent.

When the hardcover version hit #1 on the *New York Times* bestseller list, a friend observed that at last Donald Trump and I had something in common. The difference between us is, of course, that I wrote every word of *my* book.

As there is no better iteration of Trump, no improvement is ever possible. Like heat entropy, Trump naturally devolves into more chaos, more static, and more failure. You're now reading the paper-back version because it seemed imperative to poke the monster again, to remind him not only of the scope of his shortcomings but also of the continued, vexing presence of Americans not tainted by his vulgarian indecency and corruption.

It's good to be right, even when the subject one is right about is so wrong, so I would be remiss if I didn't take a victory lap.

TRUMP, THE "MAN"

The presidency always illuminates the real character of the man who holds the office. Action, affect, policy, rhetoric, and politics combine to paint a vivid picture of every president's leadership. Dorian Orange must have a portrait in a closet somewhere in the White House Residence showing a fit, virile, and handsome man of wisdom, dignity, temperament, and compassion, because the creature on our every screen most certainly has none of those qualities.

Unstable on the best of days, his temperament has become even more outrageously unhinged and undignified. His just-under-the-surface anger breaches the water like a rabid orange whale almost daily, his tweeted ragestorms immolating the targets of his boundless enmity. Trump's daily whining is both petty and vainglorious, a constant, grating static on every screen and every social media platform.

Trump's physical frame has continued to edge closer and closer to parody. The absurd claims that he clocks in at 239 pounds, that his fierce updo is real, and that he's a paragon of masculine virtues have grown all the more laughable. His KFC-fed booty, quivering FUPA, and enormous, gravid chin-mass resist even the most heroic efforts of Spanx, makeup, and lighting. We're one idiot advisor short of Trump traveling by palanquin from the Residence to the Oval Office.

It seems a small thing, but one of Trump's repeated conceits during the 2016 campaign was the constant chest-beating talk of his strength, stamina, energy, and personal endurance. Apparently, a chilly November drizzle in France in 2018 was enough to put the lie to this particular con. Trump refused to travel to a World War I memorial event where he might suffer in the chilly rain and his umber bronzer might run down his soft, gelatinous jowls. Unlike Canada's prime minister Justin Trudeau, who, on the centennial of the Armistice that ended World War I, cast aside his umbrella, and delivered a speech in the rain to praise the courage of his nation's troops in the Great War.

Cadet Bone Spurs has also been shown, like all bullies, to be a sniveling coward. Trump's refusal to visit American troops abroad in anything close to a war zone wasn't some fifth-dimensional chess game about the ongoing wars in Afghanistan and the Middle East, but rather his pathetic physical cowardice.[1] Trump, the smack-talking, dick-swinging, faux-alpha is afraid of standing anywhere near the line of fire, unlike every single American president before him. The *Washington Post* reported, "He's never been interested in going. He's afraid of those situations. He's afraid people want to kill him."

THE BEST PEOPLE

Since the publication of the hardcover version of *Everything Trump Touches Dies*, the churn in Trump White House personnel has been like watching a rat in a blender. You may not *like* rats, but what the blender does to them is bloody and horrific. The pattern I described in the hardcover edition has played out over and over again, an inevitable arc from lavish praise to exile.

The day after the 2018 election results were in, Trump naturally fired Attorney General Jeff Sessions. Sessions, who in every other aspect save his recusal in the Russia investigation was a perfectly obedient handmaiden for Trump's agenda, had been a dead man walking for

some time. He gleefully executed Trump's border war follies, fought
for Trump's Muslim ban, and weaponized the Justice Department for
the infamous "kids in cages" horror show.

None of it was good enough. Sessions, the ur-supporter of Team
MAGA, is a perfect example of how Trump is never satisfied. No sacrifice is *ever* sufficient; had Sessions fired his deputy, Rod Rosenstein,
to get to Robert Mueller, or had he blocked the special counsel in
some other way, the former Alabama senator would have been in clear
violation of the law and even the Trump administration's lax ethical
standards. You can almost hear Trump whining, "But why *won't* Jeff
go to jail for me? Why isn't he loyal?"

For months, Trump's legal team had cautioned him against firing Sessions, but it was all for naught. Trump's elevation of Matthew
Whitaker as acting attorney general smacked of a level of desperation
even Trump's worst enemies could hardly have imagined.

Whitaker is a walking roid-rage episode, dead-eyed, bullet-headed,
and every bit the Trumpian commissar the Donald wanted at DOJ.
Whitaker, who had made disqualifying statements on the Mueller
probe, declared he'd prosecute Hillary Clinton, and expressed an apparent desire to obstruct both large-J Justice and small-j justice, once
worked for a shady invention patent-marketing company that featured
scams like Bitcoin-powered investments in . . . wait for it . . . time
travel.[2] Armies of comedy screenwriters would labor for a generation
to write a character so reflective of our times.

The ETTD rule seems to hit attorneys attached to the Trump enterprise particularly hard. White House Counsel Don McGahn was
dismissed shortly after it was revealed that he had a brain. In August 2018, the *New York Times* reported that McGahn had provided
Mueller's team with "detailed accounts about the episodes at the heart
of the inquiry into whether President Trump obstructed justice, including some that investigators would not have learned of otherwise,
according to a dozen current and former White House officials and
others briefed on the matter."[3] McGahn, seeking to protect the institution of the presidency, found himself forced to tell the truth about

the president he served, and to the one man Trump fears most: Robert Mueller. Whoops.

It also became apparent that former Trump counsel Ty Cobb's elaborate mustache wouldn't save him from a client who is, to put it mildly, a lying liar who lies. Cobb sought to protect Trump from his habit of pathologically distorting the truth, even when perjury was on the line. After a while, he realized two things: first, Trump was always going to lie; second, he would drag down everyone around him into the mire of his deceptions, so Cobb wisely got the hell out of that blast radius.

My old boss Rudy Giuliani joined Team Trump, burning down his reputation and aping the Trump style and affect in an endless string of TV-lawyer appearances. The broad network of Giuliani alumni who have known and worked for him since even before I joined his team in 1997 have stared in shock at this iteration of Rudy. The man they once knew and admired, the hero who turned New York around in the 1990s and stood firm on 9/11 is a diminished figure in service to a corrupt and corrupting president. Trump is the kind of man Rudy the prosecutor would have put behind bars. Now he's fighting to keep Trump out of jail. It's not pretty.

John Kelly finally slipped through the ice, leaving Washington at the time of this writing obsessed with finding the next victim to serve in the most thankless job in Washington, DC. Wrangling the Toddler in Chief is an impossible task on the best days, and Kelly had no best days. By the end, he looked like a man who clocked in every day, choked down several Xanax, knocked back a fifth of Olde Ocelot, and started riding the tiger. It was exhausting just to look at him. Nick Ayers, who as one of the more politically skilled candidates for the job, had served ably as chief of staff to Vice President Mike Pence was offered the position and turned it down.

Sarah Huckabee Sanders continues to gamely mount the White House press room podium at random intervals, hewing closely to the crayon-scribbled talking points that come wafting out of the Oval Office like a fart at the opera. Her dead-eyed expression as she plays out the endless, painful kabuki of Trump's media war is a window into what she knows is an infinite future of explaining away her words and actions. When Stockholm syndrome is your best excuse for behavior, it's time to seek other employment.

Speaking of the best people, former Trump campaign chairman Paul Manafort will die in prison, particularly after he played games with Special Counsel Mueller's investigation by back-channeling information to the Trump defense team after taking a generous plea agreement from Mueller.

As we go to press, the walls are closing in fast on a host of Trump-Russia players, including Michael Cohen, Roger Stone, Jerome Corsi, and Donald Trump Jr. Go long on popcorn stocks.

PROMISES AND PROSPECTS

Remember when Obama's trillion-dollar deficits were an existential threat to the nation, an immediate, looming crisis of such grim fiscal import that unless quick, punitive spending cuts were imposed we would be reduced to a country where the living would envy the dead, dogs and cats would live in sin together, and our grandchildren would pick through the ruins clothed only in primitive tunics woven out of quadrillion-dollar Amero notes? That was before the King of Debt became president and his obedient minions in Congress couldn't stop themselves from a hearty "MOAR!" at every spending bill.

After years of Fed-fueled economic growth, the deficit should have continued declining steadily. Instead the deficit rose for the first time in six years, hitting almost $800 billion in 2018. Given the massive tax bill's costs, Trump's massive increases in defense spending, and the economic ruin coming in the form of a trade war, the U.S. deficit and debt are on track to rise dramatically in the coming two years. The GOP's desire to be seen as the party of fiscal discipline is, to put it mildly, strained to the breaking point.[4]

For all its promises as a potent economic and political tool, the Republican tax plan for which Trump wrongly claims so much credit has led to exactly the outcomes its skeptics predicted and none of the political benefits. The perception and reality of the tax bill merged in the minds of taxpayers; it was a sugar rush for Wall Street, not Main Street.

Mere tax cuts alone aren't conservative; this bill was a crony capitalist wonderland, and voters knew it. It was the most expensive campaign stunt in history; I'm sure future generations will be grateful that hedge funds and lobbyists made out like bandits.

Coal mines, steel mills, and iron works continue to stoke some weird Trumpian fantasy about the industrial past. There's just one problem; they still aren't coming back at scale. Since the hardcover edition of *Everything Trump Touches Dies*, Trump's obsession with keeping the Upper Midwest Dying Steel Town demo in line has grown more visible, even as the delta between fantasy and reality grows wider.

Trade wars are easy to win, right? Just ask the midwestern farmers who voted for Trump in massive numbers as they face the global collapse of their markets for soybeans, corn, and hogs. The idea that the genius negotiator was going to bring China and other trading partners to heel was central to his image and, like most of his image, was an illusion. Wall Street, knowing the end of easy Fed money is upon them, is growing nervous over trade. As I write this, GM is closing plants in North America, in part because of Trump's idiotic trade war. One of the core tests of 2020 is how long Trump's hold over blue-collar workers lasts as the impacts of his policies lead to the loss of their jobs.

Trump's hatred of the NAFTA trade agreement led to endless histrionics about the Worst Deal Ever Ever Ever, constant huffing and puffing with Canada and Mexico, and finally a sweeping victory for the president. And by "sweeping victory" I mean that they rebranded the existing NAFTA deal with a new name and called it a day. It was a triumph of Trumpian bullshitting.

Oh, and there's still no Wall on American's southern border. Trump's core promise, the one item his followers could recite by heart if you woke them from a sound sleep, is still the vaporware it's always been. I suppose, in Trumpian fashion, Mexico's check is still in the mail.

THE ELECTIONS OF 2018

Elections, famously, have consequences, and the 2018 congressional races were precisely the kind of wipeout I warned my fellow Republicans would come. For the whole of 2018, Republicans merrily bent over and shoved their heads up their collective asses, pretending that Trump wasn't going to drag them under. The GOP just spent $1 billion to get pantsed by the Democrats in the 2018 elections.

Let's survey the carnage, shall we?

Remember when I warned my fellow Republicans that Trump was leading the GOP into a demographic ditch? Or that abandoning every principle to become the political lackeys, lickspittles, and handmaidens of Donald Trump would leave them vulnerable to even marginally qualified Democratic candidates stealing their lunch money, to say nothing of their seats? Suburban women, who separated from the GOP in 2016, made the divorce final in 2018. They delivered massive margins for Democrats in vital swing states for one big reason, and that reason is bloated, largely orange, and sports an exotic coif. Deus ex Kavanaugh wasn't enough to give the GOP the Red Wave that Trump promised them.

I warned Republicans that leading their Obamacare repeal efforts with a bill that struck down coverage for preexisting conditions would be a political disaster, and it was. GOP candidates spent tens of millions of dollars on television and digital ads in the closing weeks of the campaign of 2018 staring teary-eyed into the camera and promising to never, ever, ever repeal coverage for preexisting conditions. Oopsie.

The GOP's new philosophical center—culture wars, media hating, lib owning, Trump fellating, xenophobia, and mainstreaming racial separatists—unsurprisingly went over like a lead balloon. Voters cited health care as by far the central issue in the 2018 campaign; a plurality of 41% called it the most important issue, and 75% of those voters cast a Democratic ballot.

The GOP has always had an age problem, and now it's more pronounced than ever; Donald Trump's dominance at the far right of the actuarial curve is unquestioned. Younger voters in the 18-to-29 demo rose from 11% in 2014 to 13% of the electorate in 2018, and they voted Democratic by a 66–32% margin. It seems like a small rise, but for a group usually considered nonvoters, it mattered in key races nationwide.

Married women—the vaunted "soccer moms" and "security moms" and "health care moms" of prior elections—are the coveted suburban demographic that turns out to vote with enormous regularity and commitment; in 2016 Trump lost them by 2%. In 2018 Republicans lost them by 10%. Educated women have fled the GOP in waves, leading to suburban blowouts in 2018 and beyond. Something about a president at the top of a party acting like the worst first husband ever may have something to do with it. Educated women voted 59–39% Democratic, and women overall voted 59–40% Democratic. If the GOP wants to be the party of 55+ white dudes with only a high school education and a penchant for online conspiracy theories, they're well on the way.

As for Hispanics, African Americans, and Asian Americans, well, the GOP might as well just stop hiring minority outreach folks, because these groups turned out in record numbers, with results that should—but won't—give the Trump GOP pause. Despite Trump's "Why aren't you grateful to me?" message to minorities, 90% of African Americans voted Democratic, as did 69% of Hispanics and 77% of Asians.

The House

Democrats won a resounding victory in the House, with a net gain of forty seats as of press time. The doomed GOP members in swing districts went down in flames, cursed by their need to pretend Trump was mostly normal if they were to stave off primary challenges. Democrats elected a spectrum of candidates for once in their lives; it wasn't just far-left stars like Alexandria Ocasio-Cortez; Conor Lamb, the hero of the PA-18 election of 2018, won and won big, as did a number of other Democratic House candidates who were—for once—the right fit for their districts.

The blowouts in suburban districts were impressive enough, but California's political bloodbath saw the GOP there nearly collapse, and Trump is the proximate cause. Republicans lost seats in conservative Orange County and the Central Valley, once the home of Reagan Republicans.

The Senate

The GOP opened 2018 boasting they could pick up a half-dozen seats in the Senate. It was an unfortunate example of political overpromising and underperforming. The GOP won North Dakota and Missouri, two states already trending hard red in recent years, and they held on to Tennessee and Mississippi, which is unsurprising, given how Republican both states are. But after that, the news wasn't pretty.

In Texas, Beto O'Rourke gave Ted Cruz a near-death experience. Process that, friends. Cruz won, but Texas was a competitive race for the first time in a generation, and Cruz has his frenemy Donald Trump to thank for it.

In Michigan and Wisconsin, GOP Senate candidates who in a normal Republican presidency would have been highly competitive were dragged under water. In Michigan, John James was out of central casting: African American, conservative, a decorated war veteran, and a business leader. His embrace of MAGAisma was also instant political death in the suburbs of Detroit, which make up much of the vote.

Nevada's Dean Heller and Arizona's Martha McSally embraced Trump to avoid lunatic MAGA primary challengers, and both of them lost. Both states were once GOP bastions, but oddly enough, a president who loathes, insults, and demonizes Hispanics at every opportunity is a drag on Republican candidates there.

Rick Scott won a Florida seat after a grinding recount drama and spending almost $60 million of his own money in a $100 million effort. To Scott's credit, he spent millions convincing Puerto Rican voters in Florida (who, contrary to what Trump likely believes, are U.S. citizens) he was on their side.

Governors and State Legislatures

Democrats picked up seven governors' mansions in the 2018 elections, losing Florida and Georgia in the narrowest of margins.

Nevada, New Mexico, Maine, Wisconsin, Illinois, Kansas, and Michigan flipped to the Democrats. In two of those cases, the reek of the ETTD curse was truly powerful. For Governor Scott Walker of Wisconsin, a booming state economy and strong "right direction" polling numbers weren't enough to overcome the visceral, passionate hatred of Trump in the suburbs of Milwaukee, where women voters nuked him into the Stone Age.

In a delicious ETTD moment, Kris Kobach, a man who makes Stephen Miller look like a dangerous accommodationist left-wing softie on immigration, ran and lost in the Kansas gubernatorial contest. Kobach, who in full disclosure was a client once in the early 2000s, transformed himself into a more-Trump-than-Trump candidate and was rejected even in deep-red Kansas. It was the first GOP statewide loss in Kansas in 12 years.

"Kobach trusted that his regular presence on cable news, dominance in headlines and the full-throated support of Trump would carry him to victory,"[5] suggested the *Kansas City Star*. As I've written before, the Trump model of campaigns doesn't scale. Only Trump is Trump, and that's not a compliment.

More important, there were signs down the ballot that the Trump death touch had spread into races and places the GOP had long taken for granted. Nationally over 330 Republican state legislators lost their seats. The Democrats took control of the state senate chambers in Colorado, Maine, and New York, and the state house chambers in Minnesota and New Hampshire. They established supermajorities in the California, Connecticut, and Oregon senate chambers, and in the Illinois, Nevada, and Oregon house chambers, while the GOP lost supermajority status in the Michigan, Texas, and Pennsylvania senate, and in North Carolina's house and senate.

The conceit that Trump had permanently captured the swing voters of the upper Midwest in places like Michigan, Wisconsin, and Pennsylvania was shattered. Democrats overperformed in all three, winning state legislative and U.S. congressional seats in results that would make a cautious, analytical GOP step back and analyze what went wrong. Since in the era of Trump it is heresy to blame the Maximum Leader for devastating losses, you can expect them to remain silent.

DISASTERS OVERSEAS

Donald Trump's North Korean debacle was one absolutely no one could see coming, except for, well, everyone. Trump was played and played hard by Kim Jong Un, who has continued to merrily develop plutonium-enrichment facilities and long-range missiles. As if the eye-rolling wasn't bad enough when it became utterly evident how badly the wee Korean dictator had pantsed Trump, this line of Trump's took the cake: "I was really being tough and so was he. And we would go back and forth. And then we fell in love, okay? No really. He wrote me beautiful letters. And they're great letters. And then we fell in love."[6]

They. Fell. In. Love. Imagine for a hot nanosecond Barack Obama saying that. The GOP and the conservative media would have erupted into a towering volcano of outrage, calls for impeachment, and accusations that POTUS was trying to mainstream gay marriage. Predictably enough, however, the supine GOP laughed if off, even as the intelligence community exposed the scope of Trump's utter failure.

The bill for an American president adopting the corrosive and dangerous philosophy of nationalist populism came due on the 100th anniversary of the Armistice that ended World War I. It has become clear that Donald Trump is no long even *a* leader of the free world, much less *the* leader of the free world.

A single moment on the reviewing stand at the Armistice celebration spoke volumes. As Russia's kleptocratic dictator Vladimir Putin approached the assembled leaders, Trump grinned and bounced up and down like a trucker ready for his first lap dance since payday.

Putin, seeing his lackey displaying the correct attitude of obedience and deference, shot his American vassal a broad grin and a thumbs-up. Everyone should at least once in their life have a lover who looks at them the way Trump looked at Putin at that moment in Paris.

As German chancellor Angela Merkel and French president Emmanuel Macron stared at Putin with steely-eyed resolve, Trump's eyes were wide, his mouth locked in an enormous grin. It was an ironic picture: Trump, a man who seethes with a desire to be seen as the alpha male, the macho silverback gorilla, was practically erect from Putin's approval, a feat that normally requires a horse-cart of Viagra and a team of highly compensated adult-film actresses engaged in exotic gymnastics with a baby pool, a stuffed goose, gold paint, and a gimp suit.

Macron's pointed remarks that day about nationalism were a reminder of the new security architecture emerging throughout the world. Donald Trump has made America less trusted, less relevant, and weaker in the face of Russian, Chinese, and nonstate terrorist aggression in the world. His endless, juvenile bleating about defense burden-sharing and trade with Europe plays to a narrow audience back home but reduces the American president to a clownish figure, secondary and trivial in international affairs.

Trump has finally erected a Wall, but it isn't on America's southern border. The wall he built divides America from allies once bonded by a joint commitment to freedom, liberty, economic free markets, and the sovereignty of the West.

Trump's continued love of dictators, autocrats, thugs, and strongmen played out in the closing weeks of 2018, when *Washington Post* journalist Jamal Ahmad Khashoggi was lured to a meeting in Turkey and tortured, murdered, and dismembered by Saudi security forces loyal to Crown Prince Mohammed Bin Salman. The murder of Khashoggi, an American resident, was leaked by Turkish security services, confirmed by the CIA, and dismissed by Trump, who shrugged it off with his usual amoral aplomb. In secret, Trump's son-in-law Jared Kushner was advising the Saudi leader on how to "weather the storm."

More than almost any other act in the foreign policy domain, the Khashoggi murder left the world watching America for a sign, any sign, that this former bastion of freedom was still willing to draw a bright line, to defend a free press as essential and to protect its reporters from torture and murder. But the world saw only Trump excusing the Khashoggi murder by praising U.S.-Saudi arms deals—a combination of venality, cruelty, and, most disturbingly, jealousy.

A sweeping contagion of authoritarian-curious tyrants will no longer need to peer into the depths of history for role models, but can simply look to the current president of United States. They can dabble in the oppression, murder, cruelty, and cynicism the U.S. once condemned without fear of American moral or international leadership. They can kill journalists, shutter the free presses, and silence dissent. They can now point to the man who sullies the Oval Office for at least two more years, and smile, knowing Trump has adopted all the worst tropes of the bully, the tyrant, the thug, the blood-and-soil nationalists, and the desert-kingdom dictators.

WIND AND TIDE

On my book tour and on speaking engagements I've met hundreds of people who ask me some variation of this simple question: "How much longer? How can we endure this?"

I have an answer for you, and it's more cheerful than you might think. We're going to make it through Trump. He's not invulnerable, and to quote the ancient sacred texts of the movie *Predator*, "If it bleeds, we can kill it."

Take heart. The wind and tide have turned heavily against Donald Trump, and his future is far less certain or appealing than his media cheerleaders, GOP defenders, and starry-eyed cultists would have you believe. America woke up to Trump's game in 2018, and the next two years promise to be a well-deserved hell. He's a president who has never cracked 50% in approval ratings. Americans in overwhelming numbers believe that he is a chronic liar. His base is shrinking.

While Trump and his fans believe Nancy Pelosi will be an effective foil in Congress, they once again face the same problem: they have not reckoned on the loss of the majority in the House and its impacts on his presidency.

Republicans may hate Pelosi with a hot burning fire, but she's got a passionate House and a committed Democratic base and can both count and whip votes. Set aside the political utility the GOP finds in Pelosi during campaign season, and you'll discover not one smart member of the GOP caucus is optimistic they'll roll her.

On the investigatory front, Trump has nothing but trouble ahead. Robert Mueller, seeking to avoid accusations that he was trying to upset the political balance in the country, went quiet for the few weeks before the election, but his formidable machine is, at the time of this writing, rumbling to life again, to the nervous chagrin of Team Trump. They recognize there aren't many days left when the "Witch hunt!" excuse will hold up. Even his allies fear Trump's next steps and wonder how to get him to listen to any kind of legal advice at all, and specifically how to prevent him from either perjuring himself or being busted for the ongoing obstruction of justice in which he is so evidently engaged.

Mueller is careful where Trump is impetuous. Mueller is strategic where Trump is instinctive. Trump's desire is to protect his finances, his family, and his presidency, in that order. But underneath it all lies the very real fear in Trump's heart that more than his involvement with Russia will come to light; he is utterly terrified we'll learn the truth about his finances and his taxes. Trump fears revelations about his business ties and knows an offshoot of the Mueller investigation (to say nothing of the Democratic takeover of Congress) just might blow out of the water the con that is his entire reputation as a brilliant billionaire mogul. The truth is coming, and coming fast.

Playtime is over.

WHY I FIGHT

It's October 2018, and I'm in the Charlotte Airport, waiting for a delayed flight, when hunger overcomes me and I wander over to the main terminal to get something, anything that even vaguely keeps me in ketosis. I settle for BBQ. While I'm in line, a young black woman walks up and speaks to one of the women behind the counter. She had ordered something a moment before and didn't get the right side items. I wasn't paying attention until then, but her accent catches my ear.

She is wearing a food service uniform from one of the other airport restaurants: logoed polo shirt and ball cap. Her round, dark face is framed by hip glasses, and she stands all of 4-feet-10. She gets her food and gives me a two-second look. I smile, go back to placing my order, and figure that's that. A polite nod in an airport.

The dining area is slammed. There are perhaps two dozen four-seat tables, and almost every single one has just one person hogging it. I spot the one table that's open and seize it like Germany taking the Sudetenland. I sit down, cranky and very much inside my own head. I just want to eat my mediocre brisket and slaw and go back to the gate. Then she sits down across from me with this gigantic grin. We both nod, and eat silently for a few minutes.

"I know you," she says.

I go into semi-sorta-kinda not-really demi-famous guy mode and say, "Oh, thanks. Probably from me running my mouth on TV," in a joking way. She looks super-serious and says, "No, I know you because I am from Liberia and I watch you on CNN and MSNBC and I read your book. You're a pretty good man."

I'm a lot of things, but "good man" isn't on my own list of them. I'm good *at* things but largely *not* good in my own estimation or that of others. Just ask around.

Now, this just about wrecks me. I'm tired. I'm jetlagged. I've been ping-ponging from East to West coasts. I hold it in and smile and say, "Thank you so much. I truly appreciate that."

"They"—she gestures around the room—"don't remember before him. They love him here. It makes me sad. My grandmother brought me here and said I must work to be a citizen. From nine years old when I came from Liberia, she said, 'America is for everybody. You will work. You will study. You will be good and you will pass your citizenship test.' Now they want to throw all of us away. We love this country. We love it so much."

At this point, I have no appetite, all my willpower given over to holding back a big boo hoo. My eyes are watering. I'm secretly sentimental and emotional about coming-to-America stories. I'm also sick to my stomach because every fucking Trumper hates this smart girl. She's their enemy.

We talk for a bit. This kid, this immigrant, knows more about American history than the average MAGA rally yahoo could learn in a month of pecking out Google searches.

"I go to junior college. I have an apartment. I have to work here and another job, but I do. I like to work. I'm going to vote because I passed my citizenship."

At this point my normally articulate tongue is tied tight by her story. She gets it. She gets out her phone and smiles and says, "Now I need a selfie with my famous friend." Hugs me. Selfie.

And off walks the best American I saw all that day, greater in soul, spirit, and goodness than the cancerous lump currently occupying the Oval Office.

You want to know why I fight? She's why I fight.

HERE ENDETH THE LESSON

And so, gentle readers, I am once again being badgered by editors to wrap this up, for time and publishing schedules wait for no man. As I write this in the closing days of 2018, we know what lies ahead only in the broadest strokes.

Mueller's legal juggernaut is grinding closer and closer to the inner secrets of the Trump enterprises. The economy is teetering on the edge of a correction at best and a recession at worst. The White House is a political Chernobyl, and even things that look briefly normal turn out to be irradiated and dying. The 2020 presidential election looms on the near horizon, and the Democrats will of course take every chance they have to blow it. Trump fatigue is real, and growing. Like some form of evil political Flubber, Donald Trump grows more bloated and unstable by the day.

I'm still a conservative, though being a Republican is harder by the hour. For the first time in my life I didn't vote a straight ticket in November, and it wasn't because I agreed with the Democrats on the ballot on damn near anything. Partisan identification as a *reason* for casting a vote is one thing, and I get that. Partisan identification as an *excuse* for a vote is another, and one I can no longer abide. The Republican Party has lost almost everything and learned almost nothing from Trump and their embrace of his crapulous cult.

I can't tell you everything the next two years hold, but I can tell you a few things I've learned on the road this year.

First, Trump inspires the worst in *some* people and the *best* in most people. For every scumbag alt-Reich stain on the Republic, for every pipe-bomber or synagogue-shooter, he's inspired 10,000 more people willing to be the Americans we should be: connecting, talking, knocking on doors, volunteering, and lifting people a little higher. He's inspired people from vastly different ideological backgrounds to try to fumble our way toward an understanding that the United States still deserves saving, and so we'll fight out the ideological policy battles later.

The second thing I know is now approaching the status of an immutable, proven, and inevitable law: Everything Trump Touches Dies.

You guys on the Nobel Prize for Political Smartassery committee know where to find me.

NOTES

1. Vichy Republicans

1. Lachlan Markay, Asawin Suebsaeng, Kimberly Dozier, and Spencer Ackerman, "White House 'Enemies List' Drove McMaster-Bannon Feud," *Daily Beast*, 5 Aug. 2017. https://www.thedailybeast.com/white-house-enemies-list-drove-mcmasters-bannon-feud.

2. Chris Whipple, "'Who Needs a Controversy over the Inauguration?' Reince Priebus Opens Up about His Six Months of Magical Thinking," *The Hive*, Mar. 2018, https://www.vanityfair.com/news/2018/02/reince-priebus-opens-up-about-his-six-months-of-magical-thinking.

3. Molly Ball, "How Trump Humiliated Reince Priebus—and the Republican Party," *The Atlantic*, retrieved 16 May 2018, https://www.theatlantic.com/politics/archive/2017/07/the-final-humiliation-of-reince-priebus/535368/.

4. Matt Fuller, "Paul Ryan Responds to Donald Trump's Misogyny," *HuffPost*, 7 Oct. 2016, https://www.huffingtonpost.com/entry/paul-ryan-donald-trump-misogyny-silence_us_57f81f60e4b068ecb5de8a5c.

5. Hunter Walker, "Donald Trump May Be Helping Ted Cruz with His 'Endgame,'" *Business Insider*, 27 Aug. 2015, http://www.businessinsider.com/donald-trump-may-help-ted-cruzs-endgame-2015-8.

6. "Trump Tells Christie: 'Get on the Plane and Go Home,'" *The Hill*, 27 Feb. 2016, http://thehill.com/blogs/ballot-box/presidential-races/271074-trump-tells-christie-get-in-the-plane-and-go-home.

7. Melissa Bell, "Newt Gingrich's Lunar Colony Has Us Looking at the Moon," *Washington Post*, 26 Jan. 2012, https://www.washingtonpost.com/blogs/blogpost/post/newt-gingrichs-lunar-colony-has-us-looking-at-the-moon/2012/01/26/gIQAYSffTQ_blog.html.

8. Nicole Hemmer, "The Conservative War on Liberal Media Has a Long History," *The Atlantic*, 17 Jan. 2014, http://www.theatlantic.com/politics/archive/2014/01/the-conservative-war-on-liberal-media-has-a-long-history/283149/.

9. Michael Wolff, *Fire and Fury: Inside the Trump White House* (Henry Holt and Co., New York: 2018).

10. Rupert Murdoch, Twitter, 18 July 2015, twitter.com/rupertmurdoch/status/6225 58129742573568?lang=en.

11. Tom Kludt, "Frenemies with Benefits: A Brief History of the Trump-Murdoch Relationship," *CNNMoney*, 17 Jan. 2018, http://money.cnn.com/2018/01/17/media /rupert-murdoch-donald-trump/index.html.

12. Amy Chozick and Ashley Parker, "Titans Clash as Donald Trump's Run Fuels His Feud with Rupert Murdoch," *New York Times*, 22 July 2015, https://www.nytimes .com/2015/07/22/us/politics/titans-clash-as-donald-trumps-run-fuels-his-feud -with-rupert-murdoch.html.

13. Sarah Ellison, "Inside the Final Days of Roger Ailes's Reign at Fox News," *The Hive*, 22 Sept. 2016, https://www.vanityfair.com/news/2016/09/roger-ailes-fox-news -final-days.

14. Dan Senor, Twitter, 15 July 2016, https://twitter.com/dansenor/status/75399491 3830703104.

15. Alexander Burns and Maggie Haberman, "How Donald Trump Finally Settled on Mike Pence," *New York Times*, 16 July 2016, https://www.nytimes.com/2016/07/16 /us/politics/mike-pence-donald-trump-vice-president.html.

16. Ralph Z. Hallow, "In CPAC Speech, Trump Hints of White House Bid," *Washington Times*, 10 Feb. 2011, www.washingtontimes.com/news/2011/feb/10/weighing -presidential-run-trump-make-cpac-debut/.

17. Matt Wilstein, "Palin and Trump Score More CPAC Speaking Time Than Paul, Rubio and Ryan," *Mediaite*, 12 Mar. 2013, https://www.mediaite.com/online/palin -and-trump-score-more-cpac-speaking-time-than-paul-rubio-and-ryan/.

18. Matt Cover, "Donald Trump; Brought to You by the Party's Professional Activists," 23 March 2016, *Opportunity Lives*, retrieved 16 May 2018, http://opportunitylives .com/donald-trump-brought-to-you-by-the-gops-professional-activists/.

19. Matt Fuller, "Donald Trump and the Heritage Foundation: Friends with Benefits," *HuffPost*, 10 Aug. 2016, https://www.huffingtonpost.com/entry/donald-trump -heritage-foundation_us_57aa2d40e4b06e52746dfea9.

3. Running with the Devil

1. Rod Anderson, "Donald Trump's Nonchalant Christianity," *Christian Post*, 24 July 2015, https://www.christianpost.com/news/donald-trumps-nonchalant-christianity -141834/.

5. What We Lost with Trump

1. Henry Cabot Lodge, *George Washington, the Man* (Houghton Mifflin, 1917).

6. The Media

1. Andrew Marantz, "How 'Fox & Friends' Rewrites Trump's Reality," *New Yorker*, 15 Jan. 2018, https://www.newyorker.com/magazine/2018/01/15/how-fox-and-fri ends-rewrites-trumps-reality.

2. Ibid.

3. Ibid.

4. Alan Rappeport, "Republicans Learn to Love Deficit Spending They Once Loathed," *New York Times*, 8 Feb. 2018, https://www.nytimes.com/2018/02/08/us/politics /republicans-spending-deficits-debt.html.

7. The Trump Base

1. "Why Economic Anxiety Is Driving Working Class Voters to 'Trumpism,'" *PBS News Hour*, 24 Mar. 2016, http://www.pbs.org/newshour/bb/why-economic-anxi ety-is-driving-working-class-voters-to-trumpism/.

2. Colin Grabow and Scott Lincicome, "The Many Myths of Reaganite Protection-ism," Cato Institute, 30 Nov. 2017, https://www.cato.org/publications/commentary /many-myths-reaganite-protectionism.

3. "Trump Says 'Pain' from China Tariffs Will Make US 'Much Stronger,'" *The Hill*, 6 Apr. 2018, http://thehill.com/policy/finance/381933-trump-says-pain-from -china-tariffs-will-make-us-much-stronger.

4. Tom Nichols, *The Death of Expertise: The Campaign against Established Knowl-edge and Why It Matters* (New York: Oxford University Press, 2017).

5. Ann Oldenburg, "Donald Trump vs. Whoopi Goldberg on Obama Birth Certificate," *USA Today*, 23 Mar. 2011, http://content.usatoday.com/communities/entertain ment/post/2011/03/donald-trump-takes-on-whoopi-goldberg-over-obama-birth -certificate/1.

6. "Donald Trump Takes on Whoopi, 'The View' over Obama's Birth Certificate," *Fox News Insider*, 28 Mar. 2011, YouTube, https://www.youtube.com/watch?v=yfZixq YuL58.

7. Donald J. Trump, Twitter, 12 Mar. 2012, https://twitter.com/realDonaldTrump /status/179228808891731968.

8. Donald J. Trump, Twitter, 30 May 2012, https://twitter.com/realDonaldTrump /status/207875027008368640.

9. Donald J. Trump, Twitter, 12 Dec. 2013, https://twitter.com/realDonaldTrump /status/411247268763676673.

10. Donald J. Trump, Twitter, 16 Oct. 2016, https://twitter.com/realDonaldTrump /status/787699930718695425.

11. Donald J. Trump, Twitter, 17 Oct. 2016, https://twitter.com/realDonaldTrump /status/787995025527410688.

8. Limited Government

1. "Georgia Congressman Calls Obama Marxist, Warns of Dictatorship," *Politico*, re-trieved 5 June 2017, http://www.politico.com/blogs/scorecard/ (article removed).

2. "Executive Order: Border Security and Immigration Enforcement Improvements," issued 25 Jan. 2017, White House, https://www.whitehouse.gov/the-press-office /2017/01/25/executive-order-border-security-and-immigration-enforcement -improvements.

3. David Nakamura, "Trump Administration Moving Quickly to Build Up Nationwide Deportation Force," *Washington Post*, 12 Apr. 2017, https://www.washingtonpost .com/politics/trump-administration-moving-quickly-to-build-up-nationwide-de portation-force/2017/04/12/7a7f59c2-1f87-11e7-be2a-3a1fb24d4671_story.html.

4. Lloyd Grove, "Coulter Hates 'the Browning of America,'" *Daily Beast*, 26 May 2015, https://www.thedailybeast.com/articles/2015/05/26/ann-coulter-on-the-brown ing-of-america.

5. "Ann Coulter Goes There: If Military Shoots One 'Illegal' at Border, 'Maybe They'll Learn,'" Mediate.com, 6 Apr. 2018.

6. "Fiscal Conservative Offers His Take on Trump's Budget Proposal," *Morning Edition*, NPR, 13 Feb. 2018, https://www.npr.org/2018/02/13/585299056/fiscal-con servative-offers-his-take-on-trumps-budget-proposal.

7. Stan Collender, "Get Ready: Here Comes Yet Another BS* Budget Commission," *Forbes*, 4 Mar. 2018, https://www.forbes.com/sites/stancollender/2018/03/04/get -ready-here-comes-yet-another-bs-budget-commission/.

8. "Transcript: Donald Trump's Victory Speech," *New York Times*, 10 Nov. 2016, https://www.nytimes.com/2016/11/10/us/politics/trump-speech-transcript.html.

9. Marc Scribner, "The Great Infrastructure Myth," Competitive Enterprise Institute, 10 Nov. 2016, https://cei.org/blog/great-infrastructure-myth.

10. Greg Jaffe and Damian Paletta, "Trump Plans to Ask for $716 Billion for National Defense in 2019—A Major Increase," *Washington Post*, 26 Jan. 2018, https://www.wash ingtonpost.com/world/national-security/trump-plans-to-ask-for-716-billion -for-national-defense-in-2019—a-major-increase/2018/01/26/9d0e30e4-02a8 -11e8-bb03-722769454f82_story.html.

11. Public Law 103-3, 5 Feb. 1993, https://www.gpo.gov/fdsys/pkg/STATUTE-107/pdf /STATUTE-107-Pg6.pdf.

12. Seung Min Kim, "Ivanka, Rubio Find a New Project: Paid Family Leave," *Politico*, 4 Feb. 2018, http://politi.co/2nAuqeQ.

13. "Solyndra Loan 'Crony Capitalism at Its Worst,' GOP Rep Says," Fox News, 18 Sept. 2011, http://www.foxnews.com/politics/2011/09/18/solyndra-loan-crony-capital ism-at-its-worst-republican-says.html.

14. Michael Wolff, "Ringside with Steve Bannon at Trump Tower as the President-Elect's Strategist Plots 'An Entirely New Political Movement' (Exclusive)," *Hollywood Reporter*, 18 Nov. 2016, https://www.hollywoodreporter.com/news /steve-bannon-trump-tower-interview-trumps-strategist-plots-new-political -movement-948747.

15. Donald J. Trump, Twitter, 3 Jan. 2017, https://twitter.com/realDonaldTrump/sta tus/816260343391514624.

16. Andrew P. Napolitano, "Executive Order Tyranny: Obama Plans to Rule America with Pen, Phone," Fox News, 6 Feb. 2014, http://www.foxnews.com/opinion/2014/02 /06/executive-order-tyranny-obama-plans-to-rule-america-with-pen-phone.html.

17. Derek Monson, "Obama's Chief of Staff Admits They Want Tyranny," *The Federalist*, 26 Jan. 2016, http://thefederalist.com/2016/01/26/obamas-chief-of-staff-ad mits-they-want-tyranny/.

18. Joel B. Pollak, "Three Ways Obama's Executive Orders Are the Worst of Any Pres-

ident," Breitbart, 4 Feb. 2014, http://www.breitbart.com/big-government/2014/02
/04/ruth-marcus-obama-executive-order/.

19. Bruce Thornton, "Obama the Tyrant," *Frontpage Mag*, 23 Nov. 2014, https://www
.frontpagemag.com/fpm/245833/obama-tyrant-bruce-thornton.

9. The Grown-ups All Die Too

1. Lachlan Markay and Asawin Suebsaeng. "John Kelly Pushing Out Omarosa for
'Triggering' Trump," *Daily Beast*, 2 Sept. 2017, https://www.thedailybeast.com
/john-kelly-pushing-out-omarosa-for-triggering-trump.

2. Yaron Steinbuch and Ruth Brown, "Omarosa Fired, 'Physically Dragged' from the
White House," *New York Post*, 13 Dec. 2017, https://nypost.com/2017/12/13/oma
rosa-is-leaving-the-white-house/.

3. Yamiche Alcindor and Julie Davis. "Soldier's Widow Says Trump Struggled to Remember Sgt. La David Johnson's Name," *New York Times*, 23 Oct. 2017.

4. David Nakamura, "Video of 2015 Event Shows Gen. John Kelly Misrepresented
Rep. Frederica S. Wilson's Remarks," *Washington Post*, 20 Oct. 2017, https://www
.washingtonpost.com/news/post-politics/wp/2017/10/20/video-of-2015-event
-shows-gen-john-kelly-misrepresented-rep-frederica-s-wilsons-remarks/.

5. Philip Rucker, "John Kelly's Credibility Is at Risk after Defending Aide Accused
of Domestic Violence," *Washington Post*, 8 Feb. 2018, https://www.washington
post.com/politics/john-kellys-credibility-is-at-risk-after-defending-aide-ac
cused-of-domestic-violence/2018/02/08/e8e1ff06-0ccf-11e8-8890-372e2047c935
_story.html.

6. John Bowden, "Kelly Says Trump Not Likely to Extend DACA Deadline," *The Hill*,
6 Feb. 2018, http://thehill.com/homenews/administration/372536-kelly-says-trump
-likely-wont-extend-daca-deadline.

7. Andrew Restuccia and Eliana Johnson, "In New Statement, Kelly Says He Was
'Shocked' by Porter Allegations and Condemns Abuse," *Politico*, 7 Feb. 2018, http://
politi.co/2E9e0QY.

8. Josh Dawsey, Twitter, 7 Feb. 2018, https://twitter.com/jdawsey1/status/96128195
3193488384.

9. Matt Ford, "The 19 Women Who Accused Trump of Sexual Misconduct," *The Atlantic*, 7 Dec. 2017, https://www.theatlantic.com/politics/archive/2017/12/what
-about-the-19-women-who-accused-trump/547724/; "Transcript: Donald Trump's
Taped Comments about Women," *New York Times*, 8 Oct. 2016, https://www
.nytimes.com/2016/10/08/us/donald-trump-tape-transcript.html.

10. Jonathan Swan, "1 Twisted Thing: Trump Says Porter Guilty, but Defends Him
Publicly," *Axios*, retrieved 12 Feb. 2018, https://www.axios.com/newsletters/axios
-sneak-peek-4f61181c-93eb-481f-9169-275b3db91e06.html?chunk=0#story0.

11. Michael Kranish, Anne Gearan, Dan Balz, and Philip Rucker, "Trump Wasn't
Happy with His State Department Finalists. Then He Heard a New Name," *Washington Post*. 13 Dec. 2016, https://www.washingtonpost.com/politics/trump-wasnt
-happy-with-his-state-department-finalists-then-he-heard-a-new-name/2016/12
/13/0727658e-c161-11e6-8422-eac61c0ef74d_story.html.

12. Donald J. Trump, Twitter, 11 Dec. 2016, https://twitter.com/realDonaldTrump/status/807970490635743237.

13. Donald J. Trump, Twitter, 13 Dec. 2016, https://twitter.com/realDonaldTrump/status/808638507161882624.

14. Donald J. Trump, Twitter, 13 Dec. 2016, https://twitter.com/realDonaldTrump/status/808653723639697408.

15. Donald J. Trump, Twitter, 2 Feb. 2017, https://twitter.com/realDonaldTrump/status/827113926517194757.

16. "Tracking How Many Key Positions Trump Has Filled So Far," *Washington Post*, updated 4 May 2017, https://www.washingtonpost.com/graphics/politics/trump-administration-appointee-tracker/database/?utm_term=.791bd447ab48.

17. Max Bergmann, "Present at the Destruction: How Rex Tillerson Is Wrecking the State Department," *Politico*, 29 June 2017, https://www.politico.com/magazine/story/2017/06/29/how-rex-tillerson-destroying-state-department-215319.

18. Kevin Liptak, Dan Merica, Jeff Zeleny, and Elise Labott, "Tense and Difficult Meeting Preceded Tillerson's 'Moron' Comment," CNN, 11 Oct. 2017, https://www.cnn.com/2017/10/11/politics/tillerson-moron-comment/index.html.

19. Carol E. Lee, Kristen Welker, Stephanie Ruhle, and Dafna Linzer, "Tillerson's Fury at Trump Required an Intervention from Pence," NBC News, 4 Oct. 2017, https://www.nbcnews.com/politics/white-house/tillerson-s-fury-trump-required-intervention-pence-n806451.

20. "Attributing Responsibility for the Nerve Agent Attack in the U.K.," U.S. Department of State, retrieved 13 Mar. 2018, http://www.state.gov/secretary/remarks/2018/03/279201.htm (page removed).

10. Welcome to Hell

1. Eli Stokols, "Trump White House Saw Record Number of First-Year Staff Departures," *Wall Street Journal*, 28 Dec. 2017, https://www.wsj.com/articles/trump-white-house-saw-record-number-of-first-year-staff-departures-1514457002.

2. "Three-letter" agencies are parts of the intelligence community: CIA, DIA, NSA, DHA, etc.

3. Tarini Parti and Matt Berman, "Many Trump Staffers Are Trying to Leave His Out-of-Control White House," *BuzzFeed*, 1 Mar. 2018, https://www.buzzfeed.com/tariniparti/as-trump-spirals-many-of-his-staffers-are-looking-to-exit.

4. John Fund, "Trump's Skeletal Crew," *National Review*, 13 Mar. 2017, https://www.nationalreview.com/2017/03/trumps-skeletal-crew-sub-cabinet-positions-unfilled/.

5. Glenn Thrush and Maggie Haberman, "Trump and Staff Rethink Tactics after Stumbles," *New York Times*, 5 Feb. 2017, https://www.nytimes.com/2017/02/05/us/politics/trump-white-house-aides-strategy.html.

6. Lisa Rein and Abby Phillip, "Help Wanted: Why Republicans Won't Work for the Trump Administration," *Washington Post*, 17 June 2017, https://www.washingtonpost.com/politics/help-wanted-why-republicans-wont-work-for-the-trump-administration/2017/06/17/61e3d33e-506a-11e7-b064-828ba60fbb98_story.html.

7. Nancy Cook, "Trump Aides Begin Looking for the Exits," *Politico*, 22 Sept. 2017, http://politi.co/2hkDHop.

11. The Trump Family Syndicate

1. Anne Helen Petersen, "Meet the Ivanka Voter," *BuzzFeed*, 2 Nov. 2016, https://www.buzzfeed.com/annehelenpetersen/meet-the-ivanka-voter.

2. Carrie Almond, "Ivanka Trump Will Be an Asset in Her New Role at the White House," *The Hill*, 30 Mar. 2017, http://thehill.com/blogs/pundits-blog/the-administration/326539-ivanka-will-be-an-asset-in-the-trump-white-house.

3. Henry Kissinger, *White House Years* (New York: Simon & Schuster, 2011).

4. Margaret Carlson. "Jared Kushner and Ivanka Trump Came to Washington Seeking Power and Glamour. They'll Leave with Neither," *Daily Beast*, 28 Feb. 2018, https://www.thedailybeast.com/jared-kushner-and-ivanka-trump-came-to-washington-seeking-power-and-glamour-theyll-leave-with-neither.

5. Adam Entous and Evan Osnos, "Jared Kushner Is China's Trump Card," *New Yorker*, 29 Jan. 2018, https://www.newyorker.com/magazine/2018/01/29/jared-kushner-is-chinas-trump-card.

6. Shane Harris, Carol D. Leonnig, Greg Jaffe, and Josh Dawsey, "Kushner's Overseas Contacts Raise Concerns as Foreign Officials Seek Leverage," *Washington Post*, 27 Feb. 2018, https://www.washingtonpost.com/world/national-security/kushners-overseas-contacts-raise-concerns-as-foreign-officials-seek-leverage/2018/02/27/16bbc052-18c3-11e8-942d-16a950029788_story.html; Chas Danner, "Report: Kushner Requests More Intel Than Any Non-NSC Employee at White House," *New York*, 17 Feb. 2018, http://nymag.com/daily/intelligencer/2018/02/report-kushner-requests-more-intel-than-any-non-nsc-staff.html.

7. Josh Gerstein, "Ivanka Trump, Jared Kushner Are Sued over Financial Disclosures," *Politico*, 17 Dec. 2017, http://politi.co/2oxHUeq.

8. Alexander Nazaryan, "Steve Bannon and Breitbart News Want to Take Out Jared Kushner," *Newsweek*, 28 Sept. 2017, http://www.newsweek.com/steve-bannon-and-breitbart-news-want-take-out-jared-kushner-672963.

9. Gideon Resnick, "Roger Stone: Kushner Is Leaking Intel to Scarborough," *Daily Beast*, 4 Apr. 2017, https://www.thedailybeast.com/articles/2017/04/04/roger-stone-kushner-is-leaking-intel-to-scarborough.

10. Gabriel Sherman, "'You Can't Go Any Lower': Inside the West Wing, Trump Is Apoplectic as Allies Fear Impeachment," *The Hive*, 1 Nov. 2017, https://www.vanityfair.com/news/2017/11/the-west-wing-trump-is-apoplectic-as-allies-fear-impeachment.

11. David Kocieniewski and Caleb Melby, "Kushners' China Deal Flop Was Part of Much Bigger Hunt for Cash," *Bloomberg*, 31 Aug. 2017, https://www.bloomberg.com/graphics/2017-kushners-china-deal-flop-was-part-of-much-bigger-hunt-for-cash/.

12. Jessica Kwong, "John Kelly Has Cut Jared Kushner's Many White House Roles, Report Says," *Newsweek*, 22 Nov. 2017, http://www.newsweek.com/jared-kushner-john-kelly-has-clipped-his-wings-republican-says-719666.

13. Michelle Ruiz, "Look, It's Time to Collectively and Officially Give Up on Ivanka Trump," *Vogue*, 31 July 2017, https://www.vogue.com/article/ivanka-trump-inef fective-adviser-give-up-hope.

14. Michael Wolff, *Fire and Fury: Inside the Trump White House* (New York: Henry Holt and Company, 2018).

12. Team Crony

1. "Trump Administration: 2017 Inauguration Donors," Opensecrets.com, 31 May 2018.

2. "Murray Energy's 'Action Plan' for the Trump Administration," *New York Times*, 9 Jan. 2018, https://www.nytimes.com/interactive/2018/01/09/climate/document -Murray-Energy-Action-Plan.html.

3. "Subsidising Coal Production Is a Really Bad Idea," *Economist*, 14 Dec. 2017, https:// www.economist.com/news/united-states/21732571-fierce-competition-federal -governments-worst-policy.

4. Joe Romm, "Reality Sets In for the Coal Industry: Trump Is Powerless to Save It," *ThinkProgress*, 22 Feb. 2018, https://thinkprogress.org/coal-plants-now-shutting -down-faster-under-trump-than-obama-4da9d4554ec0/.

13. Clown Princes of the Trump Media

1. Heather Dockray, "This Graph Compares Trump Tweets with 'Fox & Friends,' and I'm Sorry to Even Make You Look," *Mashable*, 30 Nov. 2017.

2. Andrew Marantz, "How 'Fox & Friends' Rewrites Trump's Reality," *New Yorker*, 15 Jan. 2018, https://www.newyorker.com/magazine/2018/01/15/how-fox-and-fri ends-rewrites-trumps-reality.

3. Ibid.

4. Rick Wilson, "Conservatives Sell Their Souls to Trump over Media-Bashing," *Daily Beast*, 14 Feb. 2017, https://www.thedailybeast.com/articles/2017/02/14/conser vatives-sell-their-souls-to-trump-over-media-bashing.

5. Alan Rappeport, "Republicans Learn to Love Deficit Spending They Once Loathed," *New York Times*, 8 Feb. 2018, https://www.nytimes.com/2018/02/08/us/politics /republicans-spending-deficits-debt.html.

6. Olivia Nuzzi, "The Strange Cocoon of Trump and Hannity, Two Friends Who Like to Talk Before Bed." *Daily Intelligencer*, 13 May 2018.

7. "Top Talk Audiences," *Talkers Magazine*, May 2018.

8. Dana Milbank, "Sean Hannity, Trump's Spin 'Doctor,'" *Washington Post*, 22 Aug. 2016, https://www.washingtonpost.com/opinions/sean-hannity-trumps-spin-doctor /2016/08/22/6cb90580–689a-11e6–99bf-f0cf3a6449a6_story.html.

9. "Sean Hannity Turns Adviser in the Service of Donald Trump," *New York Times*, 22 Aug. 2016, https://www.nytimes.com/2016/08/22/business/media/sean-hann ity-turns-adviser-in-the-service-of-donald-trump.html.

10. Ibid.

11. Asawin Suebsaeng, Spencer Ackerman, and Sam Stein, "McMaster Wants to Save

the Iran Deal by Hiding It from Trump," *Daily Beast,* 12 Oct. 2017, https://www
.thedailybeast.com/mcmaster-wants-to-save-the-iran-deal-by-hiding-it-from
-trump.

12. Mary Rich, "We're Seth Rich's Parents. Stop Politicizing Our Son's Murder," *Washington Post,* 17 May 2018.

13. David French, "The Seth Rich Conspiracy Theory Is Shameful Nonsense," *National Review,* 24 May 2017, http://www.nationalreview.com/article/447903/sean-hanni
tys-seth-rich-conspiracy-theory-disgrace.

14. "Statement on Coverage of Seth Rich Murder Investigation," Fox News, 23 May 2017, http://www.foxnews.com/politics/2017/05/23/statement-on-coverage-seth
-rich-murder-investigation.html.

15. Gabriel Sherman, "A Safe Space For Trump: Inside the Feedback Loop Between the President and Fox News," *The Hive,* 2018.

16. "Cable News Fact Sheet," Pew Research Center's Journalism Project, 2017.

17. "Ann Coulter to Donald Trump: Beware the Former Trumpers," *New York Times,* 30 Mar. 2018, https://www.nytimes.com/2018/03/30/opinion/ann-coulter-trump
-former-trumpers.html.

18. Ann Coulter, Twitter, 16 Aug. 2015, https://twitter.com/AnnCoulter/status/63295
4040675078144.

19. Asawin Suebsaeng, "Ann Coulter, Stephen Miller Helped Write Trump Immigration Plan," *Daily Beast,* 10 July 2017, https://www.thedailybeast.com/ann-coulter
-stephen-miller-helped-write-trump-immigration-plan.

20. Grace Curley, "Immigration, Ann Coulter and the Wall—4.2.18 (Hour 2)," *Howie Carr Show,* 2 Apr. 2018, https://howiecarrshow.com/2018/04/02/immigration-ann
-coulter-and-the-wall-4–2–18-hour-2/.

21. Lloyd Grove, " 'Heartbroken' Trump Critic Ann Coulter: He's a 'Shallow, Lazy Ignoramus.' " *The Daily Beast,* 28 Mar. 2018.

22. McKay Coppins, *The Wilderness: Deep Inside the Republican Party's Combative, Contentious, Chaotic Quest to Take Back the White House* (New York: Back Bay Books, 2016).

23. David Horowitz. "Bill Kristol: Republican Spoiler, Renegade Jew," Breitbart, 15 May 2016, http://www.breitbart.com/2016-presidential-race/2016/05/15/bill
-kristol-republican-spoiler-renegade-jew/.

24. Gerald Warner, "Hoist It High and Proud: The Confederate Flag Proclaims a Glorious Heritage," Breitbart, 1 July 2015, http://www.breitbart.com/big-govern
ment/2015/07/01/hoist-it-high-and-proud-the-confederate-flag-proclaims-a-glo
rious-heritage/.

25. Milo Yiannopoulos, " "Would You Rather Your Child Had Feminism or Cancer?'" Breitbart, 20 Nov. 2016, www.breitbart.com/video/2016/02/19/would-you-rather
-your-child-had-feminism-or-cancer/.

26. Paul Farhi, "The Mysterious Group That Wants to Kill Breitbart's Ad Revenue, One Tweet at a Time," *Chicago Tribune,* 22 Sept. 2017, http://www.chicagotribune.com
/business/ct-sleeping-giant-breitbart-advertisers-20170922-story.html.

27. Bonnie Kristian, "Breitbart Is Reportedly Bleeding Ad Revenue." *The Week,* 21 Aug. 2017, theweek.com/speedreads/719664/breitbart-reportedly-bleeding-ad-revenue.

28. Lucia Moses, "Breitbart Ads Plummet Nearly 90 Percent in Three Months as Trump's Troubles Mount." *Media Radar*, 6 June 2017, https://resources.media radar.com/newsroom/breitbart-ads-plummet-in-three-months.

29. Katie McHugh, Twitter, retrieved 16 Mar. 2018, https://twitter.com/k_mcq/status /644354526162644992 (post removed).

30. The site dropped from 15 million unique visitors in October, per comScore, to 13.7 million in November, 9.9 million in December, 8.5 million in January, and 7.8 million in February.

31. Rosie Gray, "The Mercers Wash Their Hands of Milo," *The Atlantic*, 2 Nov. 2017, https://www.theatlantic.com/politics/archive/2017/11/the-mercers-wash-their -hands-of-milo/544877/.

32. Tanya Gold, "The Fall of Milo Yiannopoulos," *Spectator USA*, 6 Apr. 2018, https:// usa.spectator.co.uk/2018/04/the-fall-of-milo-yiannopoulos/.

14. Trump's Island of Misfit Toys

1. Donald J. Trump, Twitter, 6 Mar. 2018, https://twitter.com/realDonaldTrump/sta tus/971006379375972354.

2. Kathryn Dunn Tenpas, Elaine Kamarck, and Nicholas W. Zeppos, "Tracking Turnover in the Trump Administration," Brookings Institution, 16 Mar. 2018, https://www.brookings.edu/research/tracking-turnover-in-the-trump-admin istration/.

3. Lloyd Grove, "How Breitbart Unleashes Hate Mobs to Threaten, Dox, and Troll Trump Critics." *Daily Beast*, 1 Mar. 2016, https://www.thedailybeast.com/how -breitbart-unleashes-hate-mobs-to-threaten-dox-and-troll-trump-critics.

4. Gabriel Sherman, "'I Have Power': Is Steve Bannon Running for President?," *The Hive*, 21 Dec. 2017, https://www.vanityfair.com/news/2017/12/bannon-for-presi dent-trump-kushner-ivanka.

5. Josh Holmes, Twitter, 12 Dec. 2017, https://twitter.com/HolmesJosh/status/94 0754883451514880.

6. Rick Wilson, Twitter, 12 Dec. 2017, https://twitter.com/TheRickWilson/status/94 0786732982722560.

7. Jason Horowitz, "Steve Bannon Is Done Wrecking the American Establishment. Now He Wants to Destroy Europe's," *New York Times*, 9 Mar. 2018, https://www .nytimes.com/2018/03/09/world/europe/horowitz-europe-populism.html.

8. Ali Watkins, "A Former Trump Adviser Met With a Russian Spy," *BuzzFeed*, 3 Apr. 2017, https://www.buzzfeed.com/alimwatkins/a-former-trump-adviser-met-with -a-russian-spy?utm_term=.muevGnk38r#.yrAnG3v82j.

9. Elisa Groll, "Russian Spy Met Trump Adviser Carter Page and Thought He Was an 'Idiot.'" *Foreign Policy*, 4 Apr. 2017, foreignpolicy.com/2017/04/04/russian-spy -met-trump-adviser-carter-page-and-thought-he-was-an-idiot/.

10. Brandy Zadrozny and Asawin Suebsaeng, "Trump's Longtime Lawyer, Michael Cohen, Knows Way Too Much. So Why Is He Still in Exile?," *Daily Beast*, 26 Feb. 2018, https://www.thedailybeast.com/trumps-longtime-lawyer-michael-cohen-knows -way-too-much-so-why-is-he-still-in-exile.

11. The only candidate for this "other guy" seems to be Trump attorney Marc Kasowitz. See his Wikipedia entry: https://en.wikipedia.org/wiki/Marc_Kasowitz.

12. Maggie Haberman, "Did Roger Stone Jump, or Was He Pushed from Donald Trump's Campaign?," *New York Times*, 8 Aug. 2015, https://www.nytimes.com /politics/first-draft/2015/08/08/did-roger-stone-jump-or-was-he-pushed-from -trump-campaign/.

13. Gideon Resnick, "Roger Stone Convinced Trump to Hire Paul Manafort, Former Officials Say," *Daily Beast*, 21 Apr. 2017, https://www.thedailybeast.com/articles /2017/04/21/roger-stone-convinced-trump-to-hire-paul-manafort-former-offi cials-say.

14. Ryan Parker, "Roger Stone Banned from Twitter after Threatening CNN Anchors," *Hollywood Reporter*, 29 Oct. 2017, https://www.hollywoodreporter.com/news /roger-stone-banned-twitter-threatening-cnn-anchors-1052758.

15. Annie Karni, "The Mooch's Gift to Trump Staff: A Taxpayer-Funded Stylist," *Politico*, 7 Jan. 2018, http://politi.co/2CQwE3x.

16. David Badash, "Sarah Huckabee Sanders Went on 'The View' Today. It Didn't Go Well (Video)," New Civil Rights Movement, 6 Sept. 2017, http://www.thenewcivil rightsmovement.com/davidbadash/sarah_huckabee_sanders_went_on_the_view _today_it_didn_t_go_well_video.

17. Dan McLaughlin, "Acting FBI Director Shoots Down Media, Trump Narratives," *National Review*, 10 Oct. 2017, https://www.nationalreview.com/corner/fbi-director -testimony-shoots-down-comey-stories/.

18. Pamela Engel, "Sebastian Gorka, Trump's Combative New National Security Aide, Is Widely Disdained within His Own Field," *Business Insider*, 22 Feb. 2017, http:// www.businessinsider.com/sebastian-gorka-trump-bio-profile-2017-2.

19. Ibid.

20. Curt Devine, Drew Griffin, and Scott Bronstein, "Sebastian Gorka's PhD Adviser: 'I Would Not Call Him an Expert in Terrorism,'" CNN, 18 Aug. 2017, https://www .cnn.com/2017/08/18/politics/gorka-credentials/index.html.

21. "White House Staff Warned Not to Admit Gorka," NBC News, 28 Aug. 2017, https://www.msnbc.com/all-in/watch/exclusive-white-house-staff-warned-not -to-admit-gorka-1034672707528.

15. The Alt-Reich

1. Jonathan Mahler and Steve Eder, " 'No Vacancies' for Blacks: How Donald Trump Got His Start, and Was First Accused of Bias." *New York Times*, 27 Aug. 2016, www .nytimes.com/2016/08/28/us/politics/donald-trump-housing-race.html.

2. Ronald Reagan, "Remarks Accepting the Presidential Nomination at the Republican National Convention in Dallas, Texas." The Reagan Library, 23 Aug. 1984, https:// www.reaganlibrary.gov/sites/default/files/archives/speeches/1984/82384f.htm.

3. Eric Cortellessa, "Trump's Holocaust Day Statement Fails to Mention Jews or Anti-Semitism," *Times of Israel*, 27 Jan. 2017, http://www.timesofisrael.com/omit ting-jews-and-anti-semitism-trumps-holocaust-day-statement-causes-stir/.

4. Josh Dawsey, "Trump Derides Protections for Immigrants from 'Shithole' Coun-

tries," *Washington Post*, 11 Jan. 2018, https://www.washingtonpost.com/politics /trump-attacks-protections-for-immigrants-from-shithole-countries-in-oval-of fice-meeting/2018/01/11/bfc0725c-f711–11e7–91af-31ac729add94_story.html.

5. Nicholas Kristof, "Is Donald Trump a Racist?," *New York Times*, 24 July 2016, https://www.nytimes.com/2016/07/24/opinion/sunday/is-donald-trump-a-racist .html.

6. Woodrow Wilson, *A History of the American People* (New York: Harper, 1902).

7. Joshua Green, *Devil's Bargain: Steve Bannon, Donald Trump, and the Storming of the Presidency* (New York: Penguin, 2018), 147, Kindle edition.

8. Ibid., p. 212.

9. The "14 words" is a white nationalist/supremacist mantra: "We must secure the existence of our people and a future for white children."

10. Joseph Goldstein, "Alt-Right Gathering Exults in Trump Election with Nazi-Era Salute," *New York Times*, 21 Nov. 2016, https://www.nytimes.com/2016/11/21/us /alt-right-salutes-donald-trump.html.

11. R. J. Wolcott, "White Nationalist Richard Spencer Blames Violent Protesters for Small Crowd at MSU," *Lansing (MI) State Journal*, 5 Mar. 2018, https://www .lansingstatejournal.com/story/news/local/2018/03/05/richard-spencer-michi gan-state/397727002/; Katie Reilly, " 'We Don't Want Your Nazi Hate': Protesters Drown Out Richard Spencer's University of Florida Speech," *Time*, 19 Oct. 2017, http://time.com/4989785/richard-spencer-uf-speech-florida/.

12. C. J. Ciaramella. "Some Well-Dressed White Nationalists Gathered in DC Last Weekend," *Vice*, 29 Oct. 2013, https://www.vice.com/en_us/article/kwpadw /some-well-dressed-white-nationalists-gathered-in-dc-last-weekend.

13. Alex Thompson, "Watch Richard Spencer Rally the Alt-Right: America Is White People's 'Creation,'" *Vice*, 21 Nov. 2016, https://news.vice.com/en_ca/article/paz7 7z/watch-richard-spencer-rally-the-alt-right-america-is-white-peoples-creation.

14. Michael Kunzelman, "Anti-Semitic Troll Calls His Online Tactics 'a National Sport,'" *Times of Israel*, 30 Mar. 2017, http://www.timesofisrael.com/anti-semitic -troll-calls-his-online-tactics-a-national-sport/.

17. Trump Is Electoral Poison

1. Maura Judkis, "Donald Trump as 'Cheeto Jesus,' and the Political Legacy of a Dusty Or-ange Snack," *Washington Post*, 17 Jun. 2016, https://www.washingtonpost.com/news /food/wp/2016/06/17/donald-trump-as-cheeto-jesus-and-the-political-legacy -of-a-dusty-orange-snack/.

2. "Virginia Exit Poll and Results for 2017 Election," NBCNews.com, 16 Nov. 2017, www.nbcnews.com/politics/2017-election/VA.

3. Donald J. Trump, Twitter, 7 Nov. 2017, https://twitter.com/realDonaldTrump/sta tus/928074747316928513.

4. Haldevang, Max de, "The Likely Newest US Senator Has Likened the Koran to Mein Kampf and Blamed 9/11 on Godlessness," *Quartz*, 26 Sept. 2017, qz.com/1088001 /roy-moore-likely-to-become-the-next-senator-from-alabama-has-a-history-of -racism/.

5. "America's Choice 2012 Election Center," CNN, retrieved 6 Mar. 2018, http://www .cnn.com/election/2012/results/state/AL/president.

6. Rick Baker, *The Seamless City: A Conservative Mayor's Approach to Urban Revitalization That Can Work Anywhere* (New York: Regnery, 2011).

7. Adam C. Smith, "8 Takeaways from the St. Pete Mayor's Race," *Tampa Bay (FL) Times*, 10 Nov. 2017, http://www.tampabay.com/news/politics/Adam-C-Smith-8 -takeaways-from-the-St-Pete-mayor-s-race_162480501.

8. T. A. Frank, "Why Conor Lamb's Red-State Strategy Could Be Trump Kryptonite in 2020," *The Hive*, 13 Mar. 2018, https://www.vanityfair.com/news/2018/03/can -the-trump-kryptonite-of-conor-lamb-save-democrats-in-2020.

9. "GOP Panic Spreads to Pennsylvania," *National Journal*, retrieved 19 Mar. 2018, https://www.nationaljournal.com/s/664776?unlock=8AE9X4M288STTFFK.

10. Jacob Pramuk, "Trump's Tax Cuts Are Taking a Backseat in Critical Pennsylvania Election," CNBC, 8 Mar. 2018, https://www.cnbc.com/2018/03/08/pa-special -election-trump-tax-plan-is-taking-a-backseat.html.

11. "Dem Gains in CD18 Special," Monmouth University Polling Institute, 12 Mar. 2018, https://www.monmouth.edu/polling-institute/reports/monmouthpoll_pa _031218/.

12. Eugene Scott, "Analysis: Rick Saccone's Accusation That the Left Hates God May Be More Alienating Than Compelling," *Washington Post*, 14 Mar. 2018, https:// www.washingtonpost.com/news/the-fix/wp/2018/03/14/gop-politicians-like -ricksaccones-accusation-that-the-left-hates-god-may-be-more-alienating-than -compelling/.

13. Denis Slattery, "Ryan Says Dem Lead in Pa. Congressional Race Is 'Wake-up Call,'" *New York Daily News*, 14 Mar. 2018, http://www.nydailynews.com/news/politics /ryan-dem-lead-pa-congressional-race-wake-up-call-article-1.3874107.

14. An-Li Herring, "GOP Nominates State Rep. Rick Saccone to Replace Former Congressman Tim Murphy," WESA, 11 Nov. 2017, http://wesa.fm/post/gop-nomina tes-state-rep-rick-saccone-replace-former-congressman-tim-murphy.

15. Harry Enten, "Special Elections So Far Point to a Democratic Wave in 2018," *FiveThirtyEight*, 13 Dec. 2017, https://fivethirtyeight.com/features/special-elec tions-so-far-point-to-a-democratic-wave-in-2018/.

16. J.D., "Jeff Flake's Anti-Trump Manifesto Could Cost Him His Job," *Economist*, 19 Oct. 2017, https://www.economist.com/blogs/democracyinamerica/2017/10 /perils-conscience.

17. As of May 28, 2018.

18. "Release Detail," Quinnipiac University Poll, 20 Feb. 2018, https://poll.qu.edu/na tional/release-detail?ReleaseID=2521.

19. "Immigration a Top Problem for Republicans, Not for Democrats," Gallup, 15 Jan. 2018, http://news.gallup.com/poll/225473/immigration-top-problem-republicans -not-democrats.aspx.

20. Jennifer Agiesta, "CNN Poll: 6 in 10 Concerned Trump Isn't Doing Enough to Protect US Elections," CNN, 27 Feb. 2018, https://www.cnn.com/2018/02/27/politics /cnn-poll-trump-russia-protect-elections/index.html.

Epilogue: Post-Trump America

1. Ulysses S. Grant, *Personal Memoirs of U. S. Grant* (New York: C. L. Webster, 1885).
2. Ronald Reagan, "Ronald Reagan—Encroaching Control," 30 Mar. 1961, archive .org/details/RonaldReagan-EncroachingControl.
3. Rick Wilson, Twitter, 18 Nov. 2017, https://twitter.com/TheRickWilson/status /931947591306240000.
4. Winston Churchill, "We Shall Fight on the Beaches," Speech to the House of Commons, 4 June 1940, https://winstonchurchill.org/resources/speeches/1940-the-fin est-hour/we-shall-fight-on-the-beaches/.

A Note on the Paperback Edition

1. Josh Dawsey and Paul Sonne, "White House Discusses Possible Trump Visit to Troops in Iraq or Afghanistan," *Washington Post*, 19 Nov. 2018, https://www.washingtonpost .com/politics/white-house-discusses-possible-trump-visit-to-troops-in-iraq-or -afghanistan/2018/11/19/9f6724d8-ec2a-11e8-96d4-0d23f2aaad09_story.html.
2. Dana Milbank, "Opinion: Matthew Whitaker Is Steeped in Time Travel and Bigfoot. He's the Right Man for the Job," *Washington Post*, 13 Nov. 2018, https://www .washingtonpost.com/opinions/matthew-whitaker-is-steeped-in-time-travel-and -bigfoot-hes-the-right-man-for-the-job/2018/11/13/2ed59fc8-e785-11e8-b8dc -66cca409c180_story.html.
3. Michael S. Schmidt and Maggie Haberman, "White House Counsel, Don McGahn, Has Cooperated Extensively in Mueller Inquiry," *New York Times*, 18 Aug. 2018, https://www.nytimes.com/2018/08/18/us/politics/don-mcgahn-mueller-investigation .html.
4. Jeff Stein, "Deficit Balloons to $779 Billion in Trump's Second Year," *Washington Post*, 15 Oct. 2018, https://www.washingtonpost.com/business/2018/10/15/deficit -balloons-billion-trumps-second-year/?noredirect=on&utm_term=.564269b7c4c8.
5. Hunter Woodall and Bryan Lowry, "Inside Kris Kobach's Losing Kansas Campaign: 'Check Logic and Reason at the Door,'" *Kansas City (MO) Star*, 9 Nov. 2018, https:// www.kansascity.com/news/politics-government/election/article221350970.html.
6. Roberta Rampton, " 'We Fell in Love': Trump Swoons over Letters from North Korea's Kim," Reuters, 30 Sept. 2018, https://www.reuters.com/article/us-north korea-usa-trump-idUSKCN1MA03Q.

ACKNOWLEDGMENTS

Any list of acknowledgments will necessarily miss family, friends, advisors, and leave people out whom I will later regret not including. In this day and age it will also sadly paint a target on the backs of anyone I list.

In my long political career I have been blessed to work with the very best in the business, and some of you are still behind enemy lines, so I don't want you getting in trouble with the Trump Thought Police if I name you. I'll send a fruit basket, and you all know who you are.

I want to thank my friend of long standing John Avlon for calling me after the 2016 election and pushing me to write about the new world of Trump for *The Daily Beast*. It started as catharsis, and now look where we are.

My Florida crew have been amazing, unwavering friends, through everything. If you've been in our kitchen or on our porch, drinking, eating, and talking too loud, you know who you are, and why I treasure you. Also, "something happened in the kitchen and I love you so much."

My outstanding agent, Christy Fletcher at Fletcher and Company, made all this easier and more fun than I had any right to expect.

I also want to thank Mitchell Ivers, Jonathan Karp, Caitlyn Reuss, and Hannah Brown at Simon & Schuster for bringing this project to life, and offering me this tremendous opportunity.

To stay up to date with Rick's touring schedule, media appearances, forthcoming podcast, and general musings on politics and beyond:

Join his mailing list at www.therickwilson.com

Or follow him on:
Twitter at: @therickwilson
Instagram: @therickwilson

If you're interested in having Rick come speak at your organization, conference, or event, please contact booking@therickwilson.com.